The Saint Martin's Benedictine community gather at Lacey in 1908. (Saint Martin's Abbey Archives)

THIS PLACE CALLED
Saint Martin's
1895 – 1995

❖

A Centennial History of
SAINT MARTIN'S COLLEGE AND ABBEY
Lacey, Washington

John C. Scott, O.S.B.

THE
DONNING COMPANY
PUBLISHERS

For information, write:
THE DONNING COMPANY/PUBLISHERS
184 Business Park Drive, Suite 106
Virginia Beach, VA 23462

Steve Mull, *General Manager*
Barbara Bolton, *Project Director*
Tracey Emmons-Schneider, *Director of Research*
Richard A. Horwege, *Editor*
Kevin M. Brown, *Graphic Designer*
Dawn V. Kofroth, *Production Manager*
Tony Lillis, *Director of Marketing*
Teri S. Arnold, *Marketing Assistant*

Library of Congress Cataloging-in-Publication Data:

Scott, John Charles, 1945–
     This place called Saint Martin's, 1895–1995 : a centennial history of Saint Martin's College and Abbey, Lacey, Washington / by John C. Scott.
                p.   cm.
     Includes bibliographical references and index.
     ISBN 0-89865-982-5 (hardcover : alk. paper)
     1. Saint Martin's College (Lacey, Wash.)—History.   2. Saint Martin's Abbey (Lacey, Wash.)—History.   I. Title.
LD4819.S62S36   1997   96-36891
                                      CIP

Printed in the United States of America

4

C O N T E N T S

ACKNOWLEDGMENTS

❧

I WISH TO THANK THE MONKS OF SAINT MARtin's Abbey for confiding to me the narration of our monastic family's history. Past and present staff and faculty of Saint Martin's College, colleagues and often friends as well, have also been most encouraging. Key alumni of our schools and members of the churches our priests have pastored have also been very supportive of my work.

Archivists are essential to the making of history. Gerald D. Kirsch of Saint Martin's Abbey and Vincent G. Tegeder of Saint John's Abbey have rendered me invaluable assistance time and again over several years. I have also used with benefit the archives of Saint Vincent Archabbey and of the Catholic Archdiocese of Seattle. The photographs used in this book are mostly from Saint Martin's or Saint John's Abbey Archives. I also thank various monks, alumni and friends, and the Saint Martin's College Office of Communication for allowing me to use various photographs. Most photographic copying and printing for this volume was provided by Ted Yearian (HS '52, SMC '56). His work is truly a sight to behold! Additional copying/printing was done by Roger E. Easton (SMC '60). Photos by local professional photographers Gant W. Eichrodt, Ed FitzGerald, John Kaiser, Mike Stankus, and David Stein are also reproduced in this book with thanks! ❧

CHAPTER 1
Parochial Beginnings (1891–)

❧

Saint Martin's traces its origin to a plea for help in the spring of 1891 from a group of German-speaking Catholics in Tacoma, Washington. They had secured property and were constructing a church in the southern part of that city, but no German-speaking priest was locally available. One of their number, Stephen Tschida, suggested that they ask their bishop for permission to approach the superior of the Benedictine monastery whose monks had staffed his former parish in Saint Paul, Minnesota.

Being responsible for Catholic operations in the entire state of Washington, Bishop Aegidius Junger was well disposed to welcome any help he could obtain. He was especially anxious to get priests who could minister to non-English-speaking Catholics such as Slovenians, Poles, and Germans in his statewide Diocese of Nesqually. So, with the bishop's approval, a committee wrote to Abbot Bernard Locnikar, O.S.B., of Saint John's Abbey, Collegeville, Minnesota, asking for one of his monks to serve as the pastor of their new congregation. Both providence and circumstance determined the outcome of their petition for only a few years earlier Abbot Bernard himself had been the pastor of some of the petitioners in Saint Paul. He agreed to pay them a visit in the near future and thereafter to give them a quick decision regarding the assignment of a Saint John's Benedictine to serve as their parish priest.

During a very friendly visit to Tacoma in mid-June 1891, Abbot Bernard evaluated the prospects for the budding parish. On June 14 he met with Father Peter Hylebos, the founder and pastor of Tacoma's first Catholic congregation, Saint Leo's Church (1879). He also consulted with Bishop Junger and had extensive discussions with the city's German Catholics. Afterwards, he promised the parish committee to quickly assign one of his priests to minister to their fledgling congregation. The abbot also suggested that the new congregation be named the Church of the Holy Rosary in honor of the Blessed Virgin Mary.[1]

Left Page:
The imposing edifice of the second Holy Rosary Church (shown here in about 1940) has long dominated a section of the skyline of Tacoma, Washington. Built in the Gothic brick style in 1920–1921 on the site of the original 1891 wooden church, its tall steeple continues to call attention to the presence of an active Catholic parish church and grade school. Benedictine monks, who have staffed this parish continuously since 1891, went forth from Holy Rosary in 1895 to establish a monastery and school collectively called "Saint Martin's College" some thirty miles to the south in rural Lacey. (Saint Martin's Abbey Archives)

Abbot Bernard Locnikar, O.S.B. (1848–1894), of Saint John's Abbey in Collegeville, Minnesota, sent one of his monks to Tacoma in the summer of 1891 at the request of some Catholics seeking a German-speaking priest for their newly organized congregation. It turned out that Abbot Bernard himself had earlier been the pastor of some of the petitioners at Assumption Church in Saint Paul, Minnesota. He thus introduced Benedictine monks to the evergreen wonders of western Washington. (Saint John's Abbey Archives)

Father William Eversmann, O.S.B., forty-two, arrived in Tacoma by train from Melrose, Minnesota, on July 16, 1891, to take up his new pastoral duties. He immediately made a good impression on Father Hylebos, who the next day reported to Abbot Bernard: "The new pastor seems to be pleasing and pleased."[2] Only a few days later, however, Father William summarized his own first impressions of his new parish in a letter to his abbot:

Sunday, July 19 we had high Mass in the new Church, a good number of people being present. It seems to me that the greater number of (German) Catholics have become (indifferent) infidels. My way of living is somewhat difficult, the nearest hotel— "Hotel Rhein"—being eleven Blocks from the Church. The Committee brought me some kind of a "Record" [church account], which I could not accept yet because it is altogether deficient & doubtful. So I told the parties I would assist them to have *a proper Statement of things & then I would continue the books for them. The collection last Sunday at Mass was $50.00. Much money is needed & I don't see yet how to get at it.*

Coming as his did from pastoring a German Catholic small-town-and-rural parish in central Minnesota, Father William saw among his new parishioners what at first seemed to be both religious indifference and financial lassitude in supporting their new parish. He was especially annoyed that the organizers of the new congregation seemed to have assumed "that the Benedictines of Minnesota would pay all [debts] at once and collect their money afterwards again." The concerns expressed by Father William in his first letter from Washington State typify the problems he would face during his eight and a half years as Holy Rosary's pastor. Yet he promised Abbot Bernard that he would do his best: "With God's blessing & the prayer of the good people, I hope we will be able to do some good."[3]

In a July 29, 1891 letter, Abbot Bernard apparently described himself as being disappointed with Father William's gloomy report on conditions in Tacoma. The new pastor therefore immediately responded:

I have great hopes in Wash[ington]; my present condition is a trial of course, but I hope it will come out all right. As far as to the pioneer life, I am ready for it! I expected that! With regard to religion or non religion of the people, I cannot correct what I said but that is far from discouraging! I know that I am here to build up [their religious practice].[4]

The good people who had initiated the organization of a German Catholic parish in Tacoma had acquired some well-situated city lots and built a modest chapel, but had not entirely paid for them. Once they had been given a German-speaking pastor, they clearly hoped to settle down into the comfortable pattern of a German Catholic ethnic or "national" parish. Mass and other sacramental rites would, of course, be celebrated in Latin, the then traditional liturgical language of the Roman Catholic Church. Sermons and instructions, other devotions, and meetings of parish organizations, however, would presumably be conducted in German for the most part. Thus, both the Catholic faith and German culture of Tacoma's German-speaking Catholics would be maintained.

The Church of the Holy Rosary at Tacoma Avenue and South Thirtieth Street was dedicated on Sunday, August 9, 1891, by Bishop Junger assisted by Father William with Father Hylebos in attendance. The *Tacoma Daily Ledger* generously described it as "a very handsome edifice" and reported that "a large number" were in attendance for the ceremony. "About the dedication, I can say it was nice," the pastor reported to his abbot while also noting that the bishop's occasional sermon was "over-the-heads of the congregation." Father William himself lived in improvised quarters in the sacristy at the rear of the church for well over a year before a house adjacent to the new school building was purchased for him late in 1892.[5]

Right from the beginning, however, Father William viewed his new congregation's reputed "Germanness" with some skepticism. "Some seem to be glad of a German church, but here there is something that makes me think: The German [language] is greatly abolished!" The new pastor therefore proposed to build a stronger foundation for a German Catholic congregation in Tacoma by opening a parochial grade school at Holy Rosary. In August 1891, Father William met John Stellbrink, "a good, religious (German) man, a teacher and organist," who had recently come from Nebraska with his family. "He promised that he would help me to get a children's choir and play the organ gratis provided he would get work in Tacoma." The priest further confided to his abbot: "I must tell you what plan I fixed in my loony head last night. ('If this man don't get employment we might place a curtain in front of the church gallery and let him help me teach school on the gallery.') You will please take this as being only a spontaneous idea; but it is also certain that instruction is so very necessary, and beside prayer the most necessary thing."[6] In early September 1891, therefore, Father William opened a school for his fledgling parish. Its thirty-five pupils were taught by Mr. Stellbrink (with a little help from the pastor) in improvised quarters in the church. When Stellbrink took ill in December 1891, Father William quickly asked his abbot for prayers for his recovery because "without that man I would not know what to do at present."

The anxious pastor also shared a private opinion with his abbot: "Had they built a School house with rooms for a pastor and a hall for church purposes over it, things would be O.K." He also reported that the Visitation Sisters from Paris, Kentucky, had relocated to Tacoma and organized a school for girls and an academy. "For the boys," he added, "there is merely nothing [Catholic] done at all—Sisters refuse to teach them." Thus, he had no choice but to establish a school for the children of his parishioners: "If we are to stay here, I don't see any other way. Without this, there will never be a German Catholic Parish in Tacoma [and] we must either give up or at least speak English." He also admitted that Saint John's Abbey "would have to advance most of the necessary funds and also at least one [additional] priest" to work in Tacoma.[7]

On December 27, 1891, foundations were laid for a parochial school building forty by fifty feet and three stories high. "One floor served as a hall and meeting place for parish societies; one half of the first floor served as living quarters for the Sisters and the balance of the building was divided into [six] classrooms." It cost $2,500 and was ready for occupancy on September 5, 1892, by Benedictine Sisters Alphonse O'Donnell, Perpetua Pick, and Rosina Loecken, who had just arrived from Saint Benedict's Convent in Saint Joseph, Minnesota. Mr. Stellbrink, who continued teaching in the new parish school along with the sisters, became a mainstay of Holy Rosary Parish and remained so for the next thirty years.[8] A daughter born to the Stellbrinks on June 30, 1895, inherited her father's musical talents. She joined the Benedictine Sisters at their Minnesota motherhouse, professed vows as Sister Ositha on July 11, 1913, and years later returned to

Father William Eversmann, O.S.B. (1849–1939), arrived in Tacoma on July 16, 1891, to assume the pastoral care of a fledgling German Catholic parish. He started a parochial school and quickly secured the help of Benedictine Sisters from Minnesota. Father William liked both the Puget Sound area and the people of his parish but quickly noted their diluted "Germanness" and the need to also accommodate English-speaking worshipers and students. He spent a vigorous eight and a half years building up Holy Rosary Parish before returning to Saint John's Abbey. (Saint John's Abbey Archives)

Washington to employ her musical talents at Holy Rosary and Visitation Parishes in Tacoma until 1984. Sister Ositha died September 11, 1986.

Whether or not German was eventually to be the sole or even principal language of instruction in Holy Rosary's parish school is unclear from surviving documentation. In 1891–92, the first classes were conducted in English because so many of the children of German heritage enrolled in Holy Rosary School knew very little German. There is no evidence that German ever was the principal language of instruction.[9]

Within weeks of his arrival in Tacoma, Father William suggested to Abbot Bernard that Holy Rosary Parish and its fledgling parochial grade school eventually might serve as a stepping stone for Saint John's Abbey to establish a Benedictine Monastery and College on the Pacific Coast.[10] In 1881, in fact, Saint John's had considered making a monastic foundation in the Pacific Northwest when Archbishop Charles J. Seghers had invited the Minnesota Benedictines to assume pastoral and educational responsibility for two Indian "missions" in Oregon. At that time, the Minnesota monks were already involved in missionary and educational work among Minnesota's Native Americans.

On October 7, 1881, after having waited some months for a reply, Archbishop Seghers again prodded Abbot Alexius Edelbrock for an affirmative response to Oregon's plea for missionary monks. The Archbishop included in his letter to Saint John's abbot some attention-getting information: "There are two Benedictine Fathers of the Swiss branch of your illustrious Order looking for a suitable place in this Diocese where to locate a Mission: they will soon request me to give my views, and I candidly acknowledge that I am very anxious to consult you before coming to any agreement with them." Two weeks later, Abbot Alexius wrote Oregon's archbishop that his abbey's chapter had decided to accept his invitation "provided such arrangements could be effected as would give mutual satisfaction." He hoped to travel west within a short while "bringing one Father and probably also one Sister with me."

On the evening of December 4, 1881, Abbot Alexius and Father Edward Ginther reached Portland after a long journey by railroad from Minnesota via Omaha to San Francisco and thence up the Pacific Coast and the Columbia and Willamette Rivers on the steamer *Oregon*. While Archbishop Seghers "kindly and cordially" received them, the abbot was by then very sick with bronchitis and the cold, rainy weather did him no good during a tiring inspection visit later that week to the Grande Ronde Indian Mission some eighty miles south of Portland.

Stopping over in San Francisco en route back to Minnesota, Abbot Alexius wrote Archbishop Seghers on December 18, 1881: "For the present we concluded not to locate in your diocese for the following reasons: We are not prepared to take on Indian missions now." He also stated frankly that eastern Oregon did not look promising for a foundation. As for locating in the western part of the state, the diocese already had some Benedictines [the forebears of today's Mount Angel Abbey in Saint Benedict, Oregon]. Moreover, the abbot observed, the secular clergy of the archdiocese would not be overly pleased that Benedictines should "take away the best Missions." The abbot concluded: "All we wanted was a fair show, a place where to locate a home, which would have reasonable hopes of success. We found no such place at present in your diocese. But where to establish a College in the West? After the Northern Pacific [Railroad] is built, we may enter Oregon again and remain—if your grace consents."[11] By 1891, the Northern Pacific Railroad had established its western terminus in Tacoma and had in fact carried a representative of the Minnesota Benedictines back to "the Pacific slope."

The day after Father William had reached Tacoma in July 1891, Father Hylebos wrote to Saint John's abbot to urge him to file quickly for incorporation in the state of Washington. He

Children and adults gather in front of Holy Rosary Church before a religious service in this mid-1890s view. Makeshift arrangements in 1891–1892 for educating some of the parish children were so promising that a school building was constructed in 1892. It enrolled eighty students in its first year and was staffed by three Benedictine Sisters, who lived on the first floor in the three-story building. In just a few years the parish had become a vital center for Tacoma's German Catholics and for many others as well. (Photo courtesy Bob Tschida.)

15

strongly advised Abbot Bernard to request a charter which would allow them to carry on a wide range of religious and educational activities: *You can be incorporated here, and now is the time to do it, as the laws of our new state are very accommodating as yet, and the expense small, less than ten dollars. Allow me to suggest that it would be advisable to insert in your articles of incorporation all the objects of your order, school, colleges, etc., and for the whole State of Washington. But remember: Headquarters at Tacoma.*[12]

Already "a kind of permanent fixture" in 1890s Tacoma, as well as a man who exercised great influence in the Catholic diocese, Father Hylebos was clearly eager to help promote anything that built up Catholic institutional life in Tacoma and western Washington. Thus he freely advised Abbot Bernard about long-range possibilities for Saint John's Benedictines in the Pacific Northwest.[13] He would understandably be delighted to see Benedictine manpower and money put to good use in his city and his diocese. Years later, Father Hylebos died suddenly of complications from the notorious "Spanish flu" epidemic without leaving a will. In January 1919, Abbot Oswald Baran commented on his passing to Abbot Peter:

Once upon a time he gave me a verbal promise that Saint Martin's would be remembered in his will with a scholarship. I did not take it seriously, now all chance has vanished.[14]

Father William was soon asking that an additional priest from Saint John's Abbey be assigned to assist him with pastoral duties in Tacoma so that one of them could be "more at liberty to tend to the financial part, collect money, etc." He also wished that the Benedictine Order should spread to the coast for he had quickly decided that the Pacific Northwest was "the country to do good [in], even if the beginning is ever so hard." By April 1892, he was campaigning for the assignment of one who could speak Polish as well as German and English. Father Wolfgang Steinkogler, O.S.B., thirty-two, the Benedictine pastor of Saint Wendelin Church in rural central Minnesota, offered his services. He arrived at Holy Rosary in mid-August 1892 "and cast his lot with the settlers of the Pacific slope."[15]

Development of Holy Rosary Church as a specifically German Catholic ethnic or national parish was further hindered by the fact that there were also English-speaking Catholics, who had "contributed liberally towards building the new church," within the parish's large boundaries. Many of them quickly started to attend Mass at the new church and, of course, they preferred Catholic pastoral services without the impediment, for them, of the German language. English-speaking Catholics were collectively called "Irish" by Holy

Saint Martin's monks' involvement in staffing western Washington Catholic parishes and missions kept expanding. Benedictine Fathers Albert, Charles, and James are shown in this 1910 view of the Holy Rosary Parish complex in Tacoma. (This picture was probably taken by that church's Benedictine pastor, Father Oswald Baran.) The priests are posed with a Mr. Cameron behind Father Oswald's rectory (1907). In the background (right to left) is the parish church (1891), the school (original section 1892) and hall, and the new Sisters' convent (1903). (Saint John's Abbey Archives)

Rosary's German-American founding families, who soon complained to Abbot Bernard that their pastor favored the "Irish." Within two months of his arrival, Father William was preaching *in English* at two of his three Sunday Masses at Holy Rosary. When called upon to explain his conduct to his abbot back in Minnesota, the pastor wrote: "The 'Irish' pay." Adding insult to injury, he also stated that the parish's "Irish" boys were more dependable as altar servers.[16]

Holy Rosary's continuing failure to develop into a truly "German" parish was clearly demonstrated by a May 8, 1898 experience of Abbot Peter Engel. On yet another visit from Saint John's Abbey, he had preached in German at the principal Mass that Sunday and later attended a meeting of the Saint Joseph's Manner-Verein. Members of that German-speaking parish men's organization complained that Father William "favored the Irish more than the Germans, notwithstanding the promise of the [Saint John's Abbey] Superiors that theirs was to be a German parish." When some men suggested a change of priests at Holy Rosary, Abbot Peter "told them their parish would remain a German parish as long as the Germans supported the same." He also noted that in other regards they esteemed Father William highly. Bishop O'Dea likewise admired Tacoma's pioneer Benedictine pastor and in 1899 described him as "a model ecclesiastic [churchman] and a faithful laborer in this diocese."[17]

Another clear indication of the "mixed" ethnic status of Holy Rosary's congregation is seen in Father Matthew Britt's preparation for his own First Mass there on June 30, 1901: "Father Wolfgang told me that I should request about 500 pictures [commemorative 'holy cards'] for the occasion; 200 of which should be in German—the remainder in English." A June 1915 comment by Abbot Oswald Baran describes the limited but lingering use of the German language among Holy Rosary's parishioners: "Next Sunday I will have to attend another First Mass celebration and preach an English and German sermon in my old field of labor." In fact, "Holy Rosary never was [formally] erected as a German National Parish," as Bishop Gerald M. Shaughnessy of Seattle would have occasion to note for the record in a discussion with Abbot Lambert Burton of Saint Martin's in 1939.[18]

A very important thing to realize is that the "Germanness" of the first Benedictine endeavor in Washington was very quickly diluted. Presumably even the conversation at parish social activities was never exclusively in German, or at least not for very long. While there were women's and men's parish organizations in which German was commonly used, a second

altar society for English-speaking women was also soon established. Starting with the September 17, 1911 issue of the
weekly parish bulletin, announcements were published in
English whereas previously they had been "consistently written
in the old German script." This dramatic change demonstrates
that Holy Rosary's pastor, who was then Father Oswald Baran,
had recognized that the large majority of his parishioners used
English as their preferred language. On June 3, 1917, a terse
announcement was made that there would henceforth be no
sermons in German, "although in Lent of 1918 it was
announced that the Friday evening sermons would be in
German."[19]

Holy Rosary parish's *diluted Germanness* reflected the
social realities of Catholic life in Tacoma and western
Washington in the 1890s and early 1900s. There simply was
not a large or vital enough German-speaking Catholic population in Tacoma and vicinity to support a bona fide German
national parish.

To understand the future development of what was to
become Saint Martin's College and Abbey, it is very important
to note that the diluted Germanness which of necessity came
to characterize Tacoma's Holy Rosary Parish would immediately and permanently affect the activities the Benedictines
would undertake in Lacey. Right from the beginning an
English-speaking school and monastery would develop at the
institution which opened for business on September 11, 1895,
under the name of "Saint Martin's College."

Two other early determinants of the direction that would
be taken by the new Saint Martin's College and its community of monks need to be noted. First, most of the Minnesota
Benedictines assigned to work in western Washington quickly
came to enjoy the region's striking differences from the upper
Midwest. Father William, for example, boasted in a December
1891 letter to his confreres back in the snowbelt that he could
still dig fresh carrots from his Tacoma garden! He gamely
shrugged off the region's rainy and foggy climate with the
observation that "people have their umbrella with
cheese[cloth] and leave their hat on"! Reading about storms
and blizzards in the East in March 1892, Father William josh-
ingly reported that in Tacoma people said it was almost too
warm to work, ladies used their umbrellas to shade the hot sun
and that for the past few weeks everything had been "nice and
green."[20] The Puget Sound country's diverse natural beauty
as well as its milder climate—"the happy gray of clouds and
rain" as a later writer would describe it—also rather quickly
enchanted many of the other Benedictine newcomers.

A second early determinant that was to significantly shape Saint Martin's development was its priests' early and expanding involvement in staffing Catholic missions, parishes, and chaplaincies. Due to a shortage of Catholic priests nearly everywhere in Washington State, Benedictines from Saint John's Abbey were warmly welcomed and quickly put to work all over the western part of the state. As Father Demetrius Jueneman matter-of-factly reported in March 1898: "I have now been in most every place between Seattle and Portland West of the Cascades."[21] The Benedictine priests' modest but regular income from full-time or weekend pastoral work later would be used to shore up the finances of their fledgling Lacey foundation. During their first two decades in Washington, our Benedictines regularly ministered to Catholics not only in Tacoma and vicinity and in the Lacey-Olympia area but also in Shelton, Port Angeles, and Seattle. Saint Martin's priests also carried their ministry to the coal fields around Cle Elum, Roslyn, and Black Diamond and to seaside summer vacationers at Long Beach. And there was always *more* pastoral work to do!

Thus three key factors would shape the initial as well as the long-term development of Saint Martin's: (1) It would *not* be a German-American monastery or school in the style of its Minnesota motherhouse, Saint John's Abbey and University. (2) Most monks would quickly and happily adapt themselves to life in the gray-green rainbelt of western Washington. (3) Residential parish responsibilities and itinerant missionary work on weekends and Catholic holydays and during the College's summer vacations would take up a lot of the energy

The new institution seen here under construction in the spring of 1895 was to be both a monastery and school collectively called "Saint Martin's College." The "frame building 100 x 60 feet, furnished with all necessary modern improvements" stood on a hill fifty feet high and occupying some six acres. It was at first largely hidden by the tall trees of its future "campus" in the rural "Woodland" area some four miles east of Washington's small capital city of Olympia. SMC's mail, however, was to be addressed to "Lacey P.O." and that name was eventually applied to the district as well. (Saint John's Abbey Archives)

Saint Martin's College was intentionally built near the southern rim of its campus hill facing the tracks of the Northern Pacific Railroad's Grays Harbor branch line. Passengers and mail service used this railroad station, a quarter-mile from the college grounds, but freight was delivered to Olympia some four miles further west Father Sebastian Ruth photographed this east-bound train about 1906 at the "Lacey" station which originally had been called "Woodland." (Saint Martin's Abbey Archives)

and manpower of the Benedictine priests assigned to the young monastery and school at Lacey.

Searching for a Homeplace

The Panic of 1893, which staggered the nation's economy, also dealt the Pacific Northwest an economic body blow.[22] News of anything that promised to stimulate the local economy was therefore gladly received and much ballyhooed. On September 28, 1893, a newspaper published in Washington State's small capital city of Olympia gleefully reported the possible establishment in the local area of "a branch house" of the Benedictine Order which would be both "a monastery and a college for boys." What was wanted for the new College's site was "pretty good land for gardens, parks, meadows, and agricultural purposes" near a railroad and with plenty of water. Hyperbole decorated the editor's analysis of the impact of securing "a branch of Saint John's College" for Olympia. It would be "an institution which, for importance and benefit to be derived, would be almost if not equally as beneficial as the fact of having the capitol located here."[23]

Additional boosterish publicity appeared in print in subsequent months and, finally, a January 24, 1894 front-page story trumpeted: "University is Coming. Benedictine Fathers Will Locate in Olympia. Large Schools Assured." Breathless prose depicted future benefits. "It is now beyond all doubt. A Catholic university of gigantic proportions is absolutely certain to be built within four miles of Olympia and work will be inaugurated before the summer is large enough to wear boys' pants. It is hardly possible to realize the great benefits which will accrue to Olympia by having such an institution." The new institution's "motherhouse," Saint John's Abbey and University at Collegeville, Minnesota, was reported to be "of startling magnitude." Olympia's Catholic pastor, Father Charles Classens, who had worked with local businessmen to lure the Benedictines to the Olympia area, predicted that a colony of from one hundred to two hundred families would probably follow the monks westward from Minnesota and that people drawn from every quarter would be attracted by the new school. Happily extrapolating from those "facts," the newspaper's editor excitedly concluded: "The consumption of provisions [at the new institution] is certain to be something enormous and Olympia will, of course, be the center of supply."[24]

The actual selection of a College building site near Olympia had been complicated, however, by the monks' earlier selection and partial acquisition of acreage in rural Lewis County. Following an August 28, 1892 mandate from Abbot Bernard, Father William and Father Wolfgang sought out "a suitable place for the future" at which to establish an expanded Benedictine presence in Washington. "It seems to me," Father William observed, "that we must get out of the City [to] where we can live cheaper and earn something." After investigating several possible sites on the rural fringe of Tacoma, in mid-September Father Wolfgang had come upon a promising location on the Chehalis River about 45 miles from Tacoma. In early October, Father William sent his abbot an update on their real estate prospecting: "Rev. Wolfgang and I just returned from 'Dryad and Salal,' Lewis County, a place on the Rail Road from Chehalis to South Bend, about 12 Miles West of Chehalis. We found a place of 160 acres good land, with large timber on it . . . and the Chehalis River flows right through the land. The soil is black and heavy . . . the best that I have seen in Washington. The river has plenty of good water and fish. There is a small house and stable and some 10 or 12 fruit trees on some half-cultivated spot of about 8 acres on said land. Everything seems to grow splendidly even in a wild condition. The 160 acres are offered to us at $25.00 per acre cash." The two priests were enthusiastic about the Dryad site: "It seems that this investment can not fail to be good and more certain than any investment in a city. We would have a home then for ourselves, and with God's blessing, be sure to make a living."

Late that November, Father William signed a contract to purchase the Dryad acreage for $4,000 and temporarily used Holy Rosary Parish funds for the $750 down-payment. He promised the owner to pay the balance "as soon as we would get the money from Saint John's, Minnesota" but with the proviso that if Abbot Bernard "would object to our bargain, he had to return the money, which he consented to do." Father William also urged an immediate development of the Lewis County acreage stating that two or three brothers and a priest could properly handle that task "if they know how to save and how to operate farm affairs with advantage." He was hopeful that the farm would be "a foundation to build up a [monastic] community, although the present condition is exceedingly tough."

However, Father William was having second thoughts by January 1893: "The land in Lewis County is (seems to be) better soil and the river is convenient but for a College, Olympia would be a more central location." However, the landowner was pressing for full payment for the Dryad land claiming that it would soon be worth $100 per acre. "But in Olympia, we might soon sell some land to some good people and keep enough anyhow, and everything would be handy, near the City and State Capitol." Yet he was uncertain how much such land in Thurston County would cost. "But times are *hard*!!! And business people [in Olympia] seem to be willing to assist such undertakings. Should you and the Fathers think Olympia to be preferable you will please let us know how much we might offer per acre?"

"The location must be carefully considered. Some prefer the advantages of the Country, others of the City! We did not pay [for] the Lewis County land yet, and will wait until you answer this letter." However, a definitive answer from Saint John's was a long time coming. After much correspondence and indecision both in Minnesota and in Washington, the Saint John's Abbey Chapter again discussed the matter on December 26 and on the morning of December 27, 1893, settled the issue: "On vote Chapter decided in favor of Olympia, giving authority at the same [time] to the Rt. Rev. Abbot to exchange present property in Lewis County."[25]

The interest and energy of Father Classens, and the efforts of a committee composed of A. H. Chambers, George A. Mottman, John Byrne, and I. C. Ellis assured a capital city area location for the proposed institution. Thus, at a public auction in Olympia on April 21, 1894, a 571-acre tract in the rural Woodland area was purchased as the site for the proposed college and monastery. It was school land—that is, land set aside

for sale for the support of public schools—and appraised at from $10 to $14 per acre. As there was no competition, the bid on each of several parcels was for the appraised value. With some additional fees for harvestable timber, the total price for the acreage came to $6,920. The required initial payment of almost $1,400, which was 10 percent of the price of the land and the full price of the timber, had to be paid in cash. The balance was due in ten annual payments.[26] The Thurston County Commissioners confirmed the sale on May 24. Father William received the "contracts" for the acreage on June 9 and that same day sent a postal card to Abbot Bernard: "We must now try to make improvements *apud Sancti Martini in Silva* ['at Saint Martin's in the woods']."[27]

Would They Be Welcome?

The newspaper report that there was no competition in the bidding for the Woodland acreage raises an interesting question. In the fifty-year history of Saint Martin's, *Between the Years* (1945), which made use of the reminiscences of the last survivor from the pioneer band of monks, Father Demetrius Jueneman, overt anti-Catholic sentiment and action was reported: "The auction was to take place on the steps of the

County Courthouse in Olympia and the land was to be sold in tracts of forty acres each. When it was rumored that this property was sought for a location for a Catholic College, the organization known as the APA [American Protective Association], similar to the later KKK [Ku Klux Klan], was aroused, and planned to defeat the aim. They arranged to send a committee to the sale and to outbid Father William. On the day appointed the auctioneer announced that the sale would be a strictly cash transaction. This eliminated the opposition as they were without the necessary funds." Likewise, a month before the scheduled sale Father William reported to Abbot Bernard: "There is a rumor that the American Protective Assoc. are making plans to make it hot for us. We do not know this for certain; but we must be prepared for anything like that.—Now, if they, or any one else, will bid and raise the price we must have an ultimatum beyond which we will not go.—And I think we should not go far beyond $8,000.00 for 600 acres. That would be $13.33 1/2 per acre, i.e., wood included."[28]

A mere "rumor" of a Catholic land purchase would hardly have been necessary, however, given the fact that for the past six months Olympia newspapers had reported and celebrated the possible siting of a Catholic college in the area. Moreover, two days after the land sale Father William, writing to Abbot Bernard, stated, "APA did not molest [us] any."[29] It is impossible to establish any attempted sabotage of the Benedictines' land acquisition from existing records today.

However, overt anti-Catholic sentiment and activities had long been common currency in American society and cropped up periodically in that era especially in times of economic distress. Perhaps coincidentally, announcements of run-of-the-mill anti-Catholic programs in local Protestant churches were published in an adjacent column in the same April 1894 issue of the *Morning Olympian* which saluted the sure inauguration of a *Catholic* college in "Woodland" as "a movement of progress which will be ultimately to the benefit of the entire city." Under the rubric of "Church Services Today," the local Christian Church (Disciples of Christ) was offering a lecture on "The False Claims of the Roman Catholic Church." Likewise, it was promised that First Presbyterian Church's pastor that same night would answer questions from his congregation's "question box" including one on "Roman Catholicism."[30]

A Small Beginning

A devastating tornado touched down on the Saint John's campus in central Minnesota on June 27, 1894, and caused major damage. Among other things, it necessitated a year's delay in the opening of the proposed school and monastery in Woodland. Father Demetrius Jueneman was sent out from Minnesota in March of 1895 to superintend the construction of the new College. It was to be "a frame building 100 x 60 feet, furnished with all necessary modern improvements" and stood on a hill fifty feet high occupying some six acres. The surrounding acreage was level "but covered to a great extent with heavy timber." In the shallow basement story was located the kitchen, two dining rooms (for students and for the "faculty"), the heating apparatus and a recreation room. The chapel, music rooms, parlors, bedrooms for professors [monks], and classrooms were located on the first floor. Classrooms and study halls filled the second floor and student dormitories the third."

In the first week of August 1895, Abbot Peter and Fathers John Katzner and Oswald Baran set out for Washington "to inspect the work and make final preparations for forming the monastic community of Saint Martin's Priory." On August 15, the abbot blessed the new College and appointed Father Oswald to be the director of the school and prior.[31]

A contemporary letter describes the new College's site:

The location is not exactly picturesque. The nearest lake is about one mile distant from the building, and it is a very fine lake. Our depot (Northern Pacific Railroad) is a quarter of a mile from the college grounds. The station is called Woodland, but the post office Lacey. The town has a freight depot, a candy store, a board[ing] house, three residences and a large race track.[32]

"The early history of Saint Martin's College," a chronicler noted in 1927, "is a history of overcoming almost insurmountable difficulties, one of courage, perseverance and final victory."[33] That statement is only slightly rhetorical.

Our Patron Saint

According to Father Demetrius Jueneman, naming the new monastery and school "Saint Martin's" was suggested by Abbot Bernard "in memory of the great devotion Saint Benedict entertained for this Saint." This seems to be the most credible explanation. Many years after the fact, Father Cornelius Wittmann, an elderly monk who came to Lacey in 1896 and helped out for a decade before returning to Saint John's, advanced a dubious alternate version of our institutional "christening." Father Cornelius told an interviewer in 1930 that he had suggested his own given name of Martin for the new monastic foundation in Washington. That is certainly

an improbable claim, for the newly installed Abbot Peter Engel noted in his diary for August 12, 1895, that he had "purchased furniture in Tacoma for [the] new College which we named Saint Martin." That was fully one year before Father Cornelius first came to Lacey.[34]

The life of the man who became Saint Martin of Tours has taken on the stuff of legend. He was born circa 316 of pagan parents in a part of the Roman Empire that is now Hungary. Reared in northern Italy, he was taken into the Roman army—in which his father had served—as a youth. Later, while stationed as a young officer in France, he reportedly encountered a naked, shivering beggar. With his sword, Martin cut his large military cloak in two and gave half of it to the beggar. Some time thereafter, Martin had a vision in which that beggar revealed himself to be the Lord Jesus Christ.

Giving up military life in the still pagan Roman army in order to enter the service of the Christians' God, Martin sought instruction and baptism. He afterwards became one of Saint Hilary of Poitiers' clergy and later went on to found the first monastery in what is now France. Martin lived a simple, very austere life and worked to evangelize the rural areas of west central France. Chosen Bishop of Tours in 371, he reluctantly accepted the office but continued to live as a monk. Held in the highest regard by all around him, Martin died in 397.

The presidents of most of the member institutions of the Association of Benedictine Colleges and Universities (ABCU) met at Saint Martin's College in July 1995 to help commemorate the host institution's Centennial. Saint Martin's president, Dr. David R. Spangler, smiles proudly at the right end of the front row. A Centennial display entitled "The Faces and Places of Saint Martin's" forms the backdrop. (Photo by Paul Peck)

Saint Martin's awe-inspiring spiritual power had marked him as a holy man in his own lifetime and over the next few centuries he became one of the most venerated saints in western Europe. Saint Benedict of Nursia (circa 480–546) greatly revered Saint Martin. His sixth century *Rule for Monasteries* inspired a religious way of life that lead to the spread of Benedictine monasteries throughout western Europe during the Middle Ages. Thus, over the centuries many chapels, churches, and monasteries in Europe came to be named in honor of Saint Martin of Tours.

Our Benedictine Heritage

In the Benedictine scheme of things, each monastery is usually an autonomous monastic family. Such is the case with Saint Martin's Abbey, which, however, proudly shares in the 1,500-year heritage of the Order of Saint Benedict, whose motto is *Ora et Labora* ("Prayer and Work").

Saint Benedict, in his widely influential *Rule for Monasteries*, constituted each monastery as a sort of family unit under an abbot. A vow of stability bound monks to their monastery of profession, where their daily schedule consisted of the public worship of God, studious spiritual reading, and various assigned labors. The life of Saint Martin's monks today is similarly structured. The Benedictine spiritual program, grounded in obedience, recollection, and humility, allowed for flexibility and adaptation.

Intellectual activity quickly grafted itself onto Benedictinism and monasteries spread throughout Europe. Over several centuries, they came to serve as the sources of the Western Christian culture that developed in Medieval Europe. The Benedictine monasteries of Europe waxed and waned over many centuries until in the first decades of the nineteenth century several Catholic reformers brought about a small, but vibrant, revitalization of Benedictine ideals. The spirit and practicality of the ancient *Rule for Monasteries* was used by these reformers to reestablish old monasteries or to establish new ones in several European countries. Slowly but earnestly, and in relatively small numbers, monks of those revitalized monasteries (and their monastic sisters from similarly renewed women's communities) followed the movement of European empires and immigrants to Australia, Africa, and North America.

In 1846, Father Boniface Wimmer, O.S.B., and several candidates for the Benedictine Order left Metten Abbey in Bavaria to settle in Latrobe, Pennsylvania. Their monastery, which was the pioneer Benedictine foundation in the United States, developed into Saint Vincent Archabbey and College. Saint John's Abbey and University in Collegeville, Minnesota, was itself established by Saint Vincent's as its first branch monastery in 1856. Saint Martin's, in turn, was established by Saint John's in 1895 as its first branch.

Today, some forty abbeys and monasteries of Benedictine men, and an even larger number of communities of Benedictine women, pray and work for Church and society in the United States. Fourteen Benedictine-sponsored colleges and universities in nine states today serve several thousand students. Saint Martin's is the only Benedictine-sponsored college west of the Rockies. Other American Benedictines sponsor and work in primary and secondary schools and provide a wide variety of pastoral ministry. Both in the United States and abroad, Benedictine monasteries retain their affinity for education and ministry.

The monastic way of life Saint Martin's monks seek to faithfully follow is both ancient and contemporary. Saint Benedict established what he called "a school for the service of the Lord." Individuals enter this "school"—the monastery—in search of God. Our monks thus continue the monastic quest to know, love and serve God by following the Benedictine *Rule*, which emphasizes the Gospel command of love and the development of one's talents within the context of a permanent Christian community. In that way, our monks try to become more and more focused on Christ to help them prepare for service in both the Church and the larger human community. ✢

When Saint Martin's College opened for business on September 11, 1895, its all-purpose building loomed proudly from its rural Lacey hilltop. While the College enrolled only one student during its first weeks of operation, then and thereafter the Benedictine monks who made up the new school's faculty carefully worked to develop a serious but friendly pattern of campus life for the boys and young men who would make up the early student body. (Saint Martin's Abbey Archives)

CHAPTER 2
An Incipient College
(1895–1904)

❧

I
N THE CENTURIES-OLD BENEDICTINE TRADI-
tion, monasteries and schools have long had a natural
affinity. In nineteenth and early twentieth century
America, such schools served a three-fold function for communities of Benedictine monks. "They were not just places of
learning and a means of preserving the Catholic faith [of
natives and immigrants alike], but truly monastic schools that
would provide vocations to the priesthood and monastic
life."[35] A school, therefore, was quickly opened by most newly
founded monasteries. Such institutions were usually established in rural areas so that the monks might have the farm,
gardens and related facilities needed for them to be self-sufficient. A location suitably removed from urban distractions was
also generally preferred for a school.

Typically, a new Benedictine foundation would be operat-
ed as an extended-family business. Eventually, it was expected
that it would become financially and administratively independent of its founding monastery. Autonomy and self-sufficiency
were to be the common ways and means for the growth and
development of American Benedictine institutions. "Unlike
European abbeys, built and endowed by lay benefactors,
American abbeys had to be satisfied with small beginnings and
to grow largely on their own resources."[36] That was certainly
to be the case at Saint Martin's.

Campus Custody Expected

Keeping boys and young men on track, in school and in
life, was one of the new College's earliest and most cherished
goals. It was clearly understood that an education of mind,
heart, and character would be undertaken in a Benedictine
school.[37] The knowledge conveyed and skills developed were
to be imparted in conjunction with religious and moral
instruction and character development. From day one, the
Lacey monks were forthright as to the place and role of religion in their school: "Since the institution is conducted by a

Catholic religious body, religion and its practices enter intimately into the daily life of the student. For the sake of order, non-Catholic students are obliged to assist at all exercises of public worship but not at religious instruction."[38]

As both boys and young men would be enrolled, the school authorities acted and were expected to act *in loco parentis*. The new institution's 1895 "Prospectus" clearly stated such a policy: "Students, whether in class or at recreation, are subject to supervision at all times." The discipline would be "mild" although "reasonably strict regulations" were deemed necessary "for the observance of order." Enforcement of College rules would be on the basis of "moral and religious suasion rather than by severer methods." Prescribing what presumably all good parents would want and expect for their sons, the Benedictines promised that "good order, courtesy, manly and Christian deportment, punctuality, and attentiveness" would be insisted upon. Moreover, "their maintenance ought to be a matter of pride to the student."[39] Thus, at Saint Martin's closely watched "scholars" was the order of the day as the entire staff kept an eye on students.

SMC advertised a program of preparatory, commercial and classical education for boys and young men commencing in September 1895. "To meet the exigencies of the times," the College was prepared to enroll boys who still required instruction in educational fundamentals although recognizing that such offerings were "not properly part of a college curriculum." Thus, students below the age of fourteen or who were not sufficiently advanced to enter the classical or commercial course were admitted into the preparatory course. However, boys less than ten years of age would not be admitted "except upon very special recommendation."

Provision was also made for "worthy young men" who wished "to devote a few winter months to the pursuit of knowledge." The Preparatory Department offered such fellows "a special class system" in which individual instruction would be given "in those branches in which they are most deficient." This arrangement obviated their attendance in classes with young boys and insured "progress proportionate to their talents and application."[40]

A six-year classical course, somewhat equivalent to a modern high school and junior college curriculum, was also announced in 1895. This evidenced SMC's intention to eventually provide some training in higher branches of study for applicants who presented themselves with such needs. "The typical Benedictine college of the nineteenth century enrolled [male] students from the age of ten to twenty, some taking commercial or trade courses, others taking a more traditional liberal arts curriculum or pursuing studies for the priesthood."[41] The new SMC fit that pattern.

Starting the new school was mostly a matter of replication and improvisation. The curriculum and practices of the first monks' home institution were essentially duplicated although on a smaller scale. Thus SMC's first academic year consisted of ten months divided into two consecutive semesters running from the first week of September 1895 through the last week of June 1896. Tuition for either the classical or commercial course was $100 per five-month semester and included board, bedding, and washing and mending of linens. For an extra fee, special instruction was available in piano or organ and other musical instruments. Elective classes in drawing, painting, phonography (a form of shorthand) and typewriting as well as in telegraphy were also offered.[42]

Open for Business

When Saint Martin's College opened for business on September 11, 1895, it had some good teachers ready to teach but one small problem: Only one student showed up to register for classes! Since Angus McDonald had traveled some thirty miles from Shelton to Olympia by boat and then by wagon or train the additional four miles to the new school, he was understandably tardy. Nonetheless, Angus was duly enrolled and a full schedule of classes was taught exclusively for him during the many weeks when he was the College's sole student.[43]

Father Oswald wrote a letter to Abbot Peter on the opening day of school at the brand-new SMC: "Our attendance is *one* boarder from Shelton. We expected four or five day scholars, but they did not show up yet, they may be around tomorrow. I hope this only one [student] will not leave us, for then I'll be out of a job. There are hopes, however, that we may have twenty by the first of [next] June. It is almost best we have not too many since the building is in no way completed yet. . . . Everybody calling to visit the institution finds no fault with it except that it is not finished. They [also] cannot understand why such a beautiful building is located in the forest apart from all men."[44]

Playfully familial attention was given to young Angus, and subsequently to other students in the tiny new school, as can be seen in this humorous report sent to Abbot Peter in January 1896: "This winter there was scarcely any snow-fall. I was obliged to scrape the snow off about half an acre to accumulate enough of that rare and precious substance to fabricate a few snowballs, which were destined to locate on or near the valuable person of our solitary student, Angus McDonald."[45]

After its quiet first year, the new school's enrollment slowly increased. Early in the spring of 1896, strenuous action had been taken to improve the visibility of the College. One of the monks reported this forthright action to his abbot in Minnesota: "Many fir trees east of the building have ceased to wave their haughty heads. Our students went at them with a zeal truly admirable. The house [the all-purpose College building] can now be easily seen from the post-office and [railroad] station, and the services of a guide are, therefore, no longer indispensable."[46] Visiting the College for a second time in September 1896, Abbot Peter noted: "The Fathers are contented. The house is nicely arranged and the surroundings have been much improved since my first visit a year ago."[47]

During the late 1890s, SMC's enrollment averaged about two dozen but such students did not necessarily stay for the entire school year. On a visit to Lacey early in May 1898, Abbot Peter observed that "only thirteen students of the twenty-six enrolled this year remain." Some students were sent home for disciplinary reasons, while others had been enrolled only for such short-term purposes as preparation for receiving First Communion or Confirmation. In the early years of the twentieth century, pupils from Tacoma and Seattle, as well as from the more remote areas of the Pacific Northwest, were enrolled as boarders. The school also served "day scholars" almost from its beginning. As enrollment gradually increased (topping fifty in the 1900–1901 school year), SMC kept to its educational and custodial tasks in the personal and serious way that had quickly come to characterize its educational endeavors.

The whole Olympia area had a stake in the success of the new College, as was evidenced by the appearance of another boosterish newspaper story on October 4, 1895: "A splendid opportunity is afforded by the opening of Saint Martin's College . . . for boys and young men to acquire a higher education." Full and thorough instruction in classical, scientific, and commercial courses was promised, and the "beautiful and healthful" campus site, "accessible by rail and wagon roads," was lauded. Excellent accommodations for boarders were reported and day students were also welcomed. The "high grade of service" that SMC was offering would henceforth negate the necessity of sending youth "abroad" for higher studies.[48]

The founding faculty and staff members at the new "Saint Martin's College" were a varied bunch. Father Oswald Baran, twenty-nine, who "had for several years presided over the commercial college at Saint John's," was appointed director of the College. Father Oswald would care for the business end of the institution and also teach. He was joined by Father Wolfgang Steinkogler, thirty-five, the assistant parish priest at Holy Rosary Church in Tacoma since 1892, and Father Demetrius Jueneman, twenty-nine, who had supervised construction of the College building. Frater Benedict Schmit, twenty-three, who arrived from Minnesota that September also helped on in a variety of ways. In the new school's first sessions, the three of them seemed to have taught whatever needed to be taught. They also continued to have weekend pastoral duties off campus.

On September 4, 1895, "a small colony" arrived from Saint John's to help staff the new school.[49] Brother William Baldus, fifty-one, was to be the chief cook. He had presided over the kitchen at Saint John's for twenty-five years and in that capacity had been "second to a very few in popularity" at the large Minnesota monastery and school. "A quarter-century of hard work told on his health; he complained of rheumatism. Instead of laying down work altogether, he applied for leave to join the Fathers who were about to organize SMC in Washington." However, he "did not find the relief he had expected in the West." Brother William's departure from Lacey in September 1896 left the small, new Benedictine institution bereft of both a fine cook and the availability of a phenomenal tenor voice for choral worship services.[50]

Brother Francis (usually called Frank) Zwiesler and Brother Herman Krell, both forty, were assigned "to superintend domestic and farm work" at the new institution. Not much has been recorded about the two of them during their brief time at Lacey. Brother Herman, who had run away from Saint John's Abbey in May 1892 after eight years but had returned and been readmitted three months later, disappeared from Saint Martin's shortly after his arrival.

In February 1899, the fugitive Brother Herman wrote Abbot Peter from Salem, Oregon, stating he had left Saint Martin's of his own accord after doing what work he could do "but not only was it not satisfactory but he was hated [as he has been in Minnesota] even by his relatives and especially by the Brother Master." He then pleaded with the abbot for some financial compensation: "Entering the monastery in good

health, now physically broken and unable to do hard work," he was completely at a loss. "The world would pay me but the monastery [had] excommunicated, cursed, rejected him" after depriving him of his health and strength and now had also deprived him "of the blessings of the Catholic Church." Krell further claimed that "nobody had told him," before he made his vows, that he would not be entitled to compensation for his work as a Benedictine lay brother.

This last assertion was patently untrue for all men entering a Benedictine monastery at that time (and since) have signed legal waivers to any compensation. Johann Krell had done so before two witnesses on August 7, 1884, stipulating "That, in consideration of spiritual benefits, and also, in consideration of the board, clothing and education, which I am to receive [as "a member of the Order of Saint Benedict in Collegeville, Minnesota"], I renounce all right to demand or claim any other compensation whatsoever, for any work or service which I shall do."[51]

Apparently Father Herman Bergmann, the then Prior of Saint John's Abbey, promptly and kindly answered Krell's letter to Abbot Peter for the fugitive wrote to the prior from Salem on March 6 apologizing for his "rough, unkind letter to the abbot." Krell also stated that when he had made his vows

The eminence of Mount Rainier is stunningly visible from Saint Martin's hill and elsewhere on campus. "The Mountain," which rises in solitary splendor to 14, 411 feet about fifty miles east of Lacey, has enthralled Saint Martin's people for the past century when its commanding presence has not been obscured by clouds or rain. This late 1970s view also shows the first Sacred Heart Church (1923) in the Old Lacey neighborhood. (Photo by Blaise Feeney)

as a lay brother he knew they could be dissolved so he asked "may the abbot do what is to be done" in his case. Krell also acknowledged that "a Brother who leaves has no rights," reported that he now felt "calm and well," and asked Father Herman to pray for him.[52]

A School with a View

Frater Benedict was the youngest of the monks sent from Minnesota in 1895 to help staff the new Benedictine College and he would be assigned to SMC until December 1900. (Among Benedictines at that time, the title *Frater* designated a monk preparing for ordination to the Catholic priesthood.) "The occupations to which my time is devoted," he wrote to Abbot Peter, "are heterogeneous: stump-eradicator, college-janitor, mail-carrier, and professor are the titles of which I am justly proud."

Frater Benedict also very much enjoyed his first months living in western Washington: "Up to date, I am the happy possessor of almost perfect health. This portion of the state can truly boast of a healthful and salubrious climate. The summers are cool and delightful, there being no excess of heat; there are no cyclones, blizzards, and high winds. The so-called winters are very short and almost 'warm'!" He continued his youthful paean to his new home in a chamber of commerce-approved vein: "The scenery about our college is certainly superb and magnificent. Perpetual spring surrounds it. Its position on the 'volcanic' hill is a commanding one—a college set on a hill that cannot be hid—and overlooking the mighty picturesque forests of fir and cedar." The ardent newcomer also eulogized Mount Rainier: "Only yesterday I marched up to the [College building's] cupola, there to gaze for almost an hour at the 'Old Monarch,' clad in robes of virgin white, climbing, as it were, to

the very heavens itself." He further noted (with understandable delight) that "the grand and venerable monument of centuries" was "in plain view" from campus!

Young Frater Benedict also commented rather naively on a trait typical of newly founded institutions everywhere—namely, their seeking of funds and other help from all possible sources in order to make a success of a new undertaking: "Father Oswald, Father William, and Brother Frank are continually asking, begging, and clamoring for money, boilers, pumps, etc.," he confided to Abbot Peter, "that by this time you must be thoroughly disgusted at this constant warfare on Saint John's treasury."[53]

On February 1, 1896, Father William Eversmann updated Abbot Peter on Washington matters: "The Fathers in Saint Martin's enjoy life pretty well since they have a few more students. They have 6 now and expect a few more this week. The place looks quite nice already. I always think, it costs too much money, but, I hope, it will be for the best. When people get a little more money the students will come in all right but, I think, we should use no more money than there is just needed at present." After almost five years in Tacoma, the pastor also unburdened himself to his superior: "I have been thinking of asking for a relief for sometime. The many sicknesses of the past and continual Pioneer troubles make me often unfit to move as I should. I have always thought Tacoma were bound to be a larger place, and I believe it yet but at present poverty is great."[54]

In March, Father Oswald sent an upbeat message to his abbot in Minnesota: "This year only serves as a preparation for the next; if next year does not bring more [students] then will be time for discouragement. Meanwhile we do not have that word in our vocabulary but [rather] firm confidence in the protection of Heaven and the future prosperity of Washington and of Saint Martin's. . . ."[55]

In May 1896, Father Cornelius Wittmann, sixty-eight, an elderly monk of Saint John's, volunteered to assist his Abbey's new Washington foundation. He was soon "entirely enchanted with Washington" and marveled at the 200–250-foot-high trees in the campus forest and the stunning views of Mount Rainier. The "old man" kept himself "quite busy building altars and making statues" (the latter reminded young Father Justin Welz of Egyptian mummies!) and "clearing parts of the campus forest where the future orchard was to be planted."[56]

Later that year, when the monks had to buy more land "for expansion and for a road," Father Cornelius felt that the landowners in the vicinity "charged exorbitant prices." Despite many rainy winter days, his new location also boasted sunny warm days and flowers blooming even in December. As it was partially "for reasons of health" that he had come to Washington, with everything so green and lush Father Cornelius felt fine.[57]

He believed much more should be done to improve the monastery's farm and even urged Saint John's to found a Catholic farming settlement in nearby "Nesqually." In June 1898, Father Cornelius urged Abbot Peter "to send a Prior and Brother for urgent work awaiting attention on the farm." He frequently urged that Saint Martin's "be right away raised to an abbey" because "'Priories' including independent ones are always a failure: no real authority." It would really be too bad if Saint John's had no one to come to Washington, "which has the best climate in the USA." Its farming abundance has been proven by rich harvests.[58]

On May 4, 1898, Abbot Peter confided to his diary that "Old Father Cornelius wants the place made an abbey; the others [stationed in Washington] consider this move premature." Two years later the abbot wrote Father Cornelius telling him that he alone among the monks in Washington was suggesting immediate independence for Saint Martin's: "I shall follow Father William's advice. The Fathers who declared they would join the going-to-be-abbey will then have some more time to think it over and then make a final decision."

In July 1900, because Father Oswald had recently returned to Minnesota, the abbot instructed Father Cornelius, as the senior monk at Lacey, to call a meeting of the monks in Washington. They were to "elect a temporary superior that is one of these three: Father Andrew, Father Wolfgang, or Father Demetrius. After six months, the newcomers may be ready to decide whether they want to become independent or wait longer." The abbot also mandated "that the [monastic] choir prayer be observed at definite hours from now on as well as community meditation."[59]

Regularity of monastic prayer in common was, and is, an essential ingredient of Benedictine community life, and Abbot Peter would consider the same as proof of the new monastery's progress toward independence. Father Demetrius Jueneman was subsequently selected by Saint Martin's priests to be their prior and the abbot confirmed him in the job. After several more years of helping out at and boosting Saint Martin's, Father Cornelius returned to Saint John's in 1906. He passed to his reward in 1921.

Ten years after commencing his studies as SMC's first student, Angus McDonald was enjoying himself high "on the hog" at the 1905 Lewis and Clark Centennial Exposition in Portland, Oregon. He earned a Commercial Certificate in June 1897 and thereafter was involved in his family's mercantile business in Shelton, Washington, and other endeavors. (Photo courtesy Bob Partlow)

Abbot Peter thought enough of Saint Martin's prospects to buy forty acres of timberland adjacent to the campus for $600 on December 28, 1896.[60] Yet in 1897, SMC still had to sell itself as an institution. An advertisement that September in the *Northwest Catholic*, a periodical published in Tacoma, touted the advantages of the Benedictine College under a headline which read: "A New School for Boys That is Meeting With Success." Parents were assured that campus discipline was reasonably strict but enforced "by moral and religious persuasion rather than by severer methods." Furthermore, "good order, courtesy, manly and Christian deportment, punctuality and attentiveness" would be insisted upon and students, whether in class or at recreation, would be subject to supervision at all times.

The school's location was "healthful," the grounds afforded "ample scope for exercise and recreation," and the "commodious" College building contained "every modern convenience for light, heat, and ventilation." Easy access was provided by the Northern Pacific Railroad, which almost passed through the campus, and via Olympia "by boat from all points on Puget Sound."

The public was also reminded that the College offered a preparatory course for boys below the age of fourteen or those who were "not sufficiently advanced to enter the classical or

commercial course." The school's "theoretical and practical course" in commercial subjects led to a commercial certificate, which would admit the holder to an entry-level job in business. A six-year "classical course" was also available at the Lacey school. Board and tuition was $20 a month.[61]

As SMC had not yet procured powers from the state legislature to confer college degrees, Father Oswald put a question to Abbot Peter: "Do you think the institution can confer diplomas for Bookkeeping without conferring Degrees? Perhaps it can, and if so we will need some diplomas."[62] Apparently the abbot had not demurred for on June 23, 1897, SMC's primordial student received his own, and the school's first, Commercial Certificate. It certified that Angus McDonald had "graduated in the Theory and Practice of Double Entry Bookkeeping, Commercial Calculations and Commercial Law and Banking" which entitled him to function henceforth as "a practical accountant to the confidence of the business community." And so the first—but not the last—of our graduates was launched into the world of business!

Father Demetrius was discouraged by the West Coast's lack of popularity among Minnesota's Benedictines. On November 1, 1897, he wrote to Abbot Peter: "Washington is now *verschrieen* ["in ill repute"] in the East It has reached its lowest watermark."[63] Some ten weeks later young Father Justin wrote to a monk friend in Minnesota and shared his opinions about the nascent SMC: "As yet, the future for Saint Martin's does not look very bright. We have at present twenty-three students on the list for this school year. Of these, one has left, six are day scholars, and four are studying free of charge, which leaves us twelve paying boarders and some of these have reduced rates. Now you may figure out how we stand financially if I tell you that our meat bill, washing and groceries alone amount to $50.00 a month each. But that bothers only the 'boss' of the institution not the rest of us, although we have to get along with rather close rations in many respects." However, young Father Justin Welz quickly admitted: "I like it well at Saint Martin's!" For one thing, the monks at Lacey got to sleep until 6:00 a.m.! He had also had a bicycle since the previous October and with Frater Benedict enjoyed "a fine ride to Olympia and Tacoma from time to time." As the roads were fine and hard, "trips of 30 or 35 miles, as from Saint Martin's to Tacoma, were only fun."[64]

In March 1898, Father Demetrius reported a more optimistic evaluation of the Benedictines' work in western Washington: "Saint Martin's is also, I think, doing well [with] 26 students. I just heard that Mt. Angel [which had opened in

1882 in Oregon], which is quite an old [Benedictine] institution, has only 40 students. I look for a bright future for Washington. Saint Martin's, if properly looked out for, properly *managed*, will, with God's blessing, flourish."[65] Visiting Lacey yet again in early May 1898, Abbot Peter recorded in his diary: "Father Demetrius would prefer missionary work to teaching and does not agree with Father Oswald's views [about how to manage the College]."[66]

During the first week of August 1898, the small community of Benedictines at SMC hosted Bishop O'Dea and his diocesan clergy for their annual retreat. Afterwards one monk happily reported on the event: "For several weeks previous all of us worked to make it a success, and we have succeeded almost beyond expectation. All were more than satisfied, and

Sent west to Lacey in the summer of 1900, Frater Matthew Britt, O.S.B., was twenty-eight and a deacon needing another year of theological courses before he could be ordained a Catholic priest. Young though he was, Father Oswald had been pleading for his services as an English teacher for SMC for over five years. Frater Matthew, who would be an academic mainstay of the school for half a century, had a scholarly bent and forthright opinions on most every subject. (Saint John's Abbey Archives)

every one promised solemnly to show his gratitude by trying to procure for Saint Martin's as many students as possible. I sincerely hope that the promises will not be broken." Clerical word-of-mouth must have helped for some weeks later the same monk observed: "Judging from the number of applications received, we will have quite a number of students this year. Well, it is about time that we are making a start!"[67] Starting a few years later the annual SMC catalogs included the following acknowledgment: "The Fathers of Saint Martin's College acknowledge their heartfelt thanks to the Rt. Rev. Bishop and the Rev. Clergy of the Diocese of Nesqually, Wash., for their uniform kindness and earnest solicitude for the success of the College."[68]

An Enlarged Staff for a Growing School

Acquiring additional monks for the new College's staff and to assist with the monastery's growing pastoral responsibilities was a rather haphazard undertaking during SMC's formative years. Several Saint John's Benedictines were sent West on what usually turned out to be short-term assignments. Shortly after he arrived in 1896, a Tacoma doctor examined Brother Florian Mehren, thirty-two, and advised Abbot Peter that the monk be assigned to a high, dry climate due to his own weak state of health. Employed as a tailor at Collegeville, he put his hand to many tasks during his five years in Washington. "Sick with consumption," he returned to Saint John's just a week before his death on November 25, 1901.[69]

There always seemed to be more than enough work to be done at Saint Martin's. Father Adolph Dingmann, thirty-two, arrived in the Northwest in January 1900 and spent a year and a half busily covering various academic and pastoral jobs: "He has been working very hard during the past year, teaching, at times, more than forty hours a week and tending to Missions besides." His campus chum, Father Matthew Britt, humorously "'accused' him of chopping his foot on purpose [while out "bushwhacking" in the campus forest] in order to get a little vacation" in Olympia's Saint Peter Hospital.[70] Not to gainsay Father Adolph's reported hard work, Father Mark Wiechman reported to their abbot at the end of the following year: "I have about sufficient work to tend to, can't say that I am overburdened, nor that I have not enough to do. During this [Christmas] vacation of course, I have less to do. Still, preparing a sermon for the Sundays and feast days and looking after other little things keeps me busy."[71]

An example of a real short-termer would be Father Andrew Straub, forty-five, who arrived August 1, 1900. Always in delicate health, he found that the Pacific Northwest's climate did not afford him any relief and returned to Minnesota in 1901.[72]

After five years at Saint Martin's helm, Father Oswald asked to be relieved of his duties in Lacey in the summer of 1900. "He left for Minnesota to visit his mother and concluded to remain there."[73] That September, Frater Matthew Britt, twenty-eight, and Frater Mark Weichman, twenty-five, both still deacons, arrived from Collegeville and began what were to become long careers of service in the Northwest They also began their final year of theological studies under the supervision of Father Andrew while working at SMC.[74]

Father Oswald had been pleading for the services of Matthew Britt for over five years. He believed Matthew would be an excellent English teacher and Saint John's already had a number of the same.[75] In May 1901, Father Matthew wrote his first letter from Washington to Abbot Peter: "The land," he stated with his characteristic bluntness, "is not worth the annual taxes paid on it. If the Benedictines ever made a mistake, it was when they undertook to 'build up' a College and a Monastery on the fir-clad hills of Woodland, where the land is so poor that it requires manuring the very first year it is broken to render it productive." A few weeks later in response to a comment in a letter from his abbot that he had been exaggerating the poverty of the campus' soil, he added this trenchant remark: "In fact , the soil in this neighborhood is so poor that I really believe it has made a Solemn Vow of Poverty."[76] Father Mark offered his own agricultural observation: "Our own land is not exactly good, but 40 acres are very good, and 80 acres are passable, and with this I think more could be done than there has been to now."[77]

Father Ulric Scheffold, twenty-nine, who came to Washington in 1901, had the actual job of developing a self-sustaining farm at Saint Martin's. "Our best land is not yet cleared," he reported to Abbot Peter. "The best soil on this side of the Cascades needs much cultivation and manuring, plowing at least in fall and spring. Our farming economy is to tell the truth in a dilapidated state, our horses are hardly fit for plowing broken land, and when hay is $10 or $11 a ton and oats also very dear it hardly pays to keep animals for good looks. If we had enough manure most of our land could be made yielding, and here is the missing link." Without a barn, manure from the campus' five cows could not be collected for fertilizer. "So all pretty well turns on the manure question." A good "footing" for Saint Martin's could be achieved, Father Ulric concluded, by building a barn, obtaining a pair of strong horses, and clearing more acres.[78]

Father Matthew also expressed his strong concern about SMC being "so dependent upon Protestant patronage": "At present there are twenty-four students attending Saint Martin's; ten of them are Catholic—or rather nine are and one is thinking about becoming a Catholic."[79] This "non-Catholic majority" worried this young man from a section of the USA where a thoroughly Catholic ambiance was taken for granted. Not for the last time would a transplanted German-American Benedictine find it necessary to adjust his perspective to the Pacific Northwest's "unchurched" and predominantly non-Catholic human context.

The College's small enrollment in 1901 (thirty-two students of diverse ages) was also of concern to Father Ulric: "Truly our numbers are small at present, but I have hopes especially if we can make some effort of looking about [for students]. We must make Saint Martin's known; we could teach and accommodate 60 boys with what is here." Yet he also was very positive in evaluating monastic and school life in Lacey: "We are also blessed. We are all healthy and happy and jubilant. Not an idea of disharmony has so far found its way into our little community. Almost every evening after supper we go into the front room, Father Oswald plays the piano and we all sing every German and English song ever composed and if they give out we go to singing Glorias and Credos."

Earnest but Spread Thin

While teaching loads at SMC in its early years were not heavy in terms of actual course enrollments, the variety of subjects taught by each monk frequently was quite challenging. Yet our early faculty, while often self-taught in multiple subjects, frequently had very good classroom success. "One of the problems of the early [American] Benedictine colleges," a careful student has noted, "was that the teachers often were sorely in need of education themselves." With "numerous duties outside the classroom," some Benedictines' teaching duties " were more survival tests than specialized disciplines."[80] However, "the best of such teachers were so successful at educating themselves for the rest of their lives that they were fine teachers. Short on education, without extraordinary ability, they had only their own willingness to work unbelievably hard, confident that they were doing God's work."[81]

SMC's early faculty shared prefecting duties in supervising their "scholars" outside of class during the morning and afternoons, in the evening study-hall, and in sleeping in the boys' dormitory at night. Yet Father Ulric was optimistic: "Still Saint John's was not built up in one day, nor must Saint Martin's be; we are going ahead as well as circumstances permit, and God willing, we are willing."[82]

Father Mark also shared his observations on Saint Martin's prospects at Abbot Peter's request: "Very likely you have received the different opinions how we are out here, and probably some of them are not very pleasing. For some reason or another some persons may see things in a darker light than they are. Of course, I am inexperienced and may see things in a wrong light. Nevertheless, I think it will not be amiss to let you know my opinions."

He then directly took up the issue of Saint Martin's future: "As far as the prospects of the future college are concerned, I don't exactly know what to say; it may be that we stand [to make] a good show, and it may that it will never be much; I suppose it depends a great deal upon ourselves. Some, I think, believe that we ought to give up, but the boys are not exactly of the best kind, and I think that should be the main reason why we ought not to give up. To make the people better is what we came out here for, I think, and in that line there is certainly much to be done out here." In terms of securing a surer field for pastoral activities, Father Mark urged that Abbot Peter or his prior "come out here and settle things with the Bishop. Because if we cannot have hold of any parishes, nor even a hold to build some, then we had better quit, but if we can have some then I don't see why we should not succeed." Father Mark concluded his 1901 observations with what turned out to be prophetic words: "As far as I am concerned, I believe that I will like [this] country. It rains much but between we also have beautiful weather and that makes up for the rainy days. My health seems also to be fully as good as in Minnesota."[83] He would labor in western Washington until his death at age ninety-eight in 1973.

More Than Parochial Concerns

With the fiery exasperation of a young man, Father Matthew commented in 1901 on the necessity of obtaining self-sustaining parishes for the Benedictines' long-term success in western Washington: "We need expect nothing in the line of Parishes. The Bishop is even unwilling to give us the one-horsed missions which we out of charity have accepted 'till he gets a priest'—which will be just as soon as these missions are able to support one. It seems strange that we should allow Bishop O'Dea or any other Bishop to use us as cats-paws in this style."[84]

Religious communities of priests often sought to secure the permanent charge of certain parishes in the regions in which their members labored. This would give them bases from which to conduct their ministry as well as visibility among area Catholics. Such an arrangement would also provide opportunities to attract both potential recruits for their Order and benefactors for their undertakings. Abbot Oswald at one time considered trying to have a sizable area of southwest Washington permanently assigned to the exclusive ministry of Saint Martin's Benedictines in order to establish just such a parochial base. Exactly that development had occurred in west central North Carolina in 1910 when Belmont Abbey's superior, Abbot Leo Haid, had been named an abbot-nullius and assigned episcopal powers over Catholics in a cluster of counties.

Pastoral assistance provided by Saint Martin's priests in those early years (and since) sometimes has had amusing twists. In January 1900, Father Adolph Dingmann, thirty-one, was sent from Collegeville to SMC where he taught a full load of classes. He was soon asked by Father Oswald to go to Vancouver, Washington, that May and take charge of the Saint James Cathedral Parish. "Later on," he wrote to Abbot Peter, "I tried to back out of it because I had preached mostly in German" up to then. However, as his classes were "mostly finished" and there was no other Benedictine available, he went off to the See City of the then Diocese of Nesqually as ordered. The pastor, Father Felix Verwilghen, himself young in the ministry (just five years ordained) condescendingly told Father Adolph (but two years a priest) all the things he should not attempt to do as an inexperienced priest. However, the young monk ended up doing most of them quite well, according to his own later account.[85]

In January 1901, Bishop O'Dea asked Abbot Peter whether he had "learned anything definite about the young Polish [that is, Polish-speaking] priest you had hopes to secure for this Diocese." Apparently hoping to stimulate additional effort on the abbot's part to help secure clergy for Washington's non-English speaking Catholics, the bishop added an incentive: "As your Fathers here are short-handed, I could relieve one of them from the Francis County missions [actually, the missions including tiny Francis in Lewis County] if I can procure the services of such a priest as mentioned above." It was important that such a priest "be conversant in both German and English as well as Polish."[86]

New Personnel and Activities

In October 1901, Mr. Aloysius J. Ruth, twenty-six, first came to Lacey. A graduate of Santa Clara University in his California hometown, he had spent half a dozen years in training to become a Jesuit priest and was an experienced teacher. Both educated and energetic, he was an immediate hit with SMC's students and likewise impressed—and was impressed by—the school's Benedictines. Expressing a desire to join the monastery, he was sent in 1902–1903 to Saint John's Abbey to make his monastic novitiate. Father Ulric recognized the novice's great talents and potential for Saint Martin's: "Mr. Ruth is an able man; he seems to have extraordinary gifts for drawing, designing, photographing, music, [and is] all around willing and useful and cheerful."[87] Given *Sebastian* as his religious name at Saint John's, he returned to Lacey in 1903,

completed his theological studies under the tutelage of various monks, and in 1906 became the first priest ordained specifically for Saint Martin's. He would spend the next half-century involved in all aspects of his monastery's academic and pastoral work and in many useful "hobbies" as well.

Monks are avid practitioners of hobbies. In 1901, a "camera craze" hit Saint Martin's and young Father Matthew Britt acknowledged his complicity to Abbot Peter: "You will probably be surprised to learn that I have become very much interested in photography. I have been studying it up of late—in fact photography is a mild species of 'craze' in Saint Martin's and I am ambitious to be just as 'crazy' as the rest of them. There are at least a half dozen cameras in the house. If I had about $15, I could get a complete outfit." As the abbot himself was an accomplished photographer, this "confession" did not bring upon the young monk's head a reproof but rather advice about the virtues of different types and brands of cameras. In response, Father Matthew remarked that one of SMC's students had an Eastman pocket Kodak the same size as the abbot's but was too simple-minded to appreciate it. On the other hand, he himself was "not at all particular what kind of camera you would send me." He closed with a facetious remark: "But now I must stop talking 'camera' or you will think I am a regular crank." Father Matthew's interest in cameras continued as evidenced by his request some two years later for "a new small 'portable' camera." In return for that benefaction, the Lacey monk promised his abbot "an album of Washington pictures—all strictly First Class!"[88]

An interest in photography has persisted among our monks, as evidenced by the following description of Abbot Raphael Heider's skill in that art during the 1950s and 1960s: "He approached photography with the eye of an artist, and the results were, therefore, not just another set of travel snapshots. The camera in his hands became a way of carefully and accurately recording what he thought was memorable."[89]

Nothing in Life is Certain

In July 1900, Bishop O'Dea praised and endorsed the work of the monks at Lacey's incipient College. Writing to Abbot Peter on another matter, he commented: "I take advantage of this opportunity to testify to my appreciation for the Fathers of your Order at Lacey, and assure you that I could desire nothing more in their regards than a continuance of their same good spirit and assistance in the future as they have manifested in the past."[90] Despite the prelate's endorsement, however, at the beginning of the new century SMC's development and permanence was by no means a certainty.

The tiny institution's future was challenged both by its own limited resources and by direct competition for students from other similar schools. For example, the 1902 reopening in Portland, Oregon, of a former Methodist college as "Columbia University" under the sponsorship of the local Catholic archbishop worried the Saint Martin's monks. When it was announced early in 1903 that Holy Cross priests from the University of Notre Dame in Indiana would take over the school, SMC's small staff really felt threatened. The elderly Father Cornelius reported to Abbot Peter that Father Demetrius, the then prior at Saint Martin's, "said our situation here is not favorable since the [Holy] Cross Fathers have come to Portland and Bishop O'Dea wishes we should seek a better place."[91]

Portland's new Catholic school was similar to SMC in many ways: "Properly speaking, Columbia University during those years was not a university but a preparatory school. It began with the hope of establishing a 'Notre Dame of the West,' and although never realized, by 1922 a junior college was in effect."[92] Thus the new Catholic "University" only a hundred miles south of Lacey would be directly competing with SMC as a boarding school for Catholic boys and young men. Enjoying as it did both the support of an archbishop and the resources of the highly regarded Holy Cross Fathers, the advent of "Columbia University" [later renamed the "University of Portland"] was indeed worrisome to tiny Saint Martin's.

In March 1902, Father Herman Bergmann, the prior of Saint John's Abbey, "set out for the Pacific Coast for a rest and a change of scene." His real purpose, however, was "to visit and inspect Saint Martin's, which was still a dependency of Saint John's." Two months later, Father Mark wrote Abbot Peter saying that the prior had "showed me your letter, where you spoke of closing Saint Martin's." The young priest was philosophical about the whole matter: "Well, I do not know what is better. But I think we could get along by and by. I have not bothered myself about that. I am satisfied if I do what I am told to do. This I try to do. But certainly Father Ulric does all he can for the farm."[93]

Financial strains, slender student enrollments (attendance had increased to sixty boys and young men in November 1902)[94] and a shortage of monks for Saint Martin's growing pastoral and academic commitments had to be dealt with again and again. In a 1902 Christmas letter, Father Mark advised his

abbot: "Perhaps it would be good if you would come out . . . some seem to be waiting anxiously for you to come."[95] In May 1903 Abbot Peter once more visited Tacoma and Lacey to evaluate for himself Saint John's venture in the West. On August 21, 1903, the Saint John's Abbey Chapter "considered the western proposition—what someone styled a 'monumental folly'—and sent the community at Saint Martin's an ultimatum: either to apply for independence or disband and return to Saint John's."

Father Alexius Hoffmann, a friend and former teacher of many of the Benedictines assigned to Washington State, labeled this turn of events "a peculiar business." He thought it was clearly Abbot Peter's duty "to furnish the means" for "the western enterprise" the abbot had earlier taken in hand. Yet he also saw that independence was desirable from the viewpoint of the Minnesota monastery "because it was difficult to 'run' a place at a distance of 2,000 miles." Likewise, he thought independence was "expedient for Saint Martin's for the same reason" but he could not understand "why a kind of coercion was used to make Saint Martin's secure independence." As Father Alexius confided to his diary: "The Fathers then in the West felt the ultimatum very keenly. But the die was cast—and Saint Martin's *did* apply for independence and got it."[96]

This was not the first time the authorities at Saint John's considered granting independence to their monks laboring in Washington. Abbot Peter had raised the issue with Bishop O'Dea late in 1899: "The desire has been expressed by a few of our Fathers that steps be taken to place Saint Martin's on an independent footing by procuring its canonical erection as a Priory or an Abbey from Rome." [It is unclear whether the abbot meant that monks in *Minnesota* or in *Washington* had initiated this move toward "independence."] The bishop had replied "that yourself and the Rev. gentlemen of the College [SMC] are the better judges of its opportuneness, and I will be pleased to ratify a mutual agreement in that matter."[97]

Eventual independence of new monastic foundations has long been the rule in the Benedictine Order. The small band of monks at Lacey and Tacoma—the pioneers and newcomers alike—were determined to persevere in their venture on the Pacific Coast. ✤

*Poised to begin its second decade, Saint Martin's College
in 1905 rises above its surroundings in the still rural and
wooded Lacey district of Thurston County, Washington.
The monks who conducted the College were eager to prove
that their institution was indeed "a good cause in the West"
(as Father Oswald Baran described it) and so to secure
continued assistance from their Minnesota Benedictine
confreres as well as the public's patronage for their
growing school. (Saint Martin's Abbey Archives)*

CHAPTER 3
A Good Cause In The West
(1904–1914)

BETWEEN 1904 AND 1914, SAINT MARTIN'S sank its roots ever more deeply in western Washington. Although its new status as a conventual priory gave the Benedictine monastery a nominally independent rank according to Catholic church law, the Lacey foundation was in fact still emotionally part of the impressive institutional fabric that was Saint John's Abbey and University in Collegeville, Minnesota. Nonetheless, the Washington monks did their best to demonstrate that Saint Martin's was indeed "a good cause in the West."[98]

On March 9, 1904, under the presidency of Abbot Peter, the Benedictine priests stationed in Washington elected Father Demetrius Jueneman as their first ruling prior. The newly constituted priory consisted of Prior Demetrius, Fathers Cornelius Wittmann (who would return to Minnesota two years later), Wolfgang Steinkogler, Oswald Baran, Ulric Scheffold, Justin Welz, Matthew Britt, the cleric Sebastian Ruth, four lay brothers, and an oblate.[99] The omission of the names of the four lay brothers then at Lacey from the chronicle of Saint John's first historian is indicative of their subordinate status in the Benedictine Order of that era.

One of those "unnamed" lay brothers of 1904 was Brother Edward Karge, who at age thirty-three had come to replace Brother William Baldus as Saint Martin's cook in September 1896. "For a while he had been chief cook at Saint John's, but his health was not very good and he was sent West partly on that account." Brother Edward had been hospitalized for quite a while in Saint Peter Hospital in Olympia when Saint Martin's became an independent priory in January 1904. Abbot Peter visited him there but decided that he was too ill to consider switching his monastic affiliation to the new Lacey priory. Thus at his death that March he remained a monk of the Collegeville community, but for convenience sake was buried in the Catholic cemetery in Olympia and later reinterred in the 1920s in Saint Martin's new burial ground. He was fondly remembered as short, beardless, and "truly religious."[100]

"The first solicitude of the new prior," as Father Demetrius himself remembered it many years later, "was to increase the accommodations for students and faculty." Thus, in 1904 a forty-four-by-sixty-six-foot, four-story addition was attached to the rear or north side of the 1895 original College structure. It served to double the dining room space on the first or ground floor and provided room for a "spacious" chapel on the second level. The extra room was quickly put to good use for in 1905 the school's student body, most of whom were boarders, for the first time exceeded one hundred students. Classrooms and music rooms filled the new third-floor area and "sleeping accommodations" expanded into the fourth level. In 1903, "a special building for lay brothers and workers," designed and built by the industrious Father Ulric, had been put up some yards northeast of the original College building.[101]

Monastic Manpower

Lay brothers—nonordained Benedictines as distinct from monks who had been (or were preparing to be) ordained Catholic priests—remain the mostly unsung heroes of the 150 years of male Benedictines' prayer and work in North America. Typically, they were the "blue-collar" workers or the enlisted men, as it were, of the abbeys' ranks. Their sweat and prayers made male Benedictine monastic life and its many undertakings possible in the United States. Whether highly skilled in one or more trades or just used to working hard, the lay brothers were depended on to maintain their monasteries' farms and physical plants. When there were too few brothers, or none at all, monasteries had to hire help and such employees were more costly and sometimes less dependable.

Benedictine priests in America and those younger monks preparing for ordination, who were known as "clerics" and

addressed as "Frater," also typically enjoyed the satisfaction wrung from manual labor. However, most monks also spent a portion of each day in the mandated communal praying of the Divine Office in chapel, in providing pastoral services of various kinds usually off campus, and in such other "white collar" tasks as teaching and administration in our College.

The clerics of Saint Martin's—especially in the institution's first decades—were also tightly scheduled and frequently overworked. They taught classes, prefected study halls and dormitories, played in campus musical groups, had assigned chores, and joined the priests in the public recitation of the daily "hours" of scheduled monastic prayer. In a very real sense, the Benedictine clerics of those early years were required to finish their college and seminary education on the run. If they made their novitiates in Lacey—as most did—they usually also had campus assignments which included prefecting or teaching. "You ought to see our lists of classes," Prior Demetrius commented to Abbot Peter in 1906, "even the novice has a long list."[102] An earlier historian of Saint Martin's development had this explanatory comment: "The use of novices as teachers was recognized as a temporary expedient, a matter of sheer necessity for the young institution." The year of novitiate was supposed to be "as much separated from secular study and from contact with lay students as possible."[103] However, this "temporary expedient" lasted at Saint Martin's for over twenty years. Even for novices, on-the-job training was the order of the day for Lacey's early "apprentice monks."

The Saint Martin's Priory community gather at Lacey in 1908, left to right: Front row— Father Charles Lighthouse, Father Justin Welz, Monsignor Gustive Achtergael (visitor), Father Oswald Baran, Father Sebastian Ruth, and Father Mark Wiechman. Back row—Fathers Placidus Houtmeyers, Ulric Scheffold, George Scheffold, Francis O'Driscoll, Bernard Neary, and Matthew Britt. There was already more than enough work to go around at the College yet the monks also tried to fulfill the requests which kept coming in for additional pastoral assistance. (Saint Martin's Abbey Archives)

Helpers On Loan

New Benedictine monasteries and schools usually have had to beg and borrow necessary institutional components, including staff. In the early years of the twentieth century, additional Benedictine personnel from Saint John's Abbey periodically showed up in Washington. Their help was essential as the College's enrollment grew. It reached 125 by the 1905–1906 school year. Moreover, several of Saint Martin's priests had taken on expanded or even full-time pastoral duties away from the campus. A few of the "loaners" were to remain permanently at Saint Martin's while others offered important but temporary help.

Father Leonard Kapsner, thirty-five, had served as the director of the commercial college at Saint John's from 1902 to 1905. His religious superiors at Collegeville decided he needed a change and sent him—not entirely willingly—to help at Lacey in 1906 "pro tem." He taught twenty hours of classes a week at SMC and had care of two missions, thirty and forty miles from the campus. Noting the many pastoral tasks needing to be done on his rural missions, he admitted that "the continuous change of diet and irregular meals which traveling to the missions necessitated" occasionally bothered his "somewhat weak stomach." However, in March 1907, he reported to Abbot Peter: "I am well and am kept very busy" while also inquiring whether the abbot intended to call him home to Saint John's that summer. In August, he offered to remain in Washington for another year but said that he would object if his time at Lacey were again extended. He also expressed his irritation with the Saint Martin's monks who pestered him to transfer his affiliation to their monastery.

A December 1907 letter from Father Leonard to Abbot Peter raised a frequent concern of monasteries about their "loaned" help: "I would like to know, however, how long you would like me to stay here. You can certainly understand that it would be much better for me and Saint Martin's to know something definite about this." He then added: "You know very well that I never asked to come out here nor to stay." Not receiving an answer, he again wrote in January 1908: "Am expecting an answer soon to my last letter. The only thing I would like to know definitely is whether you intend to recall me next summer; and, if not, how long you want me to stay at Saint Martin's."

Informed in late January 1908 that he would be recalled to Minnesota that summer, in May Father Leonard—to his abbot's and perhaps to his own surprise—volunteered to stay

on at Lacey "for some time yet." While Saint John's most likely had all its slots filled for the next academic year, he reasoned, "they are continually looking for men" to staff SMC. Furthermore, he told Abbot Peter late that June that he was "now considering the pressing needs of Saint Martin's" and requested permission to "help them out another year." Frater Charles Lighthouse was due to be ordained a priest that summer and Frater Bernard Neary the next summer "so after that time they ought to be able to get along." Abbot Peter decided otherwise and appointed Father Leonard treasurer of Saint John's University starting in the fall of 1908.[104]

The College employed its first lay teacher, Mr. Charles Hoffman, from 1905 to 1909. He taught shorthand, typewriting, and penmanship and was well regarded.[105] Father George Scheffold, forty-two, at six-foot four-inches was then considered to be very tall indeed. A brother of Saint Martin's Father Ulric, he came to Lacey in September 1908 and helped out for a year teaching Latin, history, and German plus weekend pastoral assignments. His brother's tragic death from brain fever in Seattle in April 1909 probably hastened his return to Saint John's.

Homegrown Vocations

Past and present, various motives and conditions have prompted men to attempt to live a monastic life at Saint Martin's. Some have persevered; others have not. Two early cases are illustrative of the difficulty of such vocational discernment.

One man had taken his perpetual vows as a lay brother at Saint Martin's Priory on June 14, 1901. A few years later he sought and obtained permission to transfer his vows to a Trappist monastery in Oregon. He failed to become a Trappist but was unwilling to return to Lacey, claiming that Prior Demetrius had told him "that in the event of [his] return it had been resolved to kick him out." Therefore, he petitioned Abbot Peter Engel, as president of the American Cassinese Congregation of Monasteries which included Saint Martin's Priory, to be permanently dispensed from his Benedictine vows. With the approval of his two abbot "visitors" (consultors), Abbot Peter dispensed him from his vows.[106]

Late in 1908, Father Justin Welz, as the new acting superior of the monastery, interviewed a certain twenty-one-year-old "cleric" who was in his last year of studying theology at Lacey and in temporary vows as a Benedictine. It turned out that he had already *twice* applied for a dispensation from his monastic vows. Moreover, "he said he has no liking for the priesthood and that he never had any." When questioned as to why he had stayed at Saint Martin's, he said "that it was due to a sort of moral cowardice induced by the fact that he had received his education free" and "also through the influence of his mother." Father Justin reported: "He is convinced that he could never be contented and wants to return to the world. My personal observation has convinced me long ago that the man has no sense of responsibility and very little character." Father Justin left the decision of granting the requested dispensation to Abbot Peter—which he did.[107]

The monastic vocations of a few young men nurtured in Lacey during Saint Martin's early years did come to fruition. Charles Lighthouse, for example, enrolled in 1896 with New York listed as his home state. In June 1899, he won gold medals for both good conduct and highest average in the High School Department. Two years later, he was awarded another gold medal for excellence in the Classical Course. He belonged to the College's Literary and Dramatic Society and played in the Brass Band. He won both a master's of accounts diploma and a B.A. degree in June 1903.

He became a novice at our newly independent priory in 1904, pronounced his first vows in June 1905 and was ordained a priest in June 1908. All his education took place at Lacey. He would spend over thirty years successfully teaching and doing parish work until his death on May 5, 1939.

Nourishment for the Body

At Saint Martin's, as at any residential institution, food was (and is) an important aspect of campus life. Yet for several years, the best the College's early catalogs could claim for the school's fare was that it was "healthful and abundant" although "plain."[108] Brother William Baldus, Saint John's renowned long-term kitchen master, had come West in 1895 to take on the same job in Lacey but only stayed for one year. In 1896, he was replaced by Brother Edward Karge, who served in that capacity—although in declining health—until shortly before his death in March 1904.

Saint Martin's was thus fortunate to acquire, in May 1904, the services of three Benedictine Sisters from Saint Gertrude's Convent in Cottonwood, Idaho, to run its kitchen department. It is an interesting coincidence that almost simultane-

PICTURED BELOW: Benedictine Sisters from Cottonwood, Idaho, came to Lacey in May 1904 to run SMC's "kitchen department" and remained in charge of that vital component of campus life for over half a century. They also did sewing and mending for students and monks. Older monks and alumni still remember the Sisters with affection. As Abbot Oswald contentedly reported in 1917: "Our Sisters know how to economize and at the same time to keep the boys happy." (Saint Martin's Abbey Archives)

Organizations such as the "Saint Martin's Band" encouraged and displayed the musical talents of SMC's students and staff. This photo was posed in front of the campus gym about 1911 and shows the young musicians in their uniforms and Father Edward Weckert (left) and Father Sebastian Ruth in theirs! The Brass Band played for many occasions both on and off campus. (Saint Martin's Abbey Archives)

Although "serious" music was performed on liturgical and other occasions, campus residents and their guests also enjoyed more "popular" entertainments. On February 19, 1917, for example, the SMC Glee Club "staged some pleasing stunts" during a vaudeville program that was "a real hit!" Professor John Saint Onge, a well-trained Canadian musician, joined the College staff in 1915 for a long stay as director of music. Several of the early monks were also musically gifted. (Photo from Fleetwood Collection, Lacey Museum)

ously Saint John's was turning over its catering to Sisters of the Presentation from France. "The continuing difficulty of procuring suitable male hands to conduct the kitchen" had prompted both the Minnesota and the Washington monks to restaff their food service operation.[109]

Just a few yards to the northeast of the 1895 all-purpose College building, a house which had been built in 1902 to accommodate lay brothers and workers was quickly remodeled to suit the needs of newly arrived Mother Joanna, Sister Meinrada, and Sister Walburga. With very competent Benedictine Sisters in charge of the kitchen, the campus denizens breathed easily and ate well.

At the end of World War I in November 1918, Abbot Oswald noted the typical generosity of this group of sisters: "All the workmen have an increase in wages except the sisters. The superioress in Cottonwood surely is solicitous abut our welfare."[110] For over half a century, Benedictine Sisters from Saint Gertrude's would play a very important part in the life of the Saint Martin's family. They cooked, supervised the monks' and students' "refectories" or dining rooms, and also did mending and other sewing for students and monks alike. They were both frugal and popular. "Our Sisters know how to economize and at the same time how to keep the boys happy," Abbot Oswald contentedly reported in 1917.[111]

Campus Organizations

Much as with the structuring of its academic curricula, SMC developed its extracurricular student organizations simply by replicating on a smaller scale programs its faculty had been earlier involved in at Saint John's University. A 1907 *apologia* for "College Organizations" at Saint John's therefore almost certainly expressed both that institution's view and SMC's as well. It saluted "the various organizations, which, if not part of the educational curriculum, [had] in no small measure contributed to elevate the student body by cherishing the love of religion, by extending the knowledge obtained in the classroom, [and] by physical exercise calculated to preserve the vigor of the body which is so important during the years of study."[112]

During its early years, Saint Martin's was a small, self-contained institution yet even then the cultural amenities associated with a Benedictine monastery and school were not entirely lacking. The College's 1895 prospectus advertised instruction in the use of various musical instruments and the pioneer monks could put their hands or mouths to such with good

effect. The monks entertained themselves with in-house music-making and bands and vocal ensembles, composed of monks and students of varying ages and talent, were quickly assembled. Starting in 1901, the newly arrived Mr. A. J. Ruth (later Father Sebastian) was instrumental in these musical developments.

By the 1905–1906 school year, Father Sebastian's twenty-four-member Saint Cecilia's Choir was providing music for liturgical and other special occasions. In 1907 and subsequent years, an expanded ensemble "made up of the Band, Orchestra, and Choir" was calling itself the Saint Cecilia Philharmonic Society. Its purpose was "to give its members an opportunity of improving in vocal and instrumental music and to contribute to the appropriate celebration of religious, dramatic, and literary festivals."[113]

More "popular" music was also proffered to campus audiences in that era. In 1917 the campus boasted a fine Glee Club—the first of many such groups. "We had quite a musical treat [just] before Washington's Birthday," Abbot Oswald reported. "Our Glee Club, consisting of about twenty-five young men, staged some pleasing stunts. It was a general surprise the way those boys sang. I never witnessed anything like it in any College. I hope they will give us another surprise." Their program that February 19 was a vaudeville entertainment which included both vocal solos and ensemble numbers plus musical interludes by the College Band and *A Farce in One and a Half Acts*. Not exactly highbrow entertainment but quite obviously a bang-up hit at our adolescent institution![114]

Father Sebastian also led the SMC Brass Band, which enlivened such annual campus celebrations as Saint Martin's Day (November 11), the December Yule Tide [sic] entertainment, the Washington's Birthday observance (February 22), and the June Commencement Day ceremonies. The school's Dramatic Association performed at those same functions. In 1905–1906, for example, it staged a pair of two-act comedies entitled *Vacation* and *The Captain's Idea or The Living Statue*, as well as more inspirational dramas concerning *The Boys of '76* and *Edward the Confessor or Sceptre or Sword*.[115] By December 1913, members of the Dramatics Club were preparing to appear at the Olympia Opera House for the first time. Their production was a three-act comedy, *The Fatal Shot*, which had first been staged on campus a year earlier to many encores. All but two members of the original cast had returned to school and, with a pair of new players, they were "rehearsing diligently" under the direction of Father Placidus Houtmeyers.

"Both the college band and orchestra" would "play some snappy selections between acts and during the play itself."[116]

The school's Dramatic Association had as its stated object in 1905 "the cultivation of elocutionary and dramatic talent" and was committed to furnishing "suitable entertainments during the school year." A Literary and Debating Society was later established "to foster a taste for literature and eloquence." It held weekly meetings and "its exercises consist[ed] in the readings of original essays, in declamation and debates."[117] The Society also sponsored debates on such topical issues as "That Capital Punishment Is Justifiable" (December 22, 1908) and "That Woman Suffrage Be Enacted in Every State in the Union" (May 11, 1911). It is interesting to note that the latter debate was handily won by the affirmative side on our all-male campus.[118] Another student organization, the College Congress, "organized and conducted on the same plan as the United States Congress," was "intended to impart to its members a thorough knowledge of the use of parliamentary law, and at the same time frequent practice in the art of extemporaneous debate." In 1913–1914, Senate sessions of the student Congress were held every Tuesday evening, while the House convened on Friday evenings. Public sessions were also held from time to time.[119]

Professor Carpenter

An elderly man of somewhat mysterious antecedence joined the College staff in September 1898. He was listed in the school catalog through 1906 as Mr. Joseph Carpenter although he was soon commonly called "Professor." He offered classes in music, drawing, and painting, was quickly recognized as "a skilled organist and musician" and was also a gifted watercolorist

Born in Manchester, England, probably on February 10, 1828, his given name was J. F. Cutts. Some difficulty caused him to leave England, and he moved to Victoria, British Columbia, about 1889, calling himself Joseph Carpenter. After several years in that Canadian city, where he is known to have exhibited his watercolor sketches, he moved to Seattle. In the fall of 1898, he showed up at Saint Martin's offering his talents to the tiny school in exchange for a place to peacefully spend his final years.

On November 14, 1898, Father Oswald informed Abbot Peter of the College's godsend: "I have secured a good piano teacher who will hold his own. [He is] an Englishman seventy-two [*sic*] years old but still very active and vigorous. His desire is to spend the remaining days of his existence in a religious house, offering in return his services and some real estate valued at about $500. At the same time he is a painter, not exactly a master, but [he] puts up pretty fair pictures. He will undoubtedly be of great benefit when we put up our stage in the [Play Hall] and want some scenes. A large painting of his is in the chapel and adds much beauty to the same."

In the spring of 1899, Father Oswald requested the authorities at Collegeville to provide SMC with additional artist's material for Professor Carpenter to use. One of his paintings was soon displayed at the state legislature and plans were made to exhibit several of his canvases in Tacoma to advertise the College. Carpenter apparently left SMC sometime after 1906 and died in 1911. He was buried in a now unmarked grave the Olympia area's Catholic cemetery.[120]

Devotional Clubs

Other early SMC student organizations included various devotional clubs. The Sodality of the Blessed Virgin Mary (1906) fostered "a filial devotion to the Immaculate Mother of God, and the practice of virtue and piety among its members." The Saint John Berchmans' Sanctuary Society (1902) trained boys to serve in the sanctuary for various Catholic worship services "in the modesty and decorum essential to so exalted a function." Father Matthew Britt had presided over a similar student organization at Saint John's University starting 1896. In 1899, he wrote for the benefit of his Sanctuary Society members a "Ceremonial for Altar Boys," which was later revised and published nationally. When Father Matthew came west in 1900, he brought an interest in developing such a society at Lacey with him.[121]

A local chapter of The League of the Sacred Heart, Apostleship of Prayer propagated "Devotion to the Sacred Heart of Jesus" and sought to facilitate among its student members "the attainment of Virtue and Christian Piety."[122] Abbot Peter had sponsored the League's Saint John's University chapter starting in 1896 and an SMC chapter was soon sanctioned. Piety as well as knowledge was to be inculcated at Washington's Benedictine college.

Athletics with a Purpose

The College's earliest sports teams were intramural clubs which help make available the exercise so greatly need by its adolescent enrollees. In 1907, the school's formal Athletic

Association (in which membership was compulsory for all students) was describing its functions in this way: "The Baseball, Basketball, Handball, Tennis, and Bowling Clubs are controlled by a Board of Managers, whose duty it is to furnish all members with sufficient opportunities for physical development and to encourage them to participate in these healthful games and sports."[123] In 1910, a "handsome, modern" gymnasium, ninety by forty-eight feet, was built on the flats east of the hill. It had a good selection of apparatus, a full-sized handball court, and could be used for basketball and indoor baseball as a spectators' gallery was also provided. A fully equipped stage occupied the west end of the new building with furnace and dressing room situated underneath.[124]

"On the principle that a sound mind inhabits a sound body," the school's catalog stated in 1911, "the faculty encourages athletics; but at no season of the year are sports permitted to interfere with the regular routine of study and recitation." The athletic grounds covered more than twelve acres. There were three baseball diamonds, a football field, tennis courts, a track or oval (five laps to the mile), and "ample room for every

SMC's 1907 basketball players were probably as serious about their game as they themselves appear to be in this photo! Their coach (back row third from right) was the athletically gifted John Weckert, who as Father Edward later became the College's athletic director. (Saint Martin's Abbey Archives)

71

form of manly sports." By 1913, SMC had a well-articulated philosophy of athletics. It considered "athletic sports among its students" to be "a legitimate source of recreation, of healthful exercise, of generous rivalry and manly spirit." As "a useful means for the physical and moral development" of its students, the College put within their reach "whatever will help for these purposes." It also "set such restrictions as will prevent, as far as may be, the abuse of college sport, to the detriment of scholarship, manliness, and gentlemanly courtesy."

Intercollegiate athletic competition was ideally described as a contest between gentlemen. In pursuit of that ideal, "the authorities of the College have moved steadily toward the elimination of excess, commercialism, and ungenerous rivalry in an inordinate desire to win." Amateur sport was insisted upon; "anything savoring of professionalism" would not be tolerated. No "ringers" would be enrolled nor any "gratuity" provided for students "solely on account of their athletic ability." Games with outside teams were to be scheduled "only on vacation days, so as not to interfere with the regular class schedule."[125]

An earlier 1906 statement of the College's overall educational philosophy was equally forthright: *As educators, the Benedictines aim at thoroughness and solidity; they deplore the present-day tendency towards superficiality, and recognize it is one of the greatest evils in modern educational methods. The Benedictine idea of education is the full and harmonious development of the mind and heart. Even effort is made by the faculty to inculcate principles of virtue and self-respect, and to*

PICTURED LEFT:
Eveline Kenney of Lacey became SMC's first "Rally Girl" around 1908. Born in 1891, she and her twin sister, Irene, had moved to Lacey when their parents became managers of the town's hotel in 1900. Growing up in a small settlement next to an all-male campus must have been exciting for the two girls and also, as this photo suggests, a treat for SMC's lads! (Photo courtesy Corinne Schilling Farmer)

PICTURED ABOVE:
SMC's baseball teams, starting in 1906, included a very gifted player in John Weckert (first row, second from left). Known as Father Edward after joining the monastery, he was a coach and athletic director for SMC until 1930. He then spent some thirty years as a parish priest and part-time Northwest talent scout for professional baseball teams! (Saint Martin's Abbey Archives)

build up strong, manly characters who will become ornaments to society and a credit to their Alma Mater.[126]

Entertainments

During its first decades, Saint Martin's comfortably served as the entertainment center of its then rural environs. Its musical and dramatic "entertainments," along with its athletic events, were important aspects of both campus and Lacey life. "Most of the programs [were] made up exclusively of home talent, the Dramatic Clubs and Musical Organizations of the college furnishing talent for excellent amateur productions."[127] Sports were pursued with gusto and pride. Agnes Button (born 1899) was baptized in SMC's first chapel and has spent most of her life in Lacey. In her childhood and youth, she attended many religious services on campus and enjoyed participating in outdoor devotional processions. With her family, she enjoyed the College's annual athletic Field Days (which started in 1905), ice cream socials, outdoor band concerts, and, especially, baseball games. She also recalls that the College band would meet a returning team at the Lacey railroad station and march them back the quarter-mile to the hill. "Oh, yes," Mrs. Button remembers with a gleam in her eyes, "the entertainment [in those days] was Saint Martin's College!"[128]

Building Up a Library

There was a recognized need for a "library" at SMC even in its first years of operation. What was most desired in that era was a good collection of reference and textbooks. In March 1896, for example, young Frater Benedict Schmit, in order to dispel the fear "that I would immediately ask for a library," responded to a recent letter from Abbot Peter: "The fact that I do not write for a stack of books must, however, not lead you to the conclusion that they are a superfluous article in Saint Martin's." He then solicited a reliable encyclopedia and other volumes that would be useful to him in teaching classes.[129] In June 1905, Prior Demetrius wrote the Saint John's University librarian to thank him for books recently received from Collegeville for the still diminutive SMC library collection: "Our carpenter, Father Ulric, is at present making an extension to our shelving in the library [room] to receive these books. Some of these are certainly very desirable; others will interest such who have never seen an old book and the latter belong indeed to a monastery library. Numerically, they almost double our library. You can therefore see that ours is not very large yet."[130]

By 1908, the school library was described in this fashion: "A select library of choice literature is at the disposal of the students. The books required for reading in the academic and collegiate courses are obtainable from the students' library. Each student is assessed a dollar a year for the use of the library." Three years later, a reading room "conducted by the members of the Literary and Debating Society" had been set up. It was furnished with "the best literary magazines and reviews" as well as daily and weekly papers and "current numbers of scientific and technical journals."[131]

Prior Problems

Father Demetrius Jueneman was elected the first governing prior of the newly independent monastery at Lacey in March 1904. He soon came to feel crowded in the job, however, and heavily burdened by his responsibilities. In June 1905, he displayed his unease in a letter to an old friend: "Who would have thought several years ago that I would be sitting where I am, certainly not I. I hope we will soon fill the required number for an Abbey so we can have another election so I can shake off the burden."[132]

Murmuring and bickering, and the clash of personalities and temperaments, have seldom been absent from monastic life. Such predictable human frailties have shown themselves again and again at Saint Martin's. A few times such disgruntlement has turned ugly, as it certainly did during Father Demetrius' years as prior.

On May 30, 1908, Prior Demetrius wrote directly to the Benedictine Abbot Primate in Rome indicating that he was sick of his job and wished to resign. There were six months to go in his five-year term and he had no desire of being reelected. In fact, he enclosed a petition addressed to the Holy Father personally asking that he be allowed to resign his office immediately. He alluded to dissatisfaction among Saint Martin's priests, and stated that his continuing in office might make him mentally ill. Finally, he stated a longtime desire to enter the Cistercian order.

The Abbot Primate wrote to Abbot Peter of Saint John's Abbey, who was then president of the American Cassinese Congregation of monasteries, inquiring whether he had been consulted by Father Demetrius and stating that he thought the Holy Father should be spared such requests. Why should Father Demetrius simply not stick it out until the end of his term and then just not accept a second term?

Explaining his actions after the fact in a confidential letter to Abbot Peter, Father Demetrius was more specific. "There is

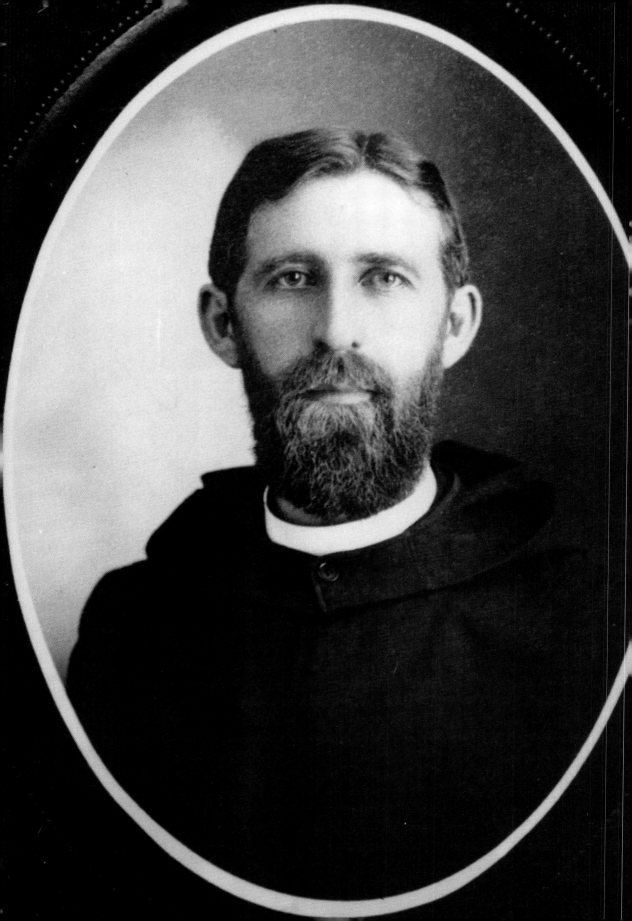

not the kind of mutual feeling among the Fathers [at Saint Martin's] that there should be and I know that I cannot improve matters but a change may do so." He admitted that when he had been in Minnesota for his mother's funeral two months earlier he had no intention of resigning, but after his return to Washington something occurred which caused him to give up.

One of the priory's neighbors, who had always had it in for Father Demetrius, had begun "to slander and calumniate me in the worst way and continues to do so." He spread reports that the prior was frequenting the company of "certain young ladies" as he made his rounds of the area buying food and feed for campus use directly from various farmers. One of the College's priests believed those reports and spread them among the other monks. This gossip had swelled to include assertions that Father Demetrius "was trying to break up the community" while in fact no one had worked harder for the betterment of Saint Martin's than he. Because "a superior must have a better name than that," he concluded that it was proper for him to resign. He asked Abbot Peter that his resignation be treated confidentially for no one at Lacey yet knew about it. He also pleaded with him to have the Abbot Primate quickly accept his resignation.[133]

Matters did not, however, move quickly in resolving the leadership problem at Saint Martin's Priory. "All the Fathers and members of Saint Martin's are still in good spirits," Father Justin reported in December 1908, "but they do begin to think that Rome is more than proverbially slow in regard to the prior affair. We sincerely hope that all will be settled soon."[134] Father Demetrius' resignation was at last accepted by the Holy See and on February 18, 1909, Father Justin was elected to a five-year term as Saint Martin's second governing prior.[135]

However, both Father Justin's narrow electoral margin— five to three over Father Ulric on the fourth ballot—and the small size of the Priory's full-fledged membership indicates the still fragile nature of Saint Martin's.

Keeping the Campus Healthy

Illness in a boarding school context can seriously jeopardize an institution if not quickly and suitably handled. In its first catalog, the College prudently notified parents and guardians that if and when their boys took ill "medical attendance and medicines" were available but "at physician's charges."[136] Starting in 1902, and for several years thereafter, SMC listed G. W. Ingham, M.D., of Olympia as its "Attending

LEFT PAGE:

In March 1904, Father Demetrius Jueneman (1866–1948) was elected the first prior of the newly independent Benedictine monastery at Lacey and thereby also became SMC's chief administrator. Financial problems frustrated Father Demetrius and personal clashes with other monks eventually made his situation unbearable. He resigned in May 1908 and went off on his own for some years but later held other pastoral assignments. When Saint Martin's celebrated its fiftieth anniversary in 1945, Father Demetrius was warmly saluted as Saint Martin's sole surviving pioneer monk. (Saint John's Abbey Archives)

Workers in 1910 use hydraulic pressure to widen creek channel for dam; bearded monk observing workers is Father Mark Wiechman.

Workers lay a foundation for the dam in the creek bed.

A monk sits atop the dam, now completed with pensto and flume.

The impoundment behind the dam was a popular swimming and diving area for students, monks, and Lacey neighbors.

Barging on the "flooded" creek was also a campus pastime.

Writing in *Between the Years* (1945), Saint Martin's fiftieth anniversary volume, Father Sebastian Ruth narrates an electrifying incident:

A copious stream [Woodland Creek] running through the northern half of the College property suggested the idea of a dam that would store sufficient water for the operation of a turbine, which in turn would furnish the power for the operation of a dynamo. The idea was followed up and a dam twenty feet high was built [in 1910] across the stream bed which had been widened and deepened. A three-foot penstock led from the lower part of the dam to the "power house" two hundred feet downstream, where, straddling the stream, was a building about twenty feet square housing the turbine, excitor and dynamo. At last the work was pronounced complete, and the gate closed and the water allowed to begin filling the dam.

A tall tree spans a deep campus section of Woodland Creek.

Disaster, however, was in store for the new project. The next morning, the south side of the dam, where the bank was of sand formation, gradually gave way, and an immense volume of water suddenly burst through, crashed down the creek bed, along the penstock, and jarred the power house from its foundations.

It was some months later, after repairs were made, that the [campus] light plant was in operation. The hydro-electric plant was not as satisfactory as had been expected [because] the supply of water varied and at times sufficient volume to activate the generator was wanting.

Although the Woodland Creek dam turned out to be unreliable in terms of generating electric power for SMC's needs, the "swimming hole" created behind the 1910 dam proved very popular with campus people and neighbors. In 1921 it was cleared of all obstructions and sand spread on its south side and for many years thereafter provided a fine swimming pool seventy-five by thirty feet and up to thirty feet deep in places The last dam on the campus section of the creek was removed in the 1950s at the insistence of the Washington State Fisheries Department.

Physician." Mr. A. J. Ruth (the future Father Sebastian), noted in his diary for 1901–1902 that a number of students were sick with "grip and colds" and one was "pretty bad." Another boy had "sprained both ankles while playing among the rafters above stage in Play Hall" and was laid up for several days. Tragedy also struck one of the two young brothers from Montesano who had only been brought to the school by Father Justin on November 4. Daniel Gleeson, age thirteen, was "very sick" by December 20 and "died at Olympia Hospital attended by Father Matthew" at 9:00 a.m. on Christmas Day.[137]

A good water supply has long been a prized asset for monasteries and schools and topped the list of requisites when the new College's campus was located in Lacey in 1894.

A good water supply has long been a prized asset for monasteries and schools. In 1904, "a wooden structure octagonal in shape and seventy feet high, on top of which rested the wooden 50,000 gallon tank," was erected on the north end of the hill. Water that was taken from the creek was not used for drinking or cooking purposes so "a smaller steel tank was located underneath the large wooden one and kept filled with fresh water from the well located below the hill in the laundry building." A decade later, Father Sebastian's "radio shack" was built just south of the water tower to house his "wireless radio" apparatus. (Saint Martin's Abbey Archives)

SMC's 1908–1909 catalog addressed the matter forthrightly: "The College is supplied with an abundance of pure water. Two water systems have been installed, one for drinking and culinary purposes, the other for bathing and laundry use and fire protection. The drinking water is pumped daily from a deep well which is scrupulously guarded from any source on contamination. To remove all doubt as to the quality of the drinking water, and to be able to assure our patrons of its superior qualities, the water has been subjected to a chemical analysis, the result of which is herewith given." According to a May 18, 1907 report from the Seattle Testing Laboratory, the campus drinking water sample submitted for testing was found to be "excellent" and "well suited for potable purposes." This endorsement was reprinted in several annual catalogs.[138] The following contemporary statement suggests that cleanliness must truly have been next to godliness at Saint Martin's in that era: "The College has a completely equipped steam laundry, and as students are expected to be always clean, no limit is placed upon the amount of laundry done for them."[139]

Following an epidemic of smallpox in June 1911, "the need of an infirmary became evident and a suitable building was erected" below and just to the west of the hill. Constructed by brothers and lay help, it measured forty feet square and provided isolated quarters for the sick in "three private rooms, a ward for four beds, a diet kitchen, dispensary and quarters for an infirmarian."[140]

Childhood diseases (such as measles or other contagious outbreaks) and predictable adolescent accidents (sports-related

In 1911, Saint Martin's lay brothers and "hired hands" constructed a campus infirmary [seen at the right in this photo] on the western slope of the hill. By isolating the sick, the infirmary helped to contain contagious diseases from spreading among the school's students. The infirmarian also provided them—and the monks—with basic medical assistance and maintained a doctor on call. In the early 1960s a new infirmary was built in "Saint Placid Hall." The old structure was burned down as a fire-fighting exercise in 1967. (Saint Martin's Abbey Archives)

or otherwise) confined many a student to the care of successive
infirmarians over the years. At certain times elderly campus
workers, who had become part of the monastery's extended
family circle, also were housed for longer or shorter periods in
the campus infirmary.

Red Letter Day at SMC

In August 1912, Lacey's Benedictine monks approved in
principle and initiated planning for a new and much larger
building for their seventeen-year-old institution. They acted
"to meet the need of proper accommodations" for an "increasing student attendance." A construction loan was secured from
the Wiegman Bank of Amsterdam, Holland. Planning and
design for the project would be supervised by a Tacoma architect, C. Frank Mahon. Ground was broken February 10, 1913,
for the construction of a four-story brick and concrete structure, two hundred by sixty feet in size, of Collegiate Gothic
style.[141] Saint John's Abbey also generously contributed
$5,000.[142]

One Olympia reporter described the completed structure
as being "pleasing in the varishaded hues" of its "dark-colored
brick" and "trimmed with terra cotta" making it "by far the
finest owned by any college in this part of the state." He also
noted with approval that is was "lighted throughout with elec-
tricity, supplied by the college hydroelectric plant" but lighting
gas was also available "in all but the sleeping rooms."[143] The
fine new building was to be the first unit of an anticipated hilltop complex optimistically called "Greater Saint Martin's."

When completed in the fall of 1913, its full basement story contained scientific labs and lecture rooms as well as two social halls. Private shower baths, a barbershop, "stationery department" and "confectionery store" were also situated on the ground floor. The first floor housed administrative offices, parlors, some guest rooms for overnight accommodation, and two large study halls. Eight "large and well-lighted" classrooms occupied the southern side of the second floor while eighteen private rooms for boarding students were situated on the northern side of that story. Two "large general dormitories," sixty by sixty feet, with adjacent toilet and washroom facilities, took up much of the third-floor area. It also contained two "spacious" and well-equipped locker rooms and several additional private bedrooms.[144]

The new structure, it was reported, was "thoroughly modern" and "fire hazard" had been "reduced to a minimum as the heating plant and boiler rooms" were "located outside the building and a complete system of fire prevention had been installed." The original 1895 multipurpose building would continue to house the campus dining rooms, kitchen, and chapel.[145] With the College's 140 students happily domiciled in the new building, the monks were grateful "that at last to some extent" they would be "able to enjoy the peace and quiet of monastic life."[146]

To pay for the $75,000 new facility, SMC's sponsoring community of monks had decided to log off the standing tim-

With the completion in the fall of 1913 of its new, four-story brick building, SMC promoted itself as "the ideal school" with modern buildings, a healthful location, picturesque surroundings and "thorough instruction" in "College, High School and Grammar Grades." (Saint Martin's Abbey Archives)

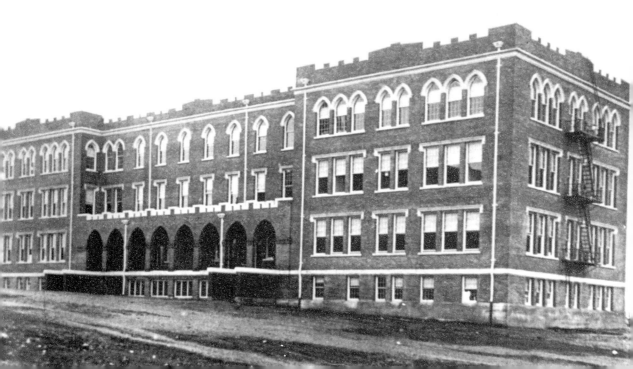

*A visitor from the past: Anthony S. "Tony" Weber visited
SMC in April 1991 and toured the Abbey Cemetery while
reminiscing with campus historian Father John Scott.
Born near Tacoma in 1899, he attended grade school classes
at Saint Martin's as a "day student" starting in 1907.
His family moved away in 1912 but Tony never forgot
the personal and caring attention he received from Father
Sebastian Ruth and others. (Photo by Deanna Partlow)*

ber on the college property. In March 1913, it was announced that the purchaser of that timber, a Mr. Raleigh W. Cady, was preparing to set up a logging camp that would probably employ from forty to seventy-five men "until late in the coming fall." The construction of a railroad spur into the campus woods from the main line would start soon. In April, it was reported that Cady had also purchased the standing timber on "several other contiguous sections" of land adjacent to the campus thus assuring logging operations continuing over several seasons.[147]

The solemn blessing and dedication of the new building took place on Sunday, November 16, 1913. It was a great day, indeed! "The largest gathering that had ever assembled in the little town of Lacey was present at the dedication" and over five hundred people signed the guest book that day. The Olympia council of the Knights of Columbus, a Catholic men's fraternal and mutual benefit society, coordinated the day's events. Bishop Edward J. O'Dea performed the solemn blessing of the new structure starting at 2:30 p.m. The "main exercises" of the afternoon began at 3:00 p.m. with various congratulatory and inspirational speeches. The College Band was in fine form, serenading and inspiring the large crowd. After the talks, the multitude inspected the not-yet fully furnished new building and enjoyed a supper prepared by the ladies of Olympia's Saint Michael's Parish.[148]

Two of the day's occasional speakers, Governor Ernest R. Lister and State Supreme Court Justice Stephen J. Chadwick, "urged the need in present-day secular education of getting back to the old standard whereby the teacher came into individual contact with his pupils."[149] That, of course, is exactly what SMC had been doing since it first opened its doors in 1895! ❧

During the institution's adolescence, the physical plant of
Saint Martin's College underwent several spurts of growth.
In the winter of 1919–1920, the west wing of an anticipated
"Greater Saint Martin's" hilltop complex was under construction. The wooden 1895 College building with its 1904
addition obscures most of the 1913 brick south wing.
Ambitious plans for a matching north wing and a short
central wing connecting to a large Abbey Church were never
realized. The cleared land below the hill extends across the
1918 Pacific Highway (now Pacific Avenue and the campus'
southern boundary) to the parallel Northern Pacific
Railroad tracks. (Photo by Albert Fisher, SMC '22)

CHAPTER 4
An Adolescent Institution
(1914–1928)

❧

AT THE TIME OF HIS ELECTION ON MAY 19, 1914, as the first abbot of the new Saint Martin's Abbey, Father Oswald Baran, O.S.B., had been away from Lacey for a decade working as a parish priest. Although he had served as the first director of Saint Martin's College from 1895 to 1900, it thus took him a while to readjust to living in a monastery and to managing a boarding school. SMC was still an adolescent institution—literally and figuratively— when Abbot Oswald again took charge. Happily, he turned out to be a modest and hardworking individual who set an upbeat tone for the new Abbey and its growing College. Both owe him a great deal.

The new abbot's letters to his friend and mentor, Abbot Peter Engel (1856–1921) of Saint John's Abbey, provide intriguing glimpses into life at Saint Martin's between 1914 and 1921. They also reveal Abbot Oswald to have been a competent, caring, and often humorous individual. Two weeks after his September 29, 1914 abbatial blessing, which Abbot Peter had attended, he reported to his mentor: "Here I am, sitting in the room I formerly occupied. I am slowly getting acquainted with my duties and trying to accustom myself to the routine of daily life. I have not yet missed any of the hours of the Choir [that is, of the scheduled periods when monks pray together]. Isn't that astonishing? I have no complaints to make. The men in the community are good and kind to me and I think we all get along well. The change from the surroundings and occupations in Tacoma [where he had served as a pastor] to the conditions here is too great to be easily made, at least for me. No doubt after some time I will feel more at home and more contented." Two months later, Abbot Oswald wrote another close friend at Saint John's, Father Alexius Hoffmann, describing his attitude toward his newly acquired position: "I [still] do not realize even at this late date that I am supposed to be a dignitary of the Church. It will take me some months or years to fully comprehend my situation and by that time I may be worn out and ready to depart from this change-

On September 29, 1914, the solemn abbatial blessing of
Abbot Oswald Baran took place in Tacoma. Holy Rosary
Church's interim worship space in the 1911 parish school was
used because Father Oswald had been pastor there at the time
of his election and the College chapel in Lacey was too small.
The blessing was conferred by Bishop Edward O'Dea of
Seattle and Oregon's Archbishop Alexander Christie deliv-
ered the occasional address. Hundreds of parishioners and
fifty-eight Catholic priests from all parts of the Northwest
were in attendance. Shown in front of the school are Abbot
Oswald (in dark robes), Bishop O'Dea and Archbishop
Christie. In the second row is the bearded Father Mark
Wiechman, the church's new pastor, and in the middle
of the third row in the dark cassock is Father Justin Welz,
who had been the prior at Lacey. (Saint Martin's Abbey
Archives)

Elected Saint Martin's first abbot by his fellow monks on May 19, 1914, Abbot Oswald Baran (1866–1928) was a modest and hard-working individual who set an upbeat tone for his new Abbey and its growing College. SMC's first director in 1895 and a popular pastor thereafter, he was a competent, caring, and often humorous individual as evidenced by his many surviving letters. (Saint Martin's Abbey Archives)

Abbot Peter Engel (1856–1921) headed Minnesota's Saint John's Abbey and University from November 1894 until his death and visited western Washington several times. Abbot Oswald frequently and confidently appealed to him for moral and material support for Lacey's Benedictine monastery and school. He also considered Abbot Peter the "true founder" of Saint Martin's because of the substantial assistance he provided the young institution over many years. (Saint John's Abbey Archives)

able world. I consider myself, as I told the [monastic] community in 'Culpa,' their companion and colaborer for the good of the Order and I hope that my actions do not belie my words."[150]

A Scheduled Life

During 1914–1915, Saint Martin's College enrolled a total of 152 boys and young men, the large majority of whom resided on campus. Most were registered in programs leading either to the eighth grade certificate or to the high school diploma, while others were taking college-level courses. The school had a Benedictine faculty of twelve priests and six clerics as well as two laymen. Meals and mending were provided by a handful of Benedictine Sisters, who usually were the only women seen on campus on a daily basis. The "Daily Routine" of the College's students was tightly scheduled and ran from a 6:00 a.m. rising to an 8:30 p.m. retiring seven days a week. The monks, however, started their days at 5:00 a.m. with morning prayers in common, and the Sisters equally early with their own regimen of devotions.

As noted earlier, recreational activities for students, including sports and musical and dramatic endeavors, were strongly encouraged and heartily joined in.[151] Custodial care and keep for boys without other options was fairly common at Saint Martin's in its early decades. One such case was reported by Abbot Oswald to his Minnesota counterpart in January 1915: "Tony Heider [who had Collegeville connections] is slowly dying in hospital in Olympia. His two boys are with us."[152] One of those boys, Albert, then aged eleven, would remain at Saint Martin's. As Father Raphael, he would be elected our third abbot in 1943.

In the first decades of the twentieth century, SMC was a small, intense and, apparently, generally happy world. "One day follows the other with the same routine," Abbot Oswald observed in November 1914: "All hands and heads seem sufficiently occupied with the daily task. Our College has over 150 students enrolled and the staff of professors just about matches the work required by this number." Thirty-five students were enrolled in the new Commercial Department. The abbot himself taught high school–level courses in Latin, business arithmetic, and algebra and also handled the institution's finances. "My voluminous correspondence is not of the poetic or sentimental kind but consists principally of the prosaic payment of the bills," he reported. Yet he also added with pleasure: "The boys seem to be much satisfied and I am surely satisfied because they will be our best advertisement."

Abbot Oswald also filed a weather report in the same November 9 letter: "Our weather conditions are good, bad, and indifferent. We have had over nine inches of rain since September. It was a blessing for us for we have electric light most of the time [from the College's hydroelectric facility on the campus section of Woodland Creek] and can save on gas" for the 1913 building's gaslights. An improvement had also recently been made to the heating system, so all the buildings on the hill were snugly steam-heated.[153]

In mid-December 1914, SMC's students "took great delight" in "wearing out the soles of their shoes skidding on the sidewalk" between the new College building and the 1895 structure which housed the monks. A happy escapee from Minnesota winters, Abbot Oswald commented: "Temperature has been about 20 degrees and excepting the kids everyone is sighing for the moisture from above, in sheets or drops, as long as it is rain."[154] The abbot was the only priest at home for Christmas as the rest of the Abbey's priests were away conducting services at parishes and missions. So "with the novices and about five clerics" (there were no brothers in the community at that time and he does not mention the Sisters), Abbot Oswald celebrated Christmas of 1914 "in a sort of primitive style" on the quiet campus. He had also come down with a bad cold: "I sang a High Mass with falsetto voice and preached, I mean whispered, a sermon of Christmas joys that nearly caused a flood of tears in the audience. Barring the miserable cold, I spent a pleasant vacation."[155]

While somewhat sequestered, Saint Martin's was not entirely disconnected from off-campus events and activities. The College's 1917–1918 catalog, for example, listed the cam-

The boys and young men who were enrolled in SMC's grammar, high school, and college programs in this era were expected by their parents to experience a scheduled and well-supervised life while on campus. Thus the College's students followed a "Daily Routine" which allowed adequate time for sleep, study, and exercise. Mass and other devotions were a daily occurrence and ample meals were served family style in the student refectory. Their Benedictine teachers conscientiously provided paternal encouragement and careful supervision along with a solid education. (Saint Martin's Abbey Archives)

Snow is usually rare enough in Lacey to be considered a treat. In this snowy panorama dated about 1921–1922, clusters of SMC students are seen enjoying a hike along the stretch of the Pacific Highway (now Pacific Avenue) that formed the southern boundary of the campus. The College buildings form an impressive "acropolis" on the hill and the surrounding evergreens a scenic palisade. (Photo by Albert Fisher, SMC '22)

pus' many connections to the larger world. "All mail matter" was to be addressed to SMC via the U.S. Post Office in Lacey, but express and freight should be sent to the local railroad express agency and "must be prepaid." Telegrams were received at the Olympia telegraph office "and phoned to the College without delay." The campus had "two long distance telephones, one installed in the Faculty Building [the monastery], the other in the College." No collect calls were accepted. The Grays Harbor branch of the Northern Pacific Railway had a Lacey station a quarter-mile from the College. "Parents, guardians or friends accompanying students to the College or visiting them during the school year" were advised that they would "find good accommodations at reasonable rates at the Woodland Hotel, situated within five minutes' walk of the College." Despite the above praise, SMC's Lacey was still "a quiet little village of about seven hundred inhabitants"[156]

Additional priests were greatly needed for the Abbey's increasing pastoral commitments: "We had the Bishop here to ordain four clerics subdeacon and deacon. They will be ordained priests at the beginning of June [1915] I think," reported Abbot Oswald. "We will need these men because the Bishop will give us some parishes." The parish at Cle Elum on the eastern slope of the Cascade Mountains was available immediately. The abbot had also asked Bishop O'Dea "for a foothold in Seattle" and had been promised one "at the proper time." Toward the end of 1916, Abbot Oswald visited the Benedictine pastor of Cle Elum and with him inspected nearby Roslyn, which Bishop O'Dea had recently offered to the monks. "It looked good to me and so I prevailed upon the [monastic] chapter to accept it. There are enough baptized miners in that coal region to keep two men busy but the best that can be said of them is that they had received the sacrament of baptism. We made a big sacrifice by sending one of our best teachers to the place but he was the only one who could speak to the different nationalities represented there. We manage to get along without him."[157]

For decades, salaries and gifts turned in by Saint Martin's Benedictine parish priests, and by those priest-teachers who served churches and missions part-time on weekends and holy days or during the summer, helped to underwrite campus operations while providing needed pastoral services to western Washington's Catholics. Such pastoral work also served to advertise SMC to prospective students and interested parents.

Father Sebastian and Campus Publications

The history of campus publications is closely associated with Father Sebastian Ruth (1875–1958). The first edition of *The Martian*, a seventy-page quarterly, appeared in January 1914 under his auspices and contained fiction and poetry as well as general campus news. Students contributed some of the stories and articles but the hand of Father Sebastian was everywhere apparent in that issue as well as in subsequent publications that appeared under his sponsorship. In 1924 *The Martian*'s format changed to a monthly four-page newspaper. In 1925, the monk-editor inaugurated a campus yearbook, the *Martian Annual*. Redubbed the *Samarco* in 1927, it served both our High School and College students until the establishment of a separate High School annual, *Samahi* (1947–1974). The College yearbook continued regular publication through 1984, and a special Centennial *Samarco* was published in 1995.

In April 1934 the *Benedictine Monachist*, edited and largely written by Father Sebastian, began bimonthly publication with the goal of stimulating further interest in things Benedictine and religious. Appearing monthly until 1950, it was a veritable gold mine of information on such topics as "Benedictiana." The magazine also fostered vocations to the Abbey and encouraged benefactors to support Saint Martin's programs. The *Monachist* was artistically laid out and printed by Father Sebastian in the campus print shop—another of his "hobbies" between 1916 to near the time of his death.[158]

Saint Martin's remained an adolescent institution even after it officially became an independent Abbey on April 18, 1914. For the next several years, Abbot Oswald frequently and confidently appealed to Abbot Peter of Saint John's Abbey, whom he thought ought to be considered the true founder of Saint Martin's, for both moral and material support: "Well, I do not think that I will have to do overmuch worrying of what we are going to eat and how we are to meet conditions if we can fall back on a resourceful parent."[159] It was simply taken for granted that Saint John's, through Abbot Peter, would lend a hand when needed to its budding Washington offspring: "From your chair you were looking westward and a vision of a growing 'son' or 'daughter', as the case may be, (at one time, I think, you called it a 'baby') appeared before you and you resolved to send an allowance to this distant child."[160]

One way Saint John's Abbey helped its "daughterhouse" was to send many of its own surplus Mass intentions to Lacey. Masses would be offered by Saint Martin's priests for the specified intentions of the donors and the attached stipends would be used to defray expenses at the Washington monastery and school. Just before Christmas in 1914, Abbot Oswald again thanked his Minnesota benefactor for sending a $100 check for Mass stipends and noted that it was "a big help."[161] Abbot Oswald thereafter frequently asked for "a good batch of intentions" because his abbey was strapped for cash or asked "to have credit again at Saint John's."[162]

By drawing on Saint Martin's "credit" at the Minnesota abbey, Abbot Oswald could obtain such items as monastic habits (at $27.50 per habit), secondhand Latin breviaries and other church-goods, or even pay off small loans. Necessity engendered humor between the two old friends: "Such a good and eloquent beggar as I am," Abbot Oswald admitted, "I guess I'm getting to be a 'money-grabber'" but "it is all for a good and worthy cause."[163] Saint John's generosity was both greatly needed and greatly appreciated by Abbot Oswald: "How these money matters prey on one's mind," he wrote in 1916, "and what a consolation when assistance is nigh. By July, Holland [this was a 1913 construction loan secured from a Dutch bank] will want nearly $6,000, annual payment and interest. This sum will devour much of what we are to get from our students. This time I have hope in [a] Divine Providence that will not forsake us in our need."[164]

Short-term loans from Saint John's were also required and received. In a typical case, Abbot Oswald reported on his allocation of a $1,500 loan: "I have been distributing wealth right and left. I paid off a mortgage of $1,275 and succeeded fairly well in removing a huge pile of bills. But new purchases had to be made. Still we do not get stuck due to your continuous assistance."[165] Ready money remained scarce, however: "Still from the first of the month," Abbot Oswald wrote tongue-in-cheek late in 1916, "my mail is quite bulky. The contents is about the same. It does not read I.O.U., but U.O.Me.!"[166] In November 1920, substantial but short-term help was once again sought from Saint John's in order to pay off the construction costs for the new west wing of the College building: "I would like to have a loan of $8,000 if you would kindly consent. Undoubtedly you can easily accommodate me since Saint John's is not building this year. Moreover, I ask for this sum for a short while only. In six months I will be able to return the money. If the authorities at Saint John's should hesitate about the loan, I will send Liberty Bonds amounting to about $5,000 as a guaranty. Will you kindly advocate this loan and help me out at a time when I need assistance?"[167]

World War I

World War I affected Saint Martin's in several ways once the United States became a belligerent in April 1917. Abbot Oswald was concerned, but not especially apprehensive, in July of that year: "The selective draft hit Saint Martin's all right. Seven names appear on the list: a workman, a brother, three clerics, one deacon, one priest, how is that for luck? I hope that we will have no trouble about [securing a deferment] for any of them."[168] In February 1918, he thought the war would soon be over and noted that "so far all our men are exempted from war service." He also reported an interesting personal situation: "I registered as an enemy alien. It may not have been necessary but I wished to avoid or preclude any trouble. I was always convinced that my father had taken out his citizenship papers but I have no proof for same. I am getting busy now to find out to what country I owe allegiance! Fine state of affairs after having voted and spent nearly all my life in the United States."[169]

A local representative of the U.S. Food Administration wanted SMC to turn over its "surplus" flour in April 1918, which caused Abbot Oswald to inquire how Saint John's was faring in terms of "substitutes for wheat." In mid-May, the Food Administration allowed SMC to keep three-months supply of wheat flour. The abbot thought that should carry the institution through until the fall harvest of wheat came on market. The campus residents were working their war gardens and hoped to raise "a good crop of spuds and vegetables." In 1918, the cherry crop was fine, hay very poor, and spuds pretty good. Necessity prompted Saint Martin's quest to be largely self-sufficient in its food production and hard work helped bring it about.

The 1917–1918 school year "came to an end with some flourish." Mid-June comméncement exercises were attended by "a good number of outsiders" including the bishop and governor. "The service flag," with about 150 stars commemorating SMC alumni in uniform, "was unfolded with appropriate exercises and patriotism." The College was "showing or at least trying to prove the proper patriotic spirit in this way and also by purchase of War Savings Stamps, Bonds, contributions to the Red Cross, etc."

That summer of 1918 it was almost impossible to get or keep laborers due to the exceptionally high wages in the shipyards. "All our young men that can be spared will be busy during vacation days," the abbot reported. "Some of the fathers" were also doing manual labor on campus when not "taking the places of priests on a vacation."[170]

Father Mathew Britt, long established as a key member of the school's faculty, suffered a recurrence of epilepsy that summer of 1918 which Abbot Oswald thought he brought on himself by overwork. "The [scholarly] work he has undertaken will bring him to the grave. It is beyond his ability but he has the tenacity of a bulldog. [Yet] if no favorable change [occurs he may] pass away unexpectedly at any time."[171]

Late in 1918, the "Spanish flu" pandemic raged across Europe and the United States. Nationwide, 500,000 to 700,000 Americans are thought to have died from that catastrophe whereas U.S. casualties in the recently ended World War totaled about 50,000. "Because of a ban on public gatherings, Thanksgiving festivities had to be canceled in some parts" of the Northwest.[172] Happily, things were generally healthy at Saint Martin's. "I think that I mentioned in my last letter," Abbot Oswald wrote to Abbot Peter, "that we are entirely rid of that unwelcome visitor, the Flu, and since he has 'flown' all is well at the college. Even the smallpox scare has vanished. A big number of boys will leave for home to eat turkey or beef on Thanksgiving day but I hope that they will not bring some sickness back with them. Usually we have to be looking for something disagreeable after some holidays. The 'Flu' has surely made inroads in Benedictine communities. How thankful we ought to be to Divine Providence that up to this time we have been immune of [sic] a single loss from our family."[173]

Fighting to be a Chaplain

Father Sebastian Ruth was a patriot who eagerly wanted to serve his country as an Army chaplain once the USA had become a belligerent in "the World's War" in April 1917. At age forty-two, however, he was too old to apply for a military commission. Therefore, he sought another route to become a military chaplain by unofficially providing Catholic ministry at newly established and rapidly growing Camp Lewis, which was located about ten miles from Lacey. Grateful "doughboys" later sent their "chaplain" a hand-lettered scroll of appreciation "for moral and spiritual services rendered during our stay at Camp Lewis" dated September 21, 1917 from "somewhere in France."[174]

In mid-October 1917, the Catholic Army and Navy Chaplain Bureau informed Father Sebastian of an opening for

Father Sebastian Ruth, O.S.B (1875–1958), was a multitalented individual who put his many skills and "hobbies" to good use at Saint Martin's. This October 13, 1919 photo depicts a handsome, middle-aged priest who worked long, hard, and effectivly to advance his monastery and its College. (Saint Martin's Abbey Archives)

a post chaplain at Camp Lewis. A local priest was desired and he was invited to apply for the job. The Knights of Columbus would pay the $1,000 annual salary, provide quarters in the K of C buildings within the military reservation, and offer all possible help to the Catholic chaplain. The Knights sponsored Catholic centers in military posts throughout the country and in Europe during the USA's active engagement in World War I. To speed things up, Father Sebastian was told to contact Bishop O'Dea of Seattle, who was endeavoring to look after the matter for the Chaplain Bureau.[175]

Bishop O'Dea, however, did not get around to formally recommending Father Sebastian for a K of C chaplaincy until September 1918, and then asked that he be assigned only to Camp Lewis or to another camp on the West Coast.[176] That same month Abbot Oswald tardily provided the requisite permission for his monk to undertake a chaplaincy, but let it be known that he too wanted his priest to stay near home for Saint Martin's was shorthanded.[177]

In late September 1918, Father Sebastian had the bittersweet experience of having his pioneering Catholic chaplaincy work at Camp Lewis officially acknowledged at the same time that another priest—a Father Dinand—was formally commissioned as an Army chaplain and appointed Camp Lewis's post chaplain![178] On October 26 Father Sebastian at last received a letter from the Army's adjutant general's office informing him that he had been designated by the secretary of war "to take the examination to determine his fitness for appointment" as an Army chaplain. He would be notified by Camp Lewis authorities when to report for that examination.[179]

Well-prepared for what he expected to be a pro forma examination and anxious to put on an Army chaplain's uniform, Father Sebastian was notified on November 4 that the chaplains' examinations would not be held until the quarantine at Camp Lewis was lifted.[180] Exactly a week later on November 11, 1918 (which also was the feast of our patron, Saint Martin of Tours), an armistice was signed ending the war.

Seldom at a loss for ideas and earnest to promote every kind of good work, the indefatigable Father Sebastian initiated a program of religious retreats for Catholic laymen at Saint Martin's in August 1918. Perhaps he borrowed the idea from Saint John's, which, "following the example of many other religious houses," began to offer such opportunities in August 1914.[181]

From 1918 to 1955, making a summer "retreat" at Lacey became an annual spiritual highlight for dozens of Catholic men. Bishop Joseph Schrembs of Toledo, Ohio, a nationally prominent churchman, directed the first Saint Martin's retreat. He and successive retreat masters, each of whom was a Catholic priest noted for his oratory as well as his piety, gave inspirational talks. In the summer of 1929, Saint Martin's

PICTURED TOP LEFT: *Religious retreats for Catholic laymen at SMC were started in 1918 by the indefatigable Father Sebastian with the assistance of the Knights of Columbus. The summer retreats continued through 1955 and were both a good pastoral service as well as an effective institutional outreach for Lacey's Benedictines in terms of promoting their College. This undated photo of a perhaps 1940s retreat shows one session's retreatants and their retreat master in front of Old Main. Father Sebastian is second row center—the elderly "black robe" on the right. (Saint Martin's Abbey Archives)*

PICTURED BOTTOM LEFT: *The younger monks waited on table during the summer retreats for laymen. In August 1943 this beaming octet of the Abbey's "clerics" or seminarians included (left to right): Fraters David Prebula, Bertrand Trautman, Andrew Mc-Hugh, William Dickerson, Conrad Rausch, Eugene Kellenbenz, Felix Wirth, and Patrick Holleran. (Saint Martin's Abbey Archives)*

new leader, Abbot Lambert, preached the laymen's retreat and also one for diocesan clergy at Lacey.[182] Mass was celebrated each day and times for personal sacramental confession of sins scheduled. Other devotions both in and out of the chapel, which eventually included a candlelight procession around the campus hill, were eagerly joined in. The retreatants were lodged in the school's dormitories or in additional improvised sleeping facilities as needed. Hearty meals prepared by the Benedictine Sisters and their helpers were served in the student refectory by the younger monks. A generous dose of the famous Benedictine hospitality was provided all retreatants.

The camaraderie among the retreatants, who at first came from all over the state, was so strong that many returned annually. The retreat program at SMC, which Father Sebastian managed for all of its thirty-eight years, had many positive results. Abbot Oswald proudly noted after only two years of retreats had been held in Lacey that "we get a lot of free and good advertising and there is no [Catholic] educational institution in the state of Washington which is so well known as Saint Martin's."[183] However, as the popularity of the laymen's retreats grew they became something of a burden for the resident monks. Eventually, three or even four sessions of retreats—typically running from Wednesday evening to the following Sunday morning—were being scheduled in late July or August. The expanded need for manpower to move furniture, make beds, clean facilities, and serve meals often severely taxed the monks' limited summer manpower.

Starting in 1956, the Archdiocese of Seattle redirected laymen's retreats to a newly opened retreat center staffed by Redemptorist priests between Tacoma and Seattle. On September 1 of that year, Father James, the Abbey's prior, expressed his relief in having had more time that summer for necessary campus repairs and maintenance: "It seems to me a lot of work has been accomplished this summer which could not have been done if we had the Laymen's Retreat. Before, very little could be done during the month of August and more, in the way of fixing up and improvements. Everybody seems to be happy about having this extra time of a month and more for work."[184] As one veteran retreatant put it in Lacey in 1955: "The retreats were instructive and inspirational [and] an important factor in Catholic action because of giving men from every part of the Archdiocese opportunities to get acquainted with one another."[185] They were indeed a good service and outreach for Saint Martin's but everything has its season.

One lasting memorial to the Laymen's Retreat program is the statute of the Sacred Heart of Jesus, mounted in the center of a twenty-eight-foot "circular plat," which has adorned the plaza in the front of Old Main's south entrance since 1919. The men who made the first retreat in August 1918 took "up a collection among themselves, and apparently enthusiastically, to place a memorial on our grounds." An eight-foot statue would be erected "on a pedestal with appropriate surroundings." The artist selected, Charles Biber of Seattle, was "a young man, a German too, and is supposed to know his business." Instead of using marble or stone, he prepared an artificial "block" on site of mixed marble dust, cement and sand "which becomes waterproof in due time." After a botched first attempt to carve the statue due to "the unsatisfactory condition of the artificial stone" a second attempt was successfully completed.[186]

"Our College is doing a rushing business," Abbot Oswald happily observed in September 1919. Two hundred and fifteen boys and young men had registered for classes "and more are on the way and others applying." A strong enrollment that year was very important for the school had begun the construction of a large addition to its modern 1913 building and there were "many worries before the same comes to a successful conclusion." (Photo from Fleetwood Collection, Lacey Museum)

Growth and Its Consequences

"We have concluded to make preparations for building an extensive addition to our college," Abbot Oswald excitedly informed Abbot Peter in May 1919. They would excavate and lay the foundation that summer, which SMC could "easily due without incurring a greater debt," and try to complete the project the next year. The school was "cramped for room" due to growing enrollment. In September 1919, the abbot again reported to Abbot Peter: "Our College is doing a rushing business. We have made room to accommodate all who apply but we must call a halt soon. At present time at least 215 boys have registered counting in day scholars and more are on the way and others are applying. We can only accept a few more and then we will be crowded. I do hope this year will be successful in every way because very much will depend upon this year. We have undertaken a big job in the construction of the addition to the College and there are many worries before the same comes to a successful conclusion." While the cost of their building project was "very high," Abbot Oswald admitted, he also believed that the College "had to seize this opportunity or others will get the best of us."[187]

The next letter Abbot Oswald directed to his Collegeville mentor was a somber one: "Well I have a story of bad luck to inform you of! Last Monday night [October 6, 1919] between 10 and 11 our gymnasium with its contents was entirely destroyed by fire. Cause is unknown but probably a match or cigarette stub did it all. We feel the loss very keenly especially at this time [of record high enrollment] when we need it so much." The $4,000 in insurance money, however, would do little more than help the College "put up a temporary concern for when we must have a place to lodge the boys during the rainy season." Seattle's Bishop O'Dea promptly issued a public statement cordially commending SMC to the public at large and urging generous support for the school's first ever public fundraising appeal.[188]

At the end of November 1919, Abbot Oswald ruminated about the role of fundraising, then a new concept and endeavor at Saint Martin's: "The drive to obtain some funds has begun. To hear our young men, inexperienced members, talk about the thousands that will come in and keep on pouring in is very amusing." Apparently a $300,000 price tag had been affixed to the new wing for which foundations had been dug that summer. A fundraising gimmick earlier decided on was the sale of "bricks." One side would have a rendering of the proposed "Greater Saint Martin's" complex while the reverse would carry the slogan, "Buy a Brick"! Every monk was supposed to sell some "bricks" so Abbot Oswald gamely asked Saint John's abbot "for a little boost in a worthy cause."[189]

When Abbot Peter quickly donated $1,000 "for the good cause," Abbot Oswald thanked him profusely while also noting that SMC's fund drive was "not materializing as well as some expected." However, he also happily reported that all who

SMC's enrollment grew rapidly in the post–World War I years. This mid-1920s scene in the hilltop courtyard shows a throng of students (boys being boys, those in front are mugging for the camera!) with a chartered "motor-coach" parked beside the new west wing. In the background is the 1923 steel water tower and, in the grove of trees, the "Log Cabin Station" used as a studio by the College's radio station, KGY. (Saint Martin's Abbey Archives)

have seen "the colored perspective" of the proposed "Greater Saint Martin's" were pleased and complimentary.[190]

Abbot Oswald was soon again requesting Abbot Peter's help but this time "to get permission from Rome to take up [that is, borrow] money amounting to $80,000" for the construction costs of the first phase of SMC's new building. Toward the end of February 1920, he noted, "a supreme effort will be made to get some money; if this don't [*sic*] bring some results the whole affair will amount to very little." On March 21, 1920, Abbot Oswald sent along his evaluation of his institution's "gigantic drive" for a "Greater Saint Martin's": "It is

In 1914–1915, this derrick was erected northeast of the campus hill by the Crescent Oil Company to test for oil. "Crowding Rockefeller off the market" was Abbot Oswald's humorous way of describing his reasons for allowing drilling on campus. His pressing concern was to marshal every possible campus asset in support of SMC's educational undertakings. Nothing came of this exploratory drilling or of later tests wells in 1940–1941. (Saint Martin's Abbey Archives)

to laugh." He thought that if the College "got one eighth of the sum" it should be satisfied. The Chamber of Commerce of Olympia had recently taken up the matter but "how soon they will take action is another question." Abbot Oswald also sadly commented that he had been "at my books nearly every day to have people pay their indebtedness to us." However, those "old accounts seem to be worthless, nearly all deadheads, or deadbeats. So you see I am worrying, planning, hoping etc. that all will be well."[191]

SMC's rapid growth in the post–World War I years and the costs of accommodating that growth first brought the College's leadership to a recognition of the urgent need for both endowment and scholarships. It published that need for the first time in the school's 1920–1921 catalog: "[T]o provide ampler and more substantial accommodations" and to widen the College's "scope as a first-class institution" there was an imperative need for an endowment. A quarter-century of excellence provided an earnest of even better things to come! "Other educational institutions, even those state-aided and already richly endowed, receive generous assistance in the[ir] work, and hesitate not to ask it." SMC's leadership understood that while "generous friends" were "not lacking" they had yet to fully understand the institution's "acute requirements." Moreover, "[t]he Faculty of the College has given its life services freely and gladly to the work. Those who would share with them in the great enterprise" could do so "most effectively" at this time "by rendering material aid and contributing funds."

Student scholarships were also urgently needed for "deserving young men of high character and aspirations" whose means did not permit them to attend SMC. It would be "clearly a noble benefaction to contribute to such a purpose" and "especially so in the case of those . . . picked young men whose future is more than ordinarily full of promise." Such admirable youths would make any sponsor proud. Two classes of scholarships could be established at SMC, "perpetual and temporary." The first would maintain one resident student "in perpetuity" including his "board, lodging, etc., tuition, textbooks" for $6,000. A temporary scholarship, which would cost $1,200, would "maintain one student at the College during the four years of his course." The school's authorities pledged that the amount contributed would be "invested in reliable securities" and the interest used to support the student. The scholarships would be named after their founders to assure "grateful remembrance."[192]

Then as now, Saint Martin's had to husband its resources and seek diligently to supplement its income. In November

1914, Abbot Oswald had reported to Abbot Peter: "We have leased our property to 'Crescent Oil Co.' This same company must begin drilling for oil within 60 days or lose the opportunity. We are not expecting very much hence will not be disappointed but if oil will be found on our land we will receive $12\frac{1}{2}$ percent royalty besides the use of all oil needed for domestic purposes. I suppose we will be crowding Rockefeller off the market before very long." He also saw the possibility of an additional benefit: "By drilling to a big depth artesian water may be had and that is what we very much need."[193]

Despite his real concerns for Saint Martin's continued growth and financial stability, Abbot Oswald was generally both prayerfully and philosophically disposed: "It is the Lord's day," he wrote on May 9, 1920, "and I feel at peace with everybody and everything this morning. It is too bad that this feeling could not continue indefinitely. All things would [then] be so pleasant. But very often when I am enjoying a happy and peaceful morning something will turn up to mar this happiness. I suppose it must be so and will remain so just to convince us [that] our earthly pilgrimage is not to be without trials and sacrifices."[194]

Logging, a Forest Fire, and Reforestation

In 1916, the campus forest was logged off in order to retire the debt on the three-year-old new College building. Saint Martin's environs were visibly changed to Abbot Oswald's wistful regret: "Well our beautiful forest is gone. How I delighted to take my walks on the roads leading through that tangle of trees and brush impenetrable to the eye. It seemed to contain mysteries or secrets. The charm is gone. It is all open now and probably means a new era of development around Saint Martin's. Instead of giant trees and shady walks and a joy for every lover of nature's work, we may find before long the common-place and prosaic spud and radishes taking root in the soil. *Sic transeat*."

Remnants of the campus forest cut that summer had become tinder-dry and on Thursday, September 14, the campus population had a real fright. While taking his morning walk, Abbot Oswald "found about an acre on fire." He sounded the alarm and by noon the fire was under control. However, "after dinner [an] immense volume of smoke and even the fire itself was visible from the hill. A strong wind had blown the sparks to rubbish near by and the fire became unmanageable for the men left to guard the same." The wind blew flames and sparks in the direction of the College's buildings on and

These 1920 photos show Father Francis O'Driscoll in a section of the logged-off area of the SMC campus and two of the SMC students who helped with reforestation efforts that year: "The boys of the College got together in a tree-planting bee among the unsightly stumps" planting two thousand two-year-old white pine trees just north of the hill. (Photos by Albert Fisher, SMC '22)

around the campus hill. "We were simply helpless," reported Abbot Oswald.

"While fighting the fire at the front other blazes would start 50 or 100 feet back of us. Towards five o'clock the wind subsided and the fire got into a space which had not been logged and where the soil was still a little moist. That saved the day. If the fire had taken the tall trees near the college, I do not know what would have happened. There were watchmen on all the buildings with fire hoses but whether we would have been successful in checking and preventing the fire from destroying the buildings remains doubtful. Since then we back fired and kept close watch day and night and probably all danger is past."

"This morning I went over the entire area of burnt logs, etc. and I could find no place where the fire could get another start and give us another scare. Thanks be to Heaven that this is over for I have been expecting something like this since the logging began." He also noted that "we can view the fire as a blessing in disguise since hundreds of dollars are saved that would have [had] to be expended to do what the fire has done," namely, to clear the debris left over from the logging.[195]

In the fall of 1920, in an effort to beautify their campus, the monks and students planted some two thousand white pine trees. As the *Washington Standard* noted, "the boys of the college got together in a tree-planting bee" to establish the young trees "among the unsightly stumps of the old logged off land just north" of the College buildings. So far as local forestry officials were aware, this was "the first time that any private owners in this part of Washington have taken steps to reforest their waste lands." The two-year-old white pines were acquired from a U.S. Forest Service Nursery at Stabler, Washington, near Cascade Locks in the Columbia River gorge. Olympia-based Forest Examiner A. A. Griffin helped in starting the planting and was confident "that in from three to five years the young pines will make a very favorable showing." Protection from livestock and fire was essential, of course, to give the young trees time to take root and flourish. Rapid growth could then be expected and "the trees will eventually make very valuable timber as well as an addition to the beauty of the college." Fathers Gregory Wall and Lawrence Piotrzkowski had unsuccessfully attempted transplanting young trees some years earlier and had finally brought in fir cones to grow trees from the seed. Some of their young firs were also planted on cutover campus acreage that fall.[196]

Big Crowd for Speech at SMC

Monday evening, October 19, 1920, found a very large crowd on campus. Some two thousand persons had come to Lacey to hear Robert Bridges, Farmer-Labor Party nominee for governor, who had been denied use of the Olympia High School auditorium. No other hall in the capital city was large enough to accommodate the anticipated crowd and the organizing committee "gladly accepted the offer of Saint Martin's for free use of the college auditorium." Free transportation had been arranged from the end of the streetcar line at Fourth and Central Streets in Olympia to the campus via a shuttle service of motor busses and volunteer cars. "The faculty and students of SMC extended every courtesy to the nominees and the auditors," it was reported. The school's facilities were provided gratis for the "sole interest" of preserving "the constitutional rights of free speech, free press, and peaceable assemblage."[197] Bridges got a fair hearing at SMC but lost the election.

Father Sebastian Ruth's amateur shortwave radio station, W7YS, first went on the air in 1914. A truly enthusiastic "Wireless fan," in 1916 he established what was believed to be "a world record in wireless telegraphy" by copying messages "for hours at a time sent from Hanover, Germany," which was "more than 6,400 miles from Lacey on a direct line." "My receiving range now," the enthusiastic priest told a reporter, "is Ketchikan on the north, Japan on the west, Panama on the south, and Germany on the extreme east. Maybe Mars will be heard from next."[198] Later billed as "The Log Cabin Station— Where the Cedars Meet the Sea," SMC's wireless station became a very popular attraction with both students and south Puget Sound area listeners.

Father Sebastian's "hobby" developed into a part-time, licensed broadcasting station in 1921 and was assigned the call letters KGY. On a weeknight in early April of that year, some three hundred SMC students, faculty, and guests gathered around the log cabin housing the campus station. At 6:30 p.m. they were treated to "the unusual event of a musical concert by radio." Arrangements had been made to pick up an hour-long broadcast of recorded music from Camp Lewis. Sgt. Neville Benoit, using the regular Army wireless phone "that had proved its worth during World War I as the ground station of airplane wireless," played fourteen selections interspersed with his own short comments. While not the first time that Camp Lewis music had been picked up by KGY, this broadcast concert was the first time locally that a large audience listened to broadcast music at the same time. A strong wind "somewhat hampered the hearing at any very great distance," but "the music and the voice could be plainly heard and understood at a distance of 200 feet." This open-air concert by radio was an experiment but its immediate success brought the promise for future broadcast concerts. It was also noted that with the acquisition of the new equipment used in this broadcast SMC now possessed "one of the finest apparatus obtainable for amateur radio purposes."[199]

Father Sebastian was issued a radio broadcast license in 1922 and he began his first "scheduled" broadcasting on April 5 of that year. Programs originated from the "Log Cabin Radio Station" (literally) on campus "Where the Cedars Meet the Sea." The license was sold to Olympia commercial interests in 1932. Today, KGY remains the oldest radio station broadcasting under its original call letters in the state of Washington. Appropriately, it broadcasts SMC men's and

Father Sebastian's "wireless" station [W]7YS first went on the air in 1914. His "hobby" developed into a part-time broadcasting station with the call letters KGY in 1921 and was fully licensed the next year. Using the slogan "Out where the Cedars meet the Sea," he took over the SMC Pep Club's log cabin for his "studio." On February 23, 1926, KGY broadcast its first regular "live" musical program from its newly acquired "Log Cabin Station." After the radio license was sold to commercial interests in Olympia in 1932, Father Sebastian resumed his "wireless" radio activities. SMC students had a longtime love affair with this monk's radio operations!

women's basketball games and otherwise continues to serve as the south Puget Sound region's flagship community radio station.

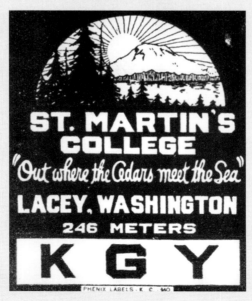

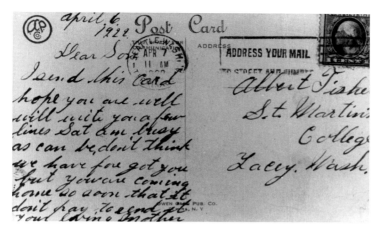

Help from Mothers' Clubs

Sixteen charter members established the Saint Martin's Mothers' Club of Seattle on October 10, 1920, under the leadership of Mary Hein, Anna Toner, and Irene Hanley. Father Bernard Neary, then director of Saint Martin's College, gave his enthusiastic approval. The ladies, as Mrs. Hein put it, hoped to be able to "get little things for the College that would increase the comfort of the Fathers and the boys." Their various fundraising activities also supported a tuition burse (scholarship) "for the education of a worthy young man to the Benedictine priesthood." Proceeds from the club's efforts also allowed them to contribute missals and chimes for campus chapels and to furnish the College's guest suite.[200]

A similar group was started in Tacoma in 1921 "to promote, by prayer and work, an increase in enrollment of worthy and deserving students at Saint Martin's."[201] The new club hosted a party "for young college men" at Tacoma's Knights of Columbus Hall in April of that year. It was strategically planned for the end of the College's Easter vacation, when students on the way back to Lacey could "share in the festivity." Seventy-five out-of-town SMC students joined their Tacoma schoolmates for dancing, whist, and general socializing. Father Bernard was a guest of honor. He and the three hundred other guests, "among them many former students of the college," took a keen interest "in helping to make the club's first dance, the beginning of an annual series, a huge success." An after-midnight supper for fifty of the college men at the Fred Ohm residence provided a "jolly and informal" conclusion to a fine evening.[202]

In the early 1920s, the southern end of Saint Martin's hilltop area was not yet effectively connected to the new (1918) paved entrance road entering the campus from the Olympia-Tacoma highway to the south. A set of steps was definitely needed to enable pedestrians to reach the impressive complex of College buildings facing the southern brow of the hill. The Tacoma Club's ardent members undertook a campaign from 1923 to 1925 to fund the building of a grand staircase in and down the south end of the campus Hill. It was constructed in 1926 at the then hefty cost of $7,000.

The founders and members of the Mothers' Clubs in the 1920s shared the Benedictine commitment to prayer and work. Their diligent and caring labors in support of our school were matched by their concern to share in the spiritual benefits of Saint Martin's religious activities. Most club members were Catholic and they naturally aspired to support vocations to the Catholic priesthood—and to our monastery—as a way of continuing and expanding their Church's ministry.

An Observant Visitor

Father Alexius Hoffmann, O.S.B., of Saint John's Abbey, after many invitations from Abbot Oswald, finally consented to conduct the Benedictine priests' and clerics' annual retreat in Lacey in June 1922. The notes and sketches in his diary covering his three-weeks stay in western Washington, which were later collected into an unpublished "Autobiography," provide a unique window into the life and times of Saint Martin's as the monastery and school began its second quarter-century.[203]

Better Education for Monk-Teachers Needed

In May 1923, Father Augustine Ogsniach wrote to the bishop of Seattle denouncing the hit-and-miss theological training Lacey's young Benedictines had been getting. Their lives during the years they studied theology at Saint Martin's were so hectic, he advised Bishop O'Dea, that the Abbey's three "neo-ordinandi" of that year were "so ignorant of the very essentials of Sacred Theology that they would not be able to pass a sample examination in catechism."[204] While these harsh comments by Lacey's first Ph.D. were probably exaggerated, he did have a point! Abbot Oswald finally did something to remedy the situation in 1928. He decided to send away his young monks to complete their bachelor's degrees at an accredited college and to have them also make their theological studies there. The abbot chose Saint Benedict's College because the Kansas school's program was accredited and it also had a well-regarded seminary. This new arrangement would give Lacey's young monks a better context in which to concentrate on their studies.

These SMC students—identified as (left to right) "Pete," "Hauser," and "'Girlie' Bourque"— appear to be makeshift minstrels as they strum their tennis rackets in 1925.

Sports and physical fitness were especially important to SMC students when most of them were young, male, and boarders. Pete Wrubles, Art McDonald, and Harry Lawrence (the future Father Alcuin, O.S.B.) look seriously fit in this 1926 lineup.

Playing without a helmet was OK during a "photo session" for one of your buddies in 1925.

Baseball was taken seriously at SMC and games always drew a crowd of campus people and Lacey neighbors. (Photos 1–3 by Bruno Rosellini; Photo 4 from Fleetwood Collection, Lacey Museum)

As SMC increased its programs and expanded its reputation as a boarding school for boys and young men, the issue of
financing the College in general and individual students' attendance came to the fore. The monks who staffed the school
received no salaries for their work and so in effect contributed
their services. They further subsidized SMC's operations by
their weekend, summer, and holy day pastoral services at
parishes and missions throughout western Washington. Part of
the salaries of Benedictines living and working away from Saint
Martin's year round also helped to subsidize the school's and
monastery's expenses, a generous underwriting which lasted
for decades. Those "parish fathers" also served as recruiters for
the College and as scouts and references for young men interested in pursuing a religious vocation as a Benedictine.

Parents settled their sons' accounts at SMC in a variety of
ways. Some few paid in full in cash while most paid in installments. In May 1915, Abbot Oswald had remarked to Abbot
Peter: "Collections, however, are slow but I have confidence
that we will be successful in obtaining the money by and by. A
number of our students are from British Columbia and financial affairs must be in a deplorable condition. It is difficult to
collect there due undoubtedly to the war. If times were pros-

perous we would not be able to accommodate the students next year."[205]

George Mitchell (alias Michels), the "potato king" of Kittitas County in central Washington, had four sons—Emmett, Carl, Jack, and Bernard—who attended SMC between 1919 and 1925. [Most of that branch of the Michels family sooner or later anglicized their surname to Mitchell.] He usually paid their school fees in kind by delivering sacks of potatoes by the carload to the Northern Pacific Railroad station in Lacey.[206]

Other students had school fees waived when their families pleaded economic distress or other contingencies. A boy in need from a distressed family was seldom denied admission or sent home. Promising students—especially those who showed some interest in pursuing a vocation as a Benedictine—were granted full or partial scholarships.

Father Justin Welz had suffered from asthma for many years. He died at Visitation Church's rectory in South Tacoma on March 23, 1923, and was buried in the new Abbey Cemetery in a quiet glade north of the hill. (Saint Martin's Abbey Archives)

Father Justin Welz

After the election of Abbot Oswald in May of 1914, Father Justin Welz, who had served as Saint Martin's second conventual prior since 1908, was named pastor of Visitation Church in South Tacoma. His health had been poor for years and in November 1918, the abbot reported that Father Justin "had a very severe spell again but that is due of course to his old ailment. It is certainly astonishing how many severe attacks he can outlive." A lifelong friend reported his final illness: "For many years" he suffered from asthma "which caused him such distress that he could do no work and required assistance" from other Benedictine priests. "Still he clung to South Tacoma for years. He was always cheerful and sociable but when the asthma attacks came on, he was down and out."[207] He died March 23, 1923, at the Visitation Parish rectory and was buried in the new Abbey Cemetery in Lacey. ✤

Saint Martin's impressive hilltop physical plant dominated the still rural Lacey area in 1937. A road was being built in a northwesterly direction to connect with the new SMC entrance off the new "Martin Highway," which was named for incumbent Governor Clarence D. Martin. Growing enrollments in its fully accredited High School and College programs augured well for the institution's future. Under Abbot Lambert Burton's strong and effective leadership, the Abbey also had a record number of young Benedictines in college, seminary, and graduate school preparing to staff its schools and parishes. (Saint Martin's Abbey Archives)

CHAPTER 5
New Leadership and Challenges (1928–1945)

⚜

IN LATE AUGUST 1928, FATHER LAMBERT Burton, O.S.B., fifty, was called west from Saint Benedict's Abbey and College in Atchison, Kansas, to become the second abbot of Saint Martin's. He was elected on the basis of his reputation as a schoolman. At Lacey, his highest academic priority would be to get the monastery's schools strengthened and fully accredited. A man of broad views and strong interests, Abbot Lambert would guide and invigorate the campus for fifteen years.

Prior to his election, Father Lambert had never been to Saint Martin's, but some of the Lacey monks had become acquainted with his educational views via their participation in the National Benedictine Educational Association of which he was a guiding light. Organized in 1918, the NBEA was a sort of "think tank" and clearinghouse for the various American Benedictine schools. Its members kept busy "studying problems and making recommendations concerning curricula, standards, and faculty training." At SMC as at Saint Benedict's College and other Benedictine schools in the United States, there was a growing perception of the need "to fit old and treasured values, and some new values, with contemporary forms." The question, of course, was "how to modernize the curriculum without losing the traditional values of educating the will as well as the intellect."[208]

In terms of modernizing the Kansas college, Saint Benedict's Abbey's new superior, Abbot Martin Veth, who was elected in November 1921, and Father Lambert "agreed on but few points regarding Saint Benedict's College." So after just three semesters as the director of the Atchison school, Father Lambert resigned in 1923 and asked "to be sent out on a parish as far away as possible." However, he was back at Saint Benedict's College in time to accept the key position as dean of men in the summer of 1928.[209] Two months later, however, he accepted his surprise election as abbot of Saint Martin's on August 28, 1928.

In large part, Lambert Burton was called to Lacey to provide new and vigorous academic leadership for Saint Martin's. In 1928, the University of Washington had withdrawn its accreditation for SMC's junior college program. Abbot Lambert, a premier leader in Benedictine educational circles in the United States, was looked to as one who could "revitalize and enhance the educational prestige of Saint Martin's." The new abbot had "two big advantages" in that he was both "possibly more objective about his task" and "without preconceived notions of the Saint Martin's [monastic] community." Most importantly, "he knew he was called [to Lacey] with a mandate to establish educational excellence or at least academic competence."[210] With amazing perseverance, in one year the new abbot regained accreditation for the junior college and then "systematically prepared the ground for the all-important full accreditation of the senior college in 1940."[211] By the mid-1930s, separately accredited High School and College programs were being offered for Saint Martin's all-male student body by a still mostly Benedictine staff.

In 1930, Abbot Lambert began a "Scholasticate" program for his new abbey which, with modifications, would last into the 1960s. Its purpose was to benefit "young men preparing to enter the Benedictine Order" at Lacey with the goal of being ordained Catholic priests. They, or their families, paid what tuition they could, and on-campus jobs provided at least some of them with a means to partially work off their fees. Otherwise, their education was subsidized by the monastery with the long-term hope of increasing the pool of candidates for its own ranks. Students considering a possible vocation as a Benedictine priest were called "scholastics." They were segregated from other SMC students "as regards study, recreation, and sleeping arrangements" but took classes with the other students and participated in campus athletics.[212]

From 1908 to 1922, Abbot Lambert had been significantly involved in a similar vocations program at his former abbey in Kansas. His "intellectual and spiritual ideals" had strongly influenced a whole generation of Saint Benedict's monks by developing in them "a desire to devote themselves to community life."[213] Saint Martin's scholasticate program had the same goal. However, the percentage of those subsidized students who entered our abbey's novitiate and were ordained to the priesthood was low.

Building Up a Strong Faculty

Between 1928 and 1940, most of Saint Martin's young monks were sent to Atchison to complete their B.A.'s and to take the prescribed four-year professional course in theology. Typically, they would come back to Lacey only after three years in Kansas—to take the final, "solemn" vows—and then, after a family vacation, would return to Saint Benedict's for a final three years of seminary training. They were of course expected to follow the full monastic schedule of prayers and chores at their host monastery along with handling their own heavy course loads. They would sometimes take education courses at Saint Benedict's College during the summer to prepare themselves for certification as high school teachers at Lacey should they later be assigned to such work. A majority of the Saint Martin's monks studying at Atchison also worked on master's degrees at Midwestern or Eastern universities during their "free" summers with the strong encouragement of their abbot.

Abbot Lambert worked to prepare SMC for a stronger future by husbanding scarce resources to support monks in their pursuit of higher academic degrees: "Well he bundled up everybody in the place and sent them off to school," Father John Raymond later recalled. "He bundled up every penny in the place and put a padlock on it for that purpose."[214] The abbot stuck with his farsighted policy even during the hard times of the Great Depression for he was both realistic and optimistic in his management of Saint Martin's. For example, in May 1937 he confidentially but forthrightly commented on the College's uncertain enrollment for the upcoming fall semester: "What the general attendance will be next year is very much of a mystery. Soaring costs of living has compelled us to raise our prices. What effect that will have on our attendance, it is impossible to say at this time. The cost of living has gone up while salaries and wages remain much the same. Just now the situation is aggravated by a [regional ferry] strike. There are several other elements which affect our situation which are better discussed viva voce than by correspondence."[215] Yet when a younger monk in 1936 alluded to his relief that "the clouds of doubt and discouragement" around Saint Martin's were beginning at last to clear, the abbot confidently replied: "I do not think there was any reason for 'doubt and discouragement.' We were having a winter season. Our fruit trees do not put forth leaves, flowers, and fruit during winter. It is spring now, and our hopes run high. May God bless them."[216]

Five Lacey Benedictines were engaged in full-time graduate studies at the Catholic University of America in

Washington, D.C., in the fall of 1936. That year's "Washington quintette" included Fathers Philip Bagan, Jerome Toner, Martin Toner, Marcel Berthon, and Leonard Feeney all of whom were "in good health and getting along first rate." They resided in Caldwell Hall, a residence for priests centrally located on campus, and paid fees of about $280 each per semester which included tuition, room, board, and use of the library.[217] When Father Leonard suggested that he would be in a better graduate program and happier studying for his doctorate at the University of Chicago (where he had earlier earned an M.A.), Abbot Lambert candidly put things in perspective for him: "You were not sent to the Catholic University because it has the best Department of English in the country, but because it is a Catholic university, has the highest rating of all Catholic universities in America, and is so recognized in educational circles in the United States. Another reason for your being sent to Washington is to strengthen our position with the hierarchy as a Catholic four-year college."[218] Despite Abbot Lambert's support and encouragement, however, only two of those five monks would successfully complete a doctorate at Catholic University.

However, two other Saint Martin's monks, Father Gerald Desmond (1904–1990) and Father Jerome Toner (1899–1977), completed their doctoral programs at Catholic University with Abbot Lambert's support and encouragement. Entering the Abbey's novitiate in 1923 after two years of studies at Lacey, both men subsequently completed college and theological studies at SMC and were ordained priests in 1930.

In 1930–1931, these young Saint Martin's monks were working on accredited bachelor's degrees or studying theology in preparation for ordination at Saint Benedict's College in Atchison, Kansas: (left to right) Fraters Meinrad Gaul, Leonard Feeney, Gabriel Donohue, Arnold Fox, Michael Contris, Alphonse Fuchs, John Raymond, Bede Ernsdorff, Damian Glenn, William O'Loane, and Anselm Lenslinger. They held much promise for their Abbey's future endeavors in academic and pastoral service. (Photo courtesy Father Arnold Fox)

Father Gerald then earned an M.A. in sociology at Catholic University and joined the SMC faculty in 1931. He served as dean of the College from 1935 through 1948 except for a couple of additional wartime years at Catholic University where he earned his Ph.D. in 1946. Father Jerome earned a B.Sc. in education in 1932 at the University of Washington and then an M.A. in economics at Catholic University in 1935. He also completed his doctorate there in 1941 with a focus on labor relations.

Father Martin Toner had earned an M.A. at the University of Washington in 1936 and continued graduate studies at Catholic University for another five years without completing his doctorate. Likewise, Father Marcel Berthon, who earned his M.A. in Romance Languages at Catholic University in 1936, spent two subsequent years at that institution without finishing his doctorate. He returned to SMC as dean of men in 1938, served as a military chaplain from 1943 to 1946, and then became principal of our High School for several years.

Father Leonard Feeney

In the fall of 1927, the future Father Leonard (1908–1980), came to Lacey from Eau Claire, Wisconsin. After working for a year following his high school graduation, the young man had confided to his pastor his great desire to study for the priesthood and his hopes to "join the Oblates down in Illinois." Father C. E. Dowd, of Eau Claire's Saint Patrick's Church, who was also of Irish heritage, told him, "I don't see how a Feeney is going to get along with those Dutchmen [that is, Germans] down there." Asked where he might then study for the priesthood, young Feeney was advised that the Benedictines in Washington "had a fine modern place and all who go there seem to be well satisfied." Sister Sylvia Stevens, O.S.B., who taught in Saint Patrick's parochial grade school for twenty-three years, also was a "loyal supporter and advocate" of Saint Martin's. It was in fact from Sister Sylvia some years earlier that little Leonard first heard about Washington's Benedictines.[219] When Feeney finally told his pastor he would go to Saint Martin's, the priest promised to write the abbot of his coming and bought him a railroad ticket to Lacey. To the surprise of his family and almost before he knew it, "I was speeding away across the prairies toward Saint Martin's and the priesthood."[220]

At Lacey, he found "the three things nearest my heart": "fresh country air and scenery" along with "the company of lots of young people with all their noise and fun," and "above

Father Leonard Feeney (1908–1980), seen here circa 1970, was a scholar as well as a man who loved "young people with all their noise and fun." His greatest goal in life was to become a Catholic priest so as to help minister to others the faith he himself held so dear. Starting in 1940, he would spend most of his Saint Martin's years working with and for the boys of the High School They were precious to him and he in turn gave them the guidance and atten-tion they needed in their adolescent years. (Saint Martin's Abbey Archives)

all the chance to study for the priesthood." He had much to keep him busy—in class and extracurricularly—and all that vital campus activity (which had eluded him earlier as a student in rural Wisconsin) "was heaven to me."[221]

After finishing a two-year college program at SMC, he entered the Abbey's novitiate where he kept Leonard as his religious name. On July 11, 1930, Frater Leonard and his novitiate classmate, Frater John Raymond, made their first vows as Benedictine monks. Abbot Lambert soon informed them that they were "both destined for Saint Benedict's" for two years of philosophy and four years of theology in prepara-tion for ordination to the priesthood.[222]

Completing his B.A. at Saint Benedict's College in 1932, Father Leonard asked his abbot for permission to go to sum-mer school and work for an M.A. in English. Abbot Lambert heartily approved his request. Indeed, he "very much urged me to go, and even gave his consent when I named expensive Chicago University as my choice of school." Father Leonard found a place to stay at Saint Bernard's Hospital and "traveled to and from campus by streetcar."[223] He received an M.A. from that prestigious university in the summer of 1935 along with another SMC alumnus, Michael J. Contris. Mike Contris, who had been in temporary vows as a Saint Martin's monk and had been a fellow student at Atchison, did not take final vows as a Benedictine. However, he returned to Lacey to join the SMC staff where he spent the remainder of his professional life.

After two years of full-time studies at Catholic University, Father Leonard completed his doctoral classwork and passed his comprehensive exams in English. However, in 1937 he had already begun to show signs of ulcers, a deterioration of the "occasional sieges of indigestion" which had afflicted him during his years at Atchison.[224] Unlucky in his quest for a satisfactory dissertation project or director, he allowed himself to be distracted by taking weekend parish assignments on a regular basis. Meanwhile, he had been away from Lacey for eight years and Abbot Lambert wanted to put him to work as an English teacher at SMC!

In June 1939, Father Leonard admitted to his abbot: "I know that it must be a disappointment to you and the rest of the Community that at least one of us did not get his degree with the class" that Catholic University graduated that month. At the end of the summer, he shamefacedly confessed: "Summer school is over and still no degree. And I don't know what I am to do. Alas, the thesis is not yet completely finished, and then there are the Orals to study for. What shall I do?"[225] He wrote his abbot again on January 14, 1940, mentioning his "utter shame" at not being able to report the "good news" of having completed the doctorate. Upon receipt of his letter, Abbot Lambert sent Father Leonard a telegram: "Start west next week. Further instructions by airmail." In reply, the embarrassed priest telegramed a frantic plea for one final extension to finish his dissertation. The abbot's response was terse: "Very sorry but your presence on the faculty for the second semester indispensable. Air mail letter gives directions about arranging to complete your work at the University for the doctorate."[226]

As things turned out, Father Leonard never completed his doctoral studies and so did not replace Mike Contris as the head of SMC's English Department upon his return to Lacey. Instead, Father Leonard spent the next thirty years working with Saint Martin's High School boys as their beloved "Pops"!

Equally happily, Mike Contris continued on the College faculty and became the heart of its English and humanities programs for some forty years.

The graduate studies of other Lacey monks did result in their being awarded doctorates. Father Leonard's novitiate classmate, Father John Raymond (1911–1974), for example, expeditiously earned his M.S. in 1934 via summer studies at the University of Iowa and after ordination in 1936 joined SMC's faculty. He then completed his Ph.D. in mathematics at the University of Washington in 1944. In the hectic years following the end of World War II, Father John served as Saint Martin's chief financial officer while also teaching math in the High School or College.

Father Bede Ernsdorff (1909–1982), a close contemporary of Father Leonard's, also successfully capped his academic

Joining SMC's science faculty in 1938, Father Bede Ernsdorff, O.S.B. (1909–1982), would develop into a demanding yet inspiring teacher of chemistry. Returning to Lacey after World War II with a Stanford doctorate in 1946, he literally built up the Chemistry Department's facilities with the labor of his students. His reputation was such that medical and dental schools generally accepted the students he recommended. A sterling teacher and trusted counselor, he was active in every aspect of the Abbey's spiritual and liturgical work. (Saint Martin's Abbey Archives)

studies with a doctorate. Sent to Atchison in the fall of 1932 after completing his novitiate at Lacey, he was awarded his B.Sc. from Saint Benedict's College in 1934. In addition to his theological studies at Atchison, Frater Bede did summer graduate work in chemistry at the University of Michigan, winning an M.Sc. in 1936. He joined the SMC faculty after his ordination in 1938. When World War II downsized the College's enrollment, Father Bede went to Stanford University to undertake doctoral work in chemistry as a DuPont Fellow and was awarded the Ph.D. in 1946. He returned to Lacey to become the mainstay of SMC's chemistry program and a much respected pre-medicine and pre-dentistry advisor over the next three decades. He also served as dean of the College and took on various leadership roles in the Abbey.

All things considered, Abbot Lambert's planning and sacrificing for Saint Martin's academic future paid great dividends. In 1940, SMC was officially accredited to award four-year degrees and in subsequent decades several of "his" well-trained Benedictine faculty were the stars of campus teaching in Lacey.

Campus Hotspots and Highjinks

On October 3, 1932, another forest fire threatened the campus. "We spent yesterday afternoon fighting a fire," wrote Abbot Lambert to a Lacey monk studying in Kansas. "It started from some unknown cause just outside of our property, and north of the spring. We did not notice it until it had spread over the lowlands west of the spring and a wind was carrying it to the uplands. Nearly everybody at Saint Martin's turned out, and staid [sic] with it until nearly six o'clock when they had it under control." A later recounting of this event was more prosaic: The fire "swept through the wooded part of the College section but was soon brought under control by the combined efforts of the Faculty and Students." Fortunately, the blaze was much less damaging than the inferno which had imperiled the campus in September 1916.[227]

One particular Lacey family had especially warm ties to Saint Martin's and its people in the 1930s. Corinne Schilling Farmer (born 1926) remembers that her childhood home, which bordered the southeast edge of the campus, was "just like a fraternity house for Saint Martin's boys." Her mother and aunt, Eveline and Irene Kenney, were twins and their family had moved to Lacey in 1900 to work at the local hotel. The twins had received their First Communion at Saint Martin's chapel in 1903 at age twelve. Eveline had been SMC's first cheerleader (circa 1908) and Lacey's postmistress at eighteen. She married Maurice Schilling in Saint Martin's chapel in

1920. Both died young, however, leaving three daughters who were to be raised by their redoubtable aunt, Irene Kenney, who because of her responsibilities as their guardian never married.

The Kenney twins started a successful a candy and ice cream shop in Olympia (eventually with branches in Aberdeen and Bremerton) which featured homemade confections. Called The Twin Shop, it was a popular in-town hangout for both Saint Martin's students and alumni. A home adjacent to campus headed by someone with such noted confectionery talent, plus three girls in residence, proved to be a big attraction for the homesick adolescent males of SMC in the 1930s!

As Corinne Farmer remembers things, "our life really revolved around Saint Martin's." Its priests, especially Fathers Sebastian Ruth, Marcel Berthon, George Monda, Leo Hansen, and Gregory Wall, were their masculine "role models." (Many years later, Mrs. Farmer named her younger son after Father Gregory.) They, and other monks and the Benedictine Sisters on the hill as well, would regularly give snacks and small gifts to the three Schilling girls.

The College's fields and forests became their playground and all three girls learned to play tennis on the summer-emptied SMC courts. During the school year, they attended many team practices as well as most games and other entertainments at "their" College. On one occasion, Aunt Irene broke up a student skirmish during a baseball game! Times were "simple but tough" in Lacey in the 1930's but people in the area helped each other out. And Saint Martin's did its share.[228]

Help from Our Mothers' Clubs

The Saint Martin's Mothers' Clubs in Seattle and Tacoma (and in Olympia starting in 1937) were a sturdy source of financial as well as personal support for both students and monks during the hard times of the Depression and World War II. The individual clubs held teas, card parties, raffles, dances, and rummage and bake sales to raise money for scholarships (a tuition "burse" was then $30 a month in the 1930s) and for special amenities for the monastery and school. Their friendly maternal concern raised the spirits of both the students and monks and helped to make campus life a little more comfortable. The abbot and other Benedictines regularly expressed Saint Martin's and their own gratitude to the ladies. Knowing that their labors of love were appreciated was important, as Imelda Bergh, secretary-treasurer of the Olympia Mothers' Club, put it so nicely in 1939: "It makes it so much easier for us to work for the good of the college when we know the fac-

Organized into Mothers'
Clubs in Seattle, Tacoma,
and Olympia starting in
the 1920s, mothers of current and former Saint
Martin's students were
mainstays of institutional
support. This undated
view shows an attractive
group of mothers of Saint
Martin's High School
and/or College students
on one of their annual
spring visits to campus.
(Saint Martin's Abbey
Archives)

The College and High
students and the monks
annually entertained
the members of various
Saint Martin's Mothers'
Clubs with a full-day
program which included
Mass, a nice meal, speeches, and a concert by cam-
pus musicians. Here
Father Sebastian conducts
a student band for an
undoubtedly appreciative
audience of moms some
time in the 1930s. (Saint
Martin's Abbey Archives)

ulty appreciates our efforts so much."[229] Abbot Lambert took the time to brief himself on how the sons (or grandsons) of Mothers' Clubs' members were doing before attending Club functions. In that way, he could have a few specific words with each parent about the son or sons she had entrusted to Saint Martin's.[230] During his first months in office in the fall of 1943 and throughout his twenty-one-year abbatial tenure, Abbot Raphael also found many occasions on which to let the mothers know that their generous aid was appreciated.[231]

The abbot and members of the SMC "faculty" (nearly all of whom were Benedictine priests or clerics in those years) were invited to attend special programs sponsored by the Mothers' Clubs. Benedictine parish priests, who usually served as spiritual directors for their local club, also attended the clubs' meetings and special events. Those events at which alumni of the College were expected to be present usually also attracted a good delegation of students and monks from campus. Current students were specifically invited to certain gatherings so they could "rise and shine" for their moms and meet and impress club members. Saint Martin's was very much a family affair in those days.

The ladies had a knack for being both gracious and practical. Regarding an upcoming annual "formal tea" at the height of the Depression, Gertrude McCoy, president of the Seattle Mothers' Club, wrote Abbot Lambert: "If you have any suggestions to offer in the way of making this occasion more enjoyable (or profitable), we surely would be pleased to get them." A few months earlier, she had written: "We again ask your prayers for another successful year. As stated before, we know this is due to prayer and our 'Object' of helping Saint Martin's and, especially, in supporting the education of Benedictine candidates for the Catholic priesthood." Later that same year Mrs. McCoy commented: "We never lose sight of the fact that our work seems blessed with success even in such strenuous times and when there are so many calls [for help] everywhere around us."[232]

Their great good will often seemed to bring good results even in hard times, as Mary E. McDermott noted in December 1937: "The Club had a lovely party . . . last Wednesday and made $54.00 net which was very good for a house party at this time of year. The cooperation and spirit of the ladies was wonderful and we were all so happy in doing it for Saint Martin's."[233] On the other hand, the Depression sometimes stalled even the best of intentions. On several occasions Mothers' Clubs' officers wrote to apologize for being in arrears on their pledged scholarship donations and to promise to be more prompt in the future.[234]

Mothers' Clubs members also had pious personal reasons for their hard work. In 1934, Teresa E. Farrell, secretary of the Seattle Club, stated: "At present more than one-half of our membership is composed of those who have no boy at the college but are anxious to belong because of the spiritual benefits derived from this membership."[235] Sick or deceased members were regularly remembered in the prayers of the monks and students. A Mass was promptly offered at the Abbey for all deceased Mothers' Clubs members and their names were listed on a plaque mounted in the lobby of Saint Martin's chapel. Abbot Lambert personally offered Mass on the First Friday of each month (a day of special devotion for many Catholics) for the current members of the Seattle Club, which "served to interest and stimulate the group."[236]

A 1938 Status Report

Over several decades one of the highlights of every school year was an annual Mothers' Day celebration on campus. Begun in 1924, it usually was held on the Tuesday following the national observance of Mothers' Day on the second Sunday of May. Faculty and students welcomed mothers of current and past students with open arms to a spruced-up and festively decorated campus.

On May 9, 1938, Abbot Lambert addressed some typically serious and sober remarks to the assembled Mothers' Day crowd. He proudly reported that the College would begin that fall offering an accredited junior year of courses. He next reasserted the great need for a Catholic atmosphere both at home and at school—something he promised that Saint Martin's provided. He then assured the contingent of mothers that they were laboring together with the Benedictines for the betterment of their children; of the school's alumni; of American society in general; and for the Catholic Church worldwide. Abbot Lambert also proclaimed the need for sacrifice at every level of society, and observed that young people too often wasted their time and money and dissipated their mental and physical abilities. Some people became really angry, he observed, when told to save and to teach sacrifice by example in the current hard times. "Other agencies offer license," he said, but "we [offer] the cross!" While society at large too often took the low road and was satisfied with low standards of achievement, SMC could not and would not do so. He closed by calling on one and all to encourage vocations to the priesthood and religious life—especially at Saint Martin's Abbey.[237]

Parish Life in the "Hard Times"

Being a pastor at any time is no easy task but when ones service occurs during "hard times" things can be even more challenging than usual. Such was to be the case during the tenure of Father Mark Wiechman at Tacoma's pioneer Benedictine parish, Holy Rosary Church, from 1914 to 1935. His long pastorate was "one filled with financial problems and building needs." After succeeding the newly-elected Abbot Oswald as the church's pastor in 1914, he held "numerous fairs, socials, festivals, and pledge drives until sufficient funds were raised to start building a new church." He also instituted an envelope system for parish collections to regularize contributions, but with indifferent results. The parish's fine new church constructed in 1920–1921 cost $200,000 and created an enormous debt which took successive pastors many years to pay off. When Father Mark was transferred to Shelton in 1935, the parish debt exceeded $135,000. The Great Depression's many setbacks hurt parishioners and thus reduced parish income. Many families could not pay the tuition for their children enrolled in the 400-student parochial school where Sister Dorothy Bretz, O.S.B., started a hot lunch program. Food and clothing were also collected for the poor of the parish.[238]

In many ways, the Depression-era experience of Visitation Parish in South Tacoma was typical of that of the several parishes then staffed by Benedictine priests from Saint Martin's. Father Anthony Hack was pastor there from September 1930 to July 1935, and under his leadership an all-

South Tacoma's Visitation Church was faced with Depression-era belt-tightening while the parish's population was rapidly expanding. The fourteen years when the Hack brothers—Father Anthony and Father Dominic— served successively as pastor were "a period of forced economizing and almost privation." Yet then and later the spirit of the parish was close-knit and vital. After World War II, Father Anselm Lenslinger (1899-1960)—shown here behind the church-rectory complex in the late 1940s—was assigned to the church as assistant to Father Gabriel Donohue. (Saint Martin's Abbey Archives)

out effort was made to reduce the parish debt and to economize in every possible way. Such "belt-tightening" was particularly difficult for it was undertaken while the parish's population was rapidly expanding. Father Dominic Hack, Father Anthony's brother, replaced him as South Tacoma's Catholic pastor in 1935, and labored there for nine years. His term was also "a period of forced economizing and almost privation." He often did his own janitorial work in order to cut costs even further. "During the depression most parishes worked just to keep up with their debts so not much work was done on improvements or additions. Then the World War II years came along and there were no materials or labor available."[239]

After leading Queen of Angels Parish in Port Angeles through the "hard times" of the Depression and World War II, Father Bernard Neary (1879–1952) finally realized his dream of building a beautiful new church for his faith community in the late 1940s. Benedictine priests from Lacey continued to serve Port Angeles and Clallam County until 1990. (Saint Martin's Abbey Archives)

An incident concerning the operation of the parochial school at Queen of Angels Parish in Port Angeles also demonstrates the financial constraints under which Benedictine (and other) parishes were forced to operate in the challenging era of the 1930s. Father Bernard Neary was appointed pastor of that scenic town's Catholic Church in September 1928, and for a quarter-century he embodied Catholicism in Clallam County,

Washington. The school had opened in 1927 and was staffed by Sisters of Saint Ann, whose motherhouse was located only a few dozen miles across the Straits of Juan de Fuca in the Canadian city of Victoria, British Columbia. The Sisters quickly noted with approval that the new pastor was "at home with children having been director of the college in Lacey for sixteen years."[240]

In the spring and summer of 1933, during one of the glummest periods of the Depression in the Northwest, funding for Queen of Angeles School reached its lowest ebb. Father Bernard's correspondence with the provincial superior of the Sisters of Saint Ann provides an acute glimpse of parochial distress:

Rev. and Dear Mother:

I do not like to ask this but I am compelled to do so on account of conditions as they are at present.

I wish you would consent to allow the parish the salary of the Sisters for the month of May.

The county [public school] teachers have done this. In fact they were compelled to do so. Their warrants are not being cashed for lack of county funds.

I have had to borrow $3000 in order to meet the demands of creditors.

I have paid the Sisters up to March 1st and am putting on a chicken dinner Sunday to help pay for March.

A portion of my salary has not been paid for 1932 also the housekeeper together with the groceries etc.

The Sisters are very devoted to their children and deserve even more than we can give them. Let us hope that God will help us to carry on. . . .

This year from Jan. 1 to date we have taken in $109 against $357 of last year and $465 of the previous year in school tuition. So you can see by this that the slump is great.

Trusting that my request will not be too much of a shock for you and wishing you God's blessing. . . .[241]

The response of the Sisters' provincial superior was equally frank and glum:

. . . your request concerning an additional reduction of our Sisters' salary is painful and unexpected. My reason for using the word "additional" is the following: According to the terms of our agreement . . . each of the Sisters is entitled to an annual salary of $350.00, and not to a monthly salary of $35.00 for a school year of nine months. Still, our records show, for the past four years, from 1928 [to] 1932, it is on this basis that our Sisters of Port Angeles have been paid, that is, they have received $315.00, or 9 months' salary, instead of $350.00, as stipulated in our agree-

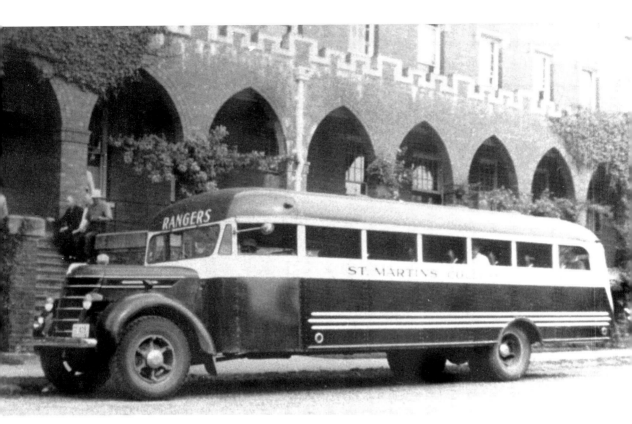

A growing campus population required new transportation for its representatives as they traveled to off-campus games or other events. Here the spiffy "Rangers" bus is parked outside the west wing of Old Main in the late 1930s. Both High School and College teams were called the "Rangers" in those days. (Saint Martin's Abbey Archives)

ment of June 22, 1927, thereby favoring the parish with $1,400.00 of their well-earned salary.

Do you not think, Reverend Pastor, that this fact should be considered now and that no further reduction should be asked for from us?

I am not exaggerating when I state that we are struggling here against many heavy difficulties and that we must depend upon the meager help of our branch houses to maintain our various works.

We, therefore, hopefully pray that you will be able with the generous co-operation of your parish to pay the nine months' salary as in past years. . . .[242]

Although this financial impasse was eventually resolved and the Sisters of Saint Ann would remain in Port Angeles until 1947, the hardships and frustration which this incident reflects was certainly repeated many times in Saint Martin's other parishes during the Depression Era.

In 1933, Abbot Lambert called on Bishop Gerald M. Shaughnessy, Seattle's then newly appointed Catholic prelate. As the bishop later remembered the exchange, the abbot "verbally and unofficially" put before him a request that Saint Martin's Abbey, by way of a *beneplacitum*, be given the permanent care of five parishes then staffed by its monks. They were Holy Rosary, Tacoma; Visitation, South Tacoma;

Assumption, Seattle; Saint Edward's, Shelton; and Queen of Angels, Port Angeles. Abbot Lambert also "mentioned his conversation with the then Apostolic Delegate" to the United States about the possibility of the Diocese of Seattle canonically confiding certain parishes to the Benedictine Fathers. When then-Bishop O'Dea had earlier queried the papal envoy about a similar comment, the latter had answered that he did not specifically remember making such a suggestion to the Abbot of Saint Martin's although he might have. After all, the Vatican diplomat admitted, such arrangements were not at all uncommon.[243] Saint Martin's Abbey never received the permanent charge of any parishes.

Coeducation for SMC?

One thing Abbot Lambert did not tell the SMC students' mothers assembled on campus in May 1938 was that the faculty the previous fall had submitted to him a resolution to introduce coeducation to the College. Arguments "of considerable weight" had been advanced in favor of the proposition but with the clear understanding "that young ladies should be only day-students, and reside off campus." However, the arguments against coeducation seemed "to be overwhelming" on account of Saint Martin's being "a boarding school, and situated in a rural district." In January 1938, the abbot had written Bishop Shaughnessy of Seattle asking for "an expression of your views, or wishes, in the matter."[244]

The following week the bishop (himself an experienced educator) responded to Abbot Lambert's query "unofficially" but at some length. He, too, could see "both the advantages and disadvantages, particularly in a school that was built only for boys." Bishop Shaughnessy also noted the "rather strange situation" of the Catholic Church's attitude toward coeducation. While the Holy Father "spoke very plainly against it" in his 1929 encyclical on the Christian education of youth, he noted, "the Pontifical University in Washington, D.C. [a.k.a. The Catholic University of America] is to all intents and purposes now coeducational." He likewise observed that "Seattle College [now Seattle University] is really coeducational, although the Jesuits have traditionally been opposed to this scheme."

Unofficially, the bishop stated that he "would interpose no objection" if SMC adopted the coeducational method. He also offered Abbot Lambert "the concrete advice" to make a careful survey "to determine what likelihood of success" there might be "if you should offer your courses to Catholic girls."

The bishop concluded his letter with a telling comment: "I have, indeed, very much at heart the educational needs of our Catholic girls, particularly in Tacoma. As is well known, they tend to enroll in sectarian institutions when faced with a lack of higher education under Catholic auspices. The question is, would coeducation in Saint Martin's College help to solve the [Tacoma] problem?"[245]

Bishop Shaughnessy's concern for the provision of Catholic-sponsored higher education in Tacoma was quite real. He had discussions with Abbot Lambert "on several occasions" about "a possible college extension course in Tacoma, to be managed by Saint Martin's College." They also discussed the feasibility of using Benedictine priests from Lacey "and some Benedictine sisters from the East, with whom the Abbot is in contact, for the faculty personnel" of a Tacoma Catholic College. On November 7, 1940, the abbot reported to the bishop that certain Midwestern Benedictine Sisters were "very receptive" to jointly providing a faculty for such an institution and that "a start might be possible perhaps in September, 1942, or maybe even in 1941."

The bishop also asked whether the Abbey might be considering buying a building in Tacoma for such a College and observed that Annie Wright Seminary was "at present in financial difficulties and perhaps could be obtained cheaper, at least if there is a foreclosure." They then discussed other possible locations after agreeing that Annie Wright was "too far from the center" of Tacoma to be practical and that another site more convenient to public transportation should be considered. Abbot Lambert also "expressed the wish that it would be a diocesan college" and reported "that he and his council felt that they could not take on any more financial commitments at the present time." That suggestion pleased Bishop Shaughnessy, who told the abbot that he was "entirely favorable and would look into the situation."

In the same conversation, Abbot Lambert reported to the bishop that he had heard from some Tacoma Catholic laymen "that the Jesuits had been planning to give up Bellarmine High School and to start a college in Tacoma." Bishop Shaughnessy replied that the Jesuits would need his permission to change from a high school to a college.[246] While nothing came of that project at that time, Saint Martin's involvement in a Tacoma Catholic College would come up for discussion again later in the 1940s.

A College freshman who began his studies at SMC in the fall of 1937 remembers that coeducation was much discussed and widely favored on campus during that academic year but that nothing concrete then came of the proposal.[247] That, however, was not for want of trying.

Despite our faculty priests' heavy academic and pastoral workloads, some scholarship was still being transacted even in the difficult 1930s. Father Matthew Britt, for example, had already published *The Hymns of the Breviary and Missal* (1922) and *A Dictionary of the Psalter* (1928). Early in 1938, he confided to an old Minnesota friend information on his ongoing scholarly pursuits: "For several years, I have been spending several hours a day in making a translation of the Psalms and a simple commentary for the people, not for Biblical experts. I am now half way through a fourth complete draft of the work. It is an excellent pastime."[248]

Provident Management

In 1914, Abbot Oswald had arranged to have exploratory drilling for oil carried out on parts of the campus but nothing had come of that venture. Likewise concerned to improve the finances of "the College," on January 23, 1931, his successor, Abbot Lambert, signed a "wildcat" gas and oil exploration lease with Olympia businessman George A. Mottman covering most areas of the campus.

It is unclear whether anything came of that 1931 venture but a decade later a similar lease was signed between SMC and Mr. Mottman. Saint Martin's as the lessor was again to have "the right to use free of charge gas or oil or both" for its "domestic or institutional purposes." Moreover, if gas or oil was not found in commercial quantities and artesian water was found, the lessor would also have "the right to use the same without cost for drilling." The use of Saint Martin's name "in any way to effect sales of stock" would void the lease immediately. No oil was discovered during the drilling period from April 1940 to mid-January 1941. In October 1941, the College took over and disassembled "the derrick which had been used for prospecting for oil on Saint Martin's grounds."[249]

Saint Martin's and World War II

As Europe plunged into war in the fall of 1939, school life at Saint Martin's High School and College, and the Benedictine monks' cycle of prayer and work, continued seemingly unabated in the quiet environs of our rural campus. The United States, after all, was a nonbelligerent and isolationism was still in the ascendancy in our country. The winds of war

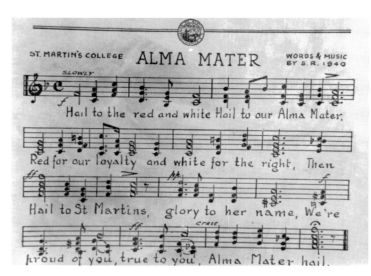

continued to swirl, however, and the Japanese Empire's attack on Pearl Harbor, Hawaii, on December 7, 1941, abruptly thrust Americans into the throes of a worldwide conflict on the side of the Allies. Many of our alumni and older students quickly rallied to the flag for national service. Several of them were very well prepared as they had participated in the SMC unit of a nationwide program to train pilots for eventual commissioning by the U.S. military.

In the summer of 1939, our then very small College joined with several larger schools in other parts of the country in an important experiment funded by the federal government's civilian aviation agency to "foster and develop" private flying and general aviation. Female and male applicants were required to be accepted on an equal basis into that program but SMC was not coeducational. Father Gerald Desmond, as dean of the College, however, prevailed upon Abbot Lambert to allow women to participate in the summer trial program. SMC offered certain aviation-related courses such as meteorology and radio communications on campus while the Buroker-Hicks Flying Service provided actual hands-on mechanical and flight instruction at and out of Olympia's municipal airfield. Buroker-Hicks provided the instructors and ground personnel, who included Herb and Gladys Buroker. Gwin Hicks served as coordinator and promoter for the program. With the advice and assistance of Jack R. Cram, an old friend and Marine Corps pilot well placed in aviation circles, Father Gerald handled campus arrangements and coordination with other schools.

Locally and nationally, 1939's summer experiment in pilot training was very successful. As legislation to further expand civilian pilot training for the sake of national defense "preparedness" worked its way through Congress, however, the proviso requiring equal access to the program for women was dropped. The intended beneficiaries of civilian-trained pilots,

In the spring of 1940, students enrolled in SMC's pilot training program received hands-on flight instruction at Olympia's municipal airfield from Buroker-Hicks Flying Service. They were part of a nationwide campus-based program to train pilots for eventual commissioning by the U.S. military. (Photo courtesy A. R. "Dick" Lewis)

Along with the rest of SMC's pilot training group, flight instructor Gladys Buroker and student-pilot Ted Sommerville moved to the Pasco, Washington airfield during the 1941–1942 Christmas holidays. Sommerville "soloed" from that field a short while later. (Photo courtesy Gladys Buroker)

the U.S. Army and Navy, were unwilling to be put in a position where they would have to accept female pilots. So when SMC and Buroker-Hicks again teamed up to participate in the federal government's expanded Civilian Pilot Training program, no women were permitted to apply.[250]

Late in the fall semester of 1939, an aviation ground school class for twenty men was offered at SMC in conjunction with Buroker-Hicks. Many of them afterwards enrolled in flight instruction courses taught by Jack Mifflin and Herb Buroker at the Olympia airport, the first of which started on January 24, 1940.

In December 1941, civilian aviation was significantly curtailed along the West Coast so SMC's pilot training students and instructors moved east of the Cascade Mountains in order to continue their flight training. Gladys Buroker remembers that redeployment: "Moving a flight operation is no small task—not only did we have planes, but tools, heavy shop machinery, office equipment, furniture—and a whole class of

students to uproot from Saint Martin's College and transport to Pasco where new arrangements for board, room, classes, and transportation had to be arranged. The students trained at Pasco during their Christmas vacation."

When the Navy announced its intention to commandeer the Pasco airport, Buroker-Hicks Flying Service signed a lease in January 1942 on Weeks Field near Coeur d'Alene, Idaho. Accompanied by Father Gerald and Father Robert Wippel, several SMC students moved to northern Idaho in the College bus to continue their flight training at Weeks Field. Ground and flight courses were taught at Weeks while students were initially housed and fed at Arnold's Auto Camp. Cheeky students erected a sign along the highway which identified Arnold's as "Buroker-Hicks Concentration Camp No. 1," which created something of an embarrassment to local business and civic leaders. Father Gerald then successfully asked local service clubs and other influential folks to help secure more appropriate room and board arrangements for the student pilots.

When the military took over the nationwide Civilian Pilot Training Program in the spring of 1942, Buroker-Hicks was notified that its current flight-school contract would terminate when those presently in training completed their course. SMC students scrambled to complete their flight training before Buroker-Hicks took on the new batch of War Training aviation students which military authorities had assigned to them for instruction. "It was a sad day," Gladys Buroker remembers, "when Saint Martin's school bus left Coeur d'Alene sending our beloved Father Gerald back to Lacey."

In Olympia, Pasco, and Coeur d'Alene, the SMC/Buroker-Hicks flight-training program taught more than four hundred students between 1939 and mid-1942. Many of "our" pilots served their country in military or naval

Father Meinrad Gaul, O.S.B. (1907–1984), seen here with some High School boys, was a campus mainstay during World War II. He taught history and other subjects, carried on a large correspondence with "my boys in the service" and noted the campus comedy associated with a boarding school for boys in his diaries. (Saint Martin's Abbey Archives)

aviation during (and after) the war. Others aided the war effort as flight instructors, glider pilots and instructors, and test pilots or by flying Air Transportation Command passenger planes or ferrying planes to our Allies.

Those few female students enrolled in SMC's aviation courses in the summer of 1939 might technically claim to be our College's first coeds. Likewise, Gladys Buroker, who was an experienced pilot as well as a patient and successful teacher of aviation skills, might claim for herself the distinction of being SMC's pioneer female instructor. She fondly remembers her teaching at Saint Martin's: "Actually, I think it was easier for me to teach the students at SMC, as most were nearer the same age level as myself, and I do not recall any apprehension except when I was told Father Gerald would be sitting in on some of my classes. I had completed my [ground school] studies and taken the tests such a short time previously to the time I started teaching that it was not difficult preparing the lesson for each class. The students were eager and excited about aviation, asking many questions, which makes teaching exciting. This was a course they wanted and not one that was required. After the first time that Father Gerald sat in on a class, I felt at ease when he attended. He was real interested in the subject being taught and expressed how pleased he was that Saint Martin's students were having the opportunity to get in on the ground floor of aviation. In talking with me, he always left me feeling encouraged and wanting to do the best job possible."

Summing up her experience at SMC, she comments: "I wasn't a Catholic and my main concern was the fact that I was teaching at a non-coed college. It always seemed as I left my car and headed for my classroom that I was in a sea of men. After a few days though, Fathers and students no longer gave me the look of 'what are you doing here?' They had discovered that I had a legitimate reason for being there."

At a time when SMC's faculty was composed almost entirely of Benedictine priests, some campus denizens waggishly referred to Mrs. Buroker in her teaching capacity as an "Assistant Father"! "Teaching at Saint Martin's College," she recalled half a century later, "was one of my most memorable experiences. I have never worked with anyone during my life that I enjoyed more than my association with Father Gerald. It also broadened my religious views."[251]

Meanwhile, Back on Campus

During the war the College's enrollment dwindled to a handful while Saint Martin's High School became more attractive for families with absent fathers. This shrinkage of enrollment is evidenced by the program for SMC's Fiftieth Commencement on June 8, 1945, which listed just three College and sixteen High School graduates. Moreover, due to wartime conditions two College and six High School graduates were absent "but three had Mothers here to replace them."[252]

While the distant war was a major backdrop for everything that occurred, the everyday life of school and monastery proceeded on of necessity. Father Meinrad described the hectic start of the 1944–1945 school year: "We have a fair capacity house, with a total registration of near 170—about 140 boarders. It is a great job to try to keep them busy with an ever lessening faculty—and together with an almost negative [that is, nonexistent] corps of prefects. If the place holds together through this year it will be some sort of minor miracle." The High School students were "very unhappy about the[ir] curtailed privileges—town only once a week, but more to do here!" He admitted, however, that his "whole outlook" was "colored by several things" including his own very heavy teaching load and the pending death—after a long, hard illness—of his mother.[253]

The usual campus comedy associated with a boarding high school for boys continued as before. Sports, campus movies (carefully chosen 16 mm. features such as *The Crusades* and *A Wing and a Prayer*), occasional dances, nominal and severe disciplinary actions, and the dreaded academic grind occupied our students and their teachers. When grade point averages were down, the faculty groused; when they rose, Father Meinrad, the registrar, worried to his diary that the students were either "getting good, or profs soft!"[254]

Our students kept up with the war news and were taught by old Father Sebastian to identify enemy aircraft should any appear in the skies overhead. Although such hazards were but a distant threat, preparedness was the watchword of the day. On May 22, 1945, for example, Washington State Patrolman Stacey Mattson visited campus to lecture our students on Japanese fire-balloon dangers.[255]

At the end of 1944, old Father Matthew finally got proof for the validity of one of his pet peeves. He had long considered the institution's classrooms, study halls, and choir chapel to be seriously underlighted. Abbot Raphael finally agreed to get "the Light Co. to bring a light meter out to the college to do a bit of testing." An adequately lighted room would register fifty on the meter, but "a slightly lower reading" would pass. The meter reading in the two big study halls (one of which had just been made into the Library) was seven and in the monks' choir chapel thirteen. It was "utterly impossible to put light bulbs sufficiently large" in those rooms because the building's wiring could not carry the load so white fluorescent lamps were "the only solution." Father Matthew claimed that had for years tried to get Father James to buy a $10 light meter, "but he was not interested, and apparently no one else was." He ended with a self-satisfied assertion: "We have been guilty of criminal negligence since 1913," which was the year the first wing of the new College building had been occupied by students. "No wonder," he added, that "so many of our students could not pass the eye tests of the Navy!"[256]

Father Meinrad also did his best to keep in touch with "my boys in the service." He regularly sent about 150 newsy "hectographed" letters to servicemen with Saint Martin's connections and also boosted an alumni war bond drive. In his diaries, he noted with pleasure the many letters he received from alumni in the military services and his enjoyment of their visits en route to or returning from training or overseas duty. He also mourned them when they were reported missing in action or killed. His May 30, 1945 diary notation read: "Decoration Day opened with Solemn Requiem Mass for Gold Star [killed in action] Alumni—26."[257]

Carrying On as Normally as Possible

Father Raphael Heider was elected Saint Martin's third abbot on September 1, 1943, some three weeks after Abbot Lambert's sudden death from a heart attack on August 9. At age forty, the new abbot was fairly young for the job and admitted to friends that he felt "overwhelmed by what had been placed on my shoulders."[258] Continuity is important for

Abbot Raphael Heider (1903–1971) was fairly young when he was elected Saint Martin's third abbot in September 1943. He tried to carry on Saint Martin's academic and pastoral work in the best fashion possible given the absence of five priests serving as military chaplains and others in graduate school. He also immediately started planning improvements for the setting of his monks prayer-life. (Saint Martin's Abbey Archives)

institutions and has long been valued by Benedictines. Abbot Raphael, therefore, immediately set to work to steer a steady course for his monastery and its apostolates. One obvious way to do so was to consolidate support for Saint Martin's among its various constituencies.

On September 12, Abbot Raphael received a letter of congratulations on his election from the president of the Saint Martin's Mothers' Club of Seattle, who stated that both she and her members would "look forward with pleasure to our mutual relations and contacts in the interest of SMC." The abbot was also invited to be the guest of honor at the club's annual formal tea on October 10, 1943. He attended their fete and really enjoyed himself. In fact, Abbot Raphael always enjoyed the programs and valued the work of the Mothers' Clubs, as he explicitly stated the next spring: "It will be a pleasure, I assure you, to accept the opportunity to be with such a loyal group of friends of Saint Martin's." A charmed Seattle Club member wrote him in June 1944 complimenting him on his recent "inspiring and pleasant visit" with the mothers: "It all seemed to remind us again of the close ties which bind us all together in our great Family."[259] In September 1944, the abbot floated the suggestion of a cooperative project wherein all three Mothers' Clubs—Seattle, Tacoma, and Olympia— would sponsor a memorial on campus listing the names of alumni servicemen who had served in the ongoing war.[260]

Fiftieth Anniversary Observance

On January 25, 1945, Father Meinrad began working on what he called a "Jubilee History" of Saint Martin's but two weeks later he noted in his diary that while Abbot Raphael had given his "O.K. to the Jubilee Book only Father Sebastian will work on it also." On March 23 he remarked with pleasure: "Got *fifty* dollars unsolicited for the Jubilee Book total now over $1850, which is getting there."[261]

The Monachist, a bimonthly Abbey publication, had already recounted the story of the institution's first thirty years in regular installments written by Father Sebastian. The "greater part " of that narrative was incorporated into the fiftieth anniversary "sketch" that Father Sebastian published as *Between the Years*. The assistance of Father Demetrius, "the sole survivor of the zealous few" who had established SMC in 1895, was gratefully acknowledged. Father Meinrad provided editorial and secretarial assistance in publishing the volume. "Right now I am head over heels in work, getting out the Annual for the Jubilee year," he confided to the absent Father

Bede in January 1945. "I'm putting in quite an array of old pictures, and all in all hope it will be quite a book."[262]

The fiftieth anniversary history appeared both as part of an expanded issue of the 1945 yearbook and as a separately published ninety-six-page booklet. The abbot mailed a copy to the Benedictine Order's abbot primate in Rome that October commenting that it presented "a generally fair picture of our history and the present community."[263]

Saint Martin's held a joyful but limited observance of its fiftieth anniversary due to wartime constraints. On July 11, 1945, a Mass of Thanksgiving was celebrated in the campus chapel by Bishop Gerald M. Shaughnessy of Seattle. (Father Meinrad privately described the bishop's expeditious liturgical performance as "clear-cutting through a pontifical" but noted that the prelate preached for a half hour.) He lauded the monks for being faithful to the work of Christian education in their High School and College apostolates.

At the jubilee banquet served in the student refectory by members of the Olympia Mothers' Club, Bishop Edward J. Kelly of Boise traced the history of Saint Martin's and paid tribute to the vision, courage, and devotion of its founders and its faculty. Including Benedictines, clerical guests that day numbered two bishops and 135 priests from throughout the Northwest. Letters and telegrams of felicitation from abbots of other Benedictine institutions and from other Catholic schools and colleges were read to the banquet audience. Father Demetrius Jueneman, seventy-nine, our sole surviving pioneer monk, was heartily saluted. Jubilee contributions from alumni and friends to support the College's work were also proudly reported.[264] Abbot Raphael commented to Father Gerald, on the East Coast finishing up his doctoral dissertation, that the celebration that day "went off quite well. It was a happy day."[265]

Our Military Chaplains

Five of the Abbey's priests eventually served as chaplains stateside and/or overseas in the U.S. Army or Army Air Force between 1943 and 1947. Their enlistment made the Abbey very shorthanded. Father James Piotrzkowski, recently appointed prior of the monastery by Abbot Raphael, vividly described that shortage in a September 1943 letter. The Abbey, he wrote, was "working under a tremendous handicap" due to its "greatly decreased" number of priests. In addition to the four who had so far joined the military, two Saint Martin's priests had died and four were away at graduate school. "All of

which means that the conducting of our school and filling the places of those Fathers . . . has placed such a heavy burden on those of us who are here that we fear that some may break down from overwork."[266]

As commissioned officers, our Benedictine military chaplains were responsible for providing services and devotions for Catholic enlisted men and officers and, occasionally, for non-Catholic personnel as well. They were also required to provide regular statistical reports to the chief of chaplains listing the number of participants at the Masses, Communions, Confessions, and other sacramental and devotional services they conducted. They also tallied their ministry as supplied through office conferences, hospital visits, "morals" lectures, and welfare cases. Our monk-chaplains by and large enjoyed their work, were proud of their service to God and country, and generally got along well with non-Catholic chaplains and soldiers.[267]

Father Leo Hansen ministered at Army hospitals in Spokane and Tacoma as well as at Port Townsend's Fort Worden and its affiliated Puget Sound harbor defense sites. He obtained supplies for Army chapels from USO units in Bremerton and Olympia. He also visited and ministered to German POWs at Fort Lewis and in other detention camps in Washington and Oregon. On January 1, 1945, a supervisor described him as being full of energy and effectively carrying a heavy schedule. At war's end, he volunteered to stay on in the Army and did so for another eighteen months. War Department directives, however, eventually called for separation of older chaplains. He was fifty-six when he was discharged from the Army on September 16, 1947.

Father Alcuin Lawrence was kept very busy with diverse pastoral duties while stationed at Camp Roberts, California, in 1943–1944. It was there that he met, converted, and provisionally baptized Sergeant Ernest F. Curtis. (After the war his "convert" became a monk at Saint Martin's and later served the monastic community as Abbot Dunstan.) Transferred to Iceland, Father Alcuin was rated "a quiet, extremely reticent officer" who "spends a majority of his evenings helping men with their problems" and was much respected by both officers and enlisted men. He was also lauded by his superiors for organizing "good morale events" for the troops of both a religious and a social nature and for being cheerful, loyal, and cooperative. His twenty-seven months as an Army chaplain, he reported after being released, had been "packed with rich experiences." He promised his prayers "for the continued good work of the Chaplain Corps and that the results of their work with

Servicemen will be carried back into their daily lives as civilians and contribute to a better America."

After chaplain's school in Massachusetts in the summer of 1944, Father Jerome Toner was assigned to Fort Oglethorpe, Georgia, for some months before being sent to France in January 1945. He was later described as "a quiet officer in poor health" but "loyal and cooperative and absolutely dependable." On April 28, 1946, while stationed in the U.S. Rivieria Recreation Area, he was temporarily promoted to captain after complaining that he had been twenty-six months in the service as a first lieutenant.

Father Robert Wippel was sent to the Presidio of San Francisco in July 1943, where he witnessed many marriages. Reassigned to the Los Angeles port of embarkation, he was promoted to captain in March 1944 and served as chaplain on Army troop transport ships to Australia and India. While later serving at Vancouver Barracks and Fort Lawton, Washington, his military superiors rated him "outstanding in performance of his duties" as well as "cooperative and broad-minded" and "loyal to Army ideals."

Starting in July 1943, Father Marcel Berthon was briefly chaplain at a camp for Italian POWs in Florence, Arizona. At the end of December, he took up new duties at Dibble Army General Hospital in Menlo Park, California. Since the hospital had not yet received its full complement of staff or patients, he had plenty of time to visit Catholic institutions, clergy, and religious in the San Francisco Bay Area. He paid a call on Auxiliary Bishop Thomas A. Connolly, who after the war became Seattle's bishop. While later stationed at an Army hospital in France, he was described as "a quiet unassuming officer who is inspired by his religious and military responsibilities. He is always 'on duty' and practices 'leadership by example.'"

Father Marcel probably spoke for all of Saint Martin's military chaplains when he wrote in March 1946 to thank the Army "for the wonderful opportunities of serving God and my country. I shall always value beyond words the experiences which have come to me through this service." His letter was quickly answered by a higher-ranking Army chaplain who observed: "It is sometimes hard to see what good can come out of war, but there are many of us who suspect that it has been a quickening influence in all religious life, and that God has indeed been moving in a 'mysterious way His wonders to perform.'"[268] The postwar boom in applicants to Catholic religious orders and seminaries both worldwide and in the United States—including Saint Martin's Abbey—certainly gave evidence of such a religious "quickening."

War's End

V-E Day on May 8 and V-J Day on August 14, 1945, signaled the Allies' complete victory in both the European and Pacific Theaters of War. Peace was wildly celebrated on the American homefront and in a somewhat more subdued way on campus. Everybody wanted things to return to normal so as to get on with their lives. The end of hostilities would also bring with it big changes in American society generally as well as for Saint Martin's. ✤

*When this community photo was taken in June 1955,
the Benedictine monks of Saint Martin's Abbey had
already sponsored the educational programs of Saint
Martin's College and Saint Martin's High School for
sixty years. Pastoral and chaplaincy duties had also provided
rich opportunities for the their ministry. The monks seem
quietly confident that they were ready to face whatever the
Lord would send their way in the years and decades to come.
Abbot Raphael Heider (front and center wearing a pectoral
cross) was then Saint Martin's spiritual father and chief
administrator. (Photo by Merle Junk)*

CHAPTER 6
Growth and Opportunities (1945–1964)

WITH THE REST OF THE WORLD, SAINT Martin's in 1945 gratefully welcomed the end of the tragedy that was World War II. The institution's monks, faculty, staff, and students also entered into the beginning of an exciting but challenging postwar era. As Saint Martin's spiritual and administrative leader, Abbot Raphael Heider had a daunting task before him. His job, however, was buoyed up by his strong Christian faith and his knowledge of and respect for the enduring accomplishments of the Benedictine pattern of monastic life.

Thus, Abbot Raphael was well set up to manage the multiple commitments Saint Martin's already had taken on as well as to chart its new patterns of service. Between 1945 and 1964, the Abbey's continued financial underwriting of the operations of both its High School and College, as well as its involvement in parishes and chaplaincies, would prove to be a demanding but generally satisfying task for most Saint Martin's people.

Postwar Vocations

A monastery needs monks and so must attract to itself earnest men who are seeking to serve God via prayer and work through the vehicle of Benedictine community life. Abbot Raphael responded personally and solicitously to any inquiries about becoming a monk at Saint Martin's. He answered many letters from GIs or ex-servicemen at the end of World War II. Typical were his comments to a serviceman in France interested in becoming a Benedictine lay brother, whom his chaplain, Father Marcel Berthon, had referred to the Abbey: "Saint Benedict says in his holy rule that the whole purpose of one who comes to the abbey should be 'to truly seek God.' That is our whole objective. That one goal is ever to be kept in the forefront."

He then added: "In a Benedictine monastery we also work, since the motto of Saint Benedict is 'Pray and Work.'

Our work is to be just another form of prayer. Our work can be of any sort under the sun, so long as it contributes to our spiritual progress. Our work is secondary but very important. We can use whatever talent a man may possess. There is no end of things which need doing in a monastery. Between discovering talents on the one hand, and loving filial obedience on the other it is possible to bring about a harmonious solution for everyone concerned."[269]

In encouraging another possible brother-candidate, the abbot assured him that after he had been at Saint Martin's for a time he would "gradually fall into the spirit of religious life and all things will become clear to you. The main thing is that you be genuinely convinced that you want to devote your talents to God's honor and glory. If you have a will to follow Christ, then all will go well."[270]

When a philosophy student in an Illinois seminary inquired about becoming a priest at Lacey, Abbot Raphael summarized the essentials of the religious life in a Benedictine community. First, he stated, we truly seek God "by performing our works under obedience and thus we are guaranteed efficaciousness for our sole purpose of sanctification." Then we vow stability, "which means we become deeply attached and loyal to our own [religious] house." Thirdly, we vow conversion of morals, "which means that our striving for perfection is constant, every moment of our lives."

Stating that he would be happy to assist "in every way that is proper" if his correspondent were genuinely interested in coming to Lacey, the abbot provided a thumbnail sketch of Saint Martin's at the end of 1945: "Saint Martin's, like all abbeys, is engaged in many activities, with hopes of growing

"Our work [as monks] is to be just another form of prayer," Abbot Raphael stated in 1945. "Our work can be of any sort under the sun, so long as it contributes to our spiritual progress. Our work is secondary but very important." He is pictured here celebrating Mass assisted by Father Denis Purcell (left) and Father James Piotrzkowski (right) in the campus chapel in 1950s. (Saint Martin's Abbey Archives)

and increasing our fields of activity and enterprise. We have a High School and a College. We have fathers on parishes. We have some who are interested in missionary activity. There are forty-seven priests, six clerics, and seven brothers in our family. Each has his own particular talents and interests, and these are encouraged and used for the good of the community. There are endless possibilities and dreams of future greatness. But first of all comes our seeking perfection."[271]

An abbot also must be solicitous for the spiritual growth and contentedness of his monks. Abbot Raphael's treatment of a fretful monk taking seminary coursework at Mount Angel Abbey in Oregon shows his sensitivity and personal concern: "All that I have thus far written is on the assumption that sending you elsewhere [to complete your studies] is the only manner in which your peace of soul and mind can be restored. If . . . you are honestly convinced that a change *must* be made, then you may return here after the semester examinations are finished. Then it will be a matter of biding your time here till arrangements [for you to take up your studies at another Benedictine seminary] can be satisfactorily completed."

"I want above all that you pursue perfection and truly seek God in joy and peace of mind," he continued. "It is only for this reason that I follow a policy that is exceptional but I would regret it very much if you would throughout the rest of your life work on the theory that 'the squeaky wheel gets the grease.' Perhaps this one more concession will make for your genuine happiness in our chosen way of life. If that is so then all is well and everyone will be happy."

With prudent concern, Abbot Raphael sent a note the next day to the priest who supervised Saint Martin's young monks at the Oregon seminary: "Thank you for your letter of the 15th which throws additional light on the matter of our unhappy cleric. Yesterday I wrote to him giving him an opportunity to return here after the examinations, provided that he

In earlier years, Benedictine brothers formed a sort of sub-community within the Abbey and primarily engaged in "blue collar" tasks vital to campus life at Saint Martin's. Brother Brendan Kelly (1897–1971) was a skilled craftsman who repaired and refurbished chalices and other "sacred vessels" used in Catholic worship. His extraordinary skills were also made use of by other Northwest institutions. (Saint Martin's Abbey Archives)

is honestly convinced that such procedure would be the only way of restoring his peace of soul. It may be that such action is the answer, but one does have misgivings about the future. May it please God to arrange that all ends well!"[272] The young man was eventually ordained but later left the monastery and finished his life as a diocesan priest in his native Wisconsin.

When one candidate for the monastery was deemed unacceptable, the abbot so informed him firmly but gently: "After much deliberation and having taken counsel, I cannot but state my frank opinion in your regard. You should entertain no hope of being accepted [as a novice] in our community. This advice on my part if offered with kindest feelings for you personally. You have good intellectual gifts which I respect. These talents must not be buried as a result of what may seem to be a harsh judgment on may part. It seems to me the best thing for you is to finish your college work, and commit yourself to the program of making yourself a useful apostle in the lay state."[273]

Benedictinism in Context

Writing from Saint Meinrad's Abbey in southwest Indiana on August 16, 1952, Abbot Raphael explained to his prior his decision to remain there for a monastic meeting and thus to miss the funeral of their venerable confrere, Father Bernard Neary: "It promises to be important for us as Benedictines," he explained, "that we, among ourselves, can come to grips with the problems which face us in our pursuit of the Benedictine way." The abbot had just come from a very large Congress of Religious held at the University of Notre Dame. While many of the papers read at the Congress were excellent, he admitted, there was not much place for real discussion in the vast proceedings. There was also a lack of consideration about matters specifically monastic.

"During these days here I am working on policies and procedures in respect to the Brothers," he added. "All the houses are aware of a new challenge in the matter of the Brotherhood in our monasteries. I had a good talk with Father Pascal Botz (he is Brother Director at Saint John's) yesterday morning. Next week I hope to have another bull session with him and any other Brother Director who may happen to come to the meeting. There should be some, since the meeting will be appealing to the novice masters and any who deal with the spiritual progress of Benedictines—Sisters too."

Always an eager student of things monastic, Abbot Raphael further reported: "I have been doing a little research on monastic horaria [schedules] so that I will have some facts and reactions when we might desire to re-study our program. There are some interesting arrangements in various monasteries."[274]

Matters Liturgical

Abbot Raphael had a fine appreciation of liturgy and of the importance for suitably embellished liturgical space. Thus, early in his term as abbot he set about planning liturgical improvements for Saint Martin's Chapel. "Father Abbot is planning extensive renovations in the Students' Chapel and, of course, The Organ," one senior monk reported. In late 1944, the sanctuary area was lowered to be "on a level with the floor of the Chapel" and widened some ten feet, a "beautiful curtain" hung back of the altar, and the altar "table" itself enhanced with new alderwood candlesticks, crucifix, and wood-sheathed tabernacle. The entire sanctuary floor as well as the steps and platform of the altar were carpeted in red and black. "In my opinion," Father Matthew observed, "the sanctuary has been greatly improved. Next the organ!"[275] Prior James likewise applauded the "strictly liturgical" altar and "very roomy" new sanctuary. "Eventually," he noted, "the [monks'] choir stalls will be installed on both sides of the altar."[276] A comment of Abbot Raphael's on the newly "re-done chapel" is quite revealing: "I suspect the job meets with the moderate approval of most interested persons. I hope above all it pleases the Lord, for whom it is being done."[277]

The Chapel's new pipe organ was "used for the first time—even though not all finished"—on July 11, 1945, during the Mass that day celebrating the institution's fiftieth anniversary. Abbot Raphael described the "grand celebration" to three of his aunts back in Minnesota and commented on the renovated Chapel: "The men worked late the evening before in order to have the organ ready for the solemn pontifical Mass. Now our organ is completed and everyone is very happy

with the results. The whole chapel has been redone since you saw it."278

Throughout 1945 Brother Jerome Keppers, an uncle of Abbot Raphael's who came to Lacey in 1930 as a middle-aged widower and became a lay brother two years later, worked hard on finishing up new choir stalls. He got some added help late that year and on the evening of November 30 the monks moved their "choir" into the old Students' Chapel so that they might "begin a new church year under different conditions." Abbot Raphael scheduled "a practice session on recitation, in order to pick up a few loose ends of rubrics and manners for choir." He afterwards noted with pleasure that "there was considerable improvement immediately—and now the problem will be not to slide back into former ways." There were, of course, "a few bugs to iron out" and "many improvements" yet to come but overall he was satisfied with the new location and style of his monastery's common prayer.279 By Christmas the abbot also hoped "to install six new altars in a Mass Chapel for the fathers" at the site of the old choir chapel to relieve crowded conditions. With concern but also hope, he confided to one of his military chaplains overseas: "Soon we will also need to be thinking of more living space. Just how and when to do the job is still in question."280

On Sunday, December 31, 1944, the Abbey's clerics, who were home from seminary studies for the holidays, took over the partially renovated Chapel "and demonstrated how High

Mass should be sung." Father Leonard Feeny celebrated the Mass and preached. Father Matthew greatly appreciated the young monks efforts and noted approvingly that Frater Michael Feeney was "quite a prime mover in all matters pertaining to Gregorian [chant]" and that he had "several good helpers" among the clerics. "Some day when our scattered exiles return," the old man hoped, "we ought to have a good choir."[281]

Father Vincent Carey had tried "to start a choir going, and keep it going" but without success. However, he said that "Father Bede can see what he can do when he gets home" from graduate studies. Frater Eugene Kellenbenz passed that news on to Father Bede in March 1945 and, importantly, offered his own help in corralling a choir when they were both home in Lacey that next fall.

The musically very talented Frater Eugene suggested a choir-building scheme for Saint Martin's: Father Bede with his influence at Lacey "could push through the idea of getting six or eight fellows . . . on scholarships to form the members of a choir." They could repay their scholarships "by spending an hour a day on singing." He added reasonably enough: "If they have fine voices, they would most probably be very interested in their singing." With daily practice, "they could soon sing beautiful programs of Gregorian and Polyphonic" and would provide a core "permanent membership" for a campus sacred choir.

The young cleric was sure that the time was ripe to easily push through such a plan to build up a permanent basis for a Saint Martin's Choir in the new era of postwar growth that the College would soon be experiencing. Moreover, the monks, who had "suffered so for the past two years for lack of any choir," would be quite enamored with the idea. Abbot Raphael, moreover, clearly seemed well disposed to all manner of liturgical embellishment and he was overseeing the introduction of a pipe organ to the Chapel that summer.

Father Bede would be very busy, of course, with his chemistry teaching and other obligations but the soon-to-be-ordained Frater Eugene could be his understudy and assistant in terms of coaching the scholarship choir members. He would be quite willing "to take care of a lot of the musical drudgery" while Father Bede could work with the choir on the overall interpretation of the music and give it "the polish and finesse

Father Eugene Kellenbenz (1917–1982) was musically gifted. Seen here in 1945 at the console of the chapel's new pipe organ, he worked with Father Bede to build up the quality of the monks' singing at Saint Martin's. Father Eugene would also develop a fine SMC Men's Chorus and other ensembles which performed both sacred and secular works. (Saint Martin's Abbey Archives)

it should have." While admittedly ambitious, this choir-building project seemed to Frater Eugene "to be the only way out of the present [musical] dilemma" at Saint Martin's.[282]

Abbot Raphael also instructed Frater Clement Pangratz "to learn all that you can of making candles of excellent quality" while he was studying at Mount Angel Seminary so that he might bring that very useful talent back to Lacey: "So learn all the tricks of the trade and we shall have a good candle-making department."[283] Candles had long embellished Catholics' sacred liturgy and a good and cheap supply of them would help to further enrich the Abbey's liturgical worship.

In the summer of 1951, Father James sent a happy report to his abbot at a conference back East: "Monday Father Paul [Kucera] brot [sic] over a beautiful and expensive Ostensorium, two Missals, chalice, ciborium, cruets, and a set of black vestments—a donation from the Providence Sisters—came from California. The haul was engineered by his Sister (a nun). You should see the Ostensorium! The most beautiful I have ever seen. Brother Brendan says it's worth over a M [thousand] dollars. I told Father Paul you would write a letter of thanks to his Sister and two other Sisters of Providence who made the haul for us."[284]

Abbot Raphael was also concerned that his abbey be actively involved in promoting the growing Catholic liturgical movement In 1943, he instructed Father James to get Kaufer's, a Seattle-based Catholic supplies emporium, to back-order copies of "the six-year course in liturgy for study clubs" as soon as possible.[285] Liturgical education and enrichment was important for monk and layman alike.

Revamping the College

Plans for handling postwar College enrollment began in earnest on June 9, 1945, when Abbot Raphael appointed Father Meinrad Gaul "to concentrate on the College and its problems." His principal tasks—as "Dean of College Faculties"—were to prepare additional housing in Saint Placid Hall for September enrollees and to plan an expanded curriculum for returning and prospective ex-GI students. So Father Meinrad settled into a "routine of teaching, office work, and painting" Placid Hall alias "College Hall." That September, he registered 22 College students including 9 boarders along with 145 High School boys of whom 117 lived on campus.[286]

The Saint Martin's Library had been relocated to the west end of the main or second floor of the south wing at the end of 1944. On New Year's Day 1945, Father Matthew com-

The impressive north and east facades of Old Main's two wings frame the hilltop courtyard. In this scene from about 1950 vehicles outline the new central lawn and shrubs in front of the Benedictine Sisters' Convent fill the foreground. (Saint Martin's Abbey Archives)

mented on the relocation to the absent Father Bede: "The Library is now duly installed in the west study hall. Of course there is much work to be done in arranging the books, but the big moving is over." Prior James gave Father Bede some additional details about the move: "The library was moved during the Christmas vacation to the large west study hall. Just had to have more room for all the books, and the new location is ample and it is an ideal place for the library. Father Luke [O'Donnell, the newly appointed librarian] certainly worked hard for it [was] an immense job to move all the books from upstairs. Of course, the good Clerics helped, for without them it could not have been done in so short a time."[287] The SMC Library still uses that space along with the adjacent area of the former Chapel.

Abbot Raphael also significantly involved himself in the reestablishment of a college program at Lacey. In mid-September 1945, he shared some pertinent observations with one of the Abbey's military chaplains: "Next semester promises a substantial increase and the future is going to require immediate solutions to some major problems. Among others are first the *faculty* and secondly *housing*. We have no time to lose on the whole matter. Action is necessary, and cooperation to make what promises to be a fine school."[288]

Abbot Raphael was also very concerned to assemble a strong College faculty and so wrote to four Saint Martin's priests serving as military chaplains asking them "to initiate procedures for discharge" under a new federal directive which gave institutions of higher education "a chance to clear professors." During the war, he noted, we cared for our soldiers as chaplains and now in peace "we desire as much to provide for their moral and intellectual growth." Moreover, "the veterans have begun to return to their books and their presence here indicates that we must immediately solve our great problem of staffing the faculty." Fathers Alcuin Lawrence, Jerome Toner,

Robert Wippel, and Marcel Berthon were informed that their help was needed "in conducting a first rate college" by January, or at the very latest, September 1946.[289]

"With the return of Veterans to school, we find it a joy and a job to make provisions for great increases in enrollments," Abbot Raphael noted in February 1946. About forty veterans had already enrolled in the new term starting the previous month. "Come next September we will be more than filled up."[290] Father Meinrad quickly set to work compiling an extensive but provisional list of 1946–1947 courses into a "Veterans' Bulletin" for the College to use as a student recruitment tool.

Meanwhile, the abbot doggedly searched for suitable laymen who might supplement the school's Benedictine faculty. He contacted SMC alumni, followed up on other individuals suggested to him and contacted placement bureaus at a number of West Coast colleges and universities.[291] Teachers for courses in economics, business, or accounting—reportedly greatly desired by the returning GIs—were much in demand. He wrote to a 1943 SMC graduate still on active duty with the U.S. Navy to ask whether he "would be interested in joining our faculty as an instructor in business administration courses." Someone "to carry on the work of the practical courses," such as elementary accounting and mathematics of finance, was needed. The possibility of future assistance from the College with his acquisition of a master's degree was proffered. "If you are inclined to accept," the abbot concluded, "I should be glad

The SMC Library's holdings were being improved in the 1950s but even then it was much too crowded. Later expansions into adjacent sections of Old Main helped a bit. Father Luke O'Donnell (standing at the check-out desk) was the librarian for a quarter-century. (Saint Martin's Abbey Archives)

to know what arrangements you suggest for salary and upkeep. Being a bachelor, so far as I know, you could find housing here."[292]

In addition, the abbot sought instructors for newly approved curricula in engineering, agriculture and aeronautics. When one applicant for athletic director and head football coach was informed that those positions had been filled, he inquired: "Might your main interest outside of coaching be in the field of agriculture or business administration? Or engineering? These are fields where we might [still] use a man."[293]

He also contacted Herb Buroker in Coeur d'Alene, Idaho, about jointly offering "aeronautics" courses for vets and other students starting in the 1946 fall semester: "I would say that we are interested in keeping contact with aviation developments, even to the extent of working with an operator as you suggest for the mutual benefit of both institution and operator." From SMC's perspective, "the operator would have to conduct all the courses, both ground instruction and flight instruction." The College would list the courses in its literature, "if they have the support and approval of government agencies," make classroom facilities available, and handle all registration and collection of fees. The fees should "be apportioned satisfactorily between operator and institution" with perhaps "a 50-50 arrangement" for ground school courses but "only a much smaller portion" for flight courses. SMC was "inclined to look with disfavor upon the granting of college credit" for such courses "but it may be that trends will change as we go along." Several weeks later, the abbot in his capacity as SMC's president sought to finalize arrangements for an aviation program on campus: "You also indicated, when here [about a month ago], that you would get the requirements of the CAA for ground school instruction. I realize that you have been busy but I should like to have the matter of our arrangements cleared up in the not too distant future."[294]

Both on his travels and through the mail, Abbot Raphael served as a sort of talent scout for possible SMC faculty and staff. En route by train to New York City in August 1947 after attending a conference in Illinois, he scheduled a stop at Saint Vincent Archabbey and College in Latrobe, Pennsylvania, for a very specific purpose. "I have heard of a Father Alcuin at Saint Vincent's who is a doctor in education," he wrote to Saint Martin's prior, Father James. "As I understand it, he is somewhat on the loose so far as his major interest is concerned. I understand also that his abbot would be inclined to respond favorably to my request that he be allowed to help us. This seems to be a good lead [for an education professor for SMC], and I would so much rather have a Benedictine than a layman. My reason for writing you airmail is that you can tell Father Gerald, so that he will hold off hiring anybody until I can find our about Father Alcuin. You might wire me at Saint Vincent's in the event any commitments have been made for a man in education."[295] Two years later the abbot ended a letter from Saint Benedict's College in Kansas with an important note: "P.S. I met our new chem[istry] prof [here] last evening. A fine man."[296]

An Imposing Impostor

A certain Dr. Robert Linton French, who showed up Lacey in July 1946 as a candidate for monastic life, was another addition to SMC's faculty for the fall semester. With great credentials, enthusiasm, and many plans to help Saint Martin's in its postwar "boom," he seemed like a prize catch. Claiming to be an M.D. as well as a professional psychologist, he was soon providing medical advice and services to campus denizens and teaching psychology to initially impressed students.

In September, Abbot Raphael joined other Benedictine leaders to celebrate the centennial of the United States' first Benedictine foundation, Saint Vincent Archabbey. While there, another abbot said something to him about a certain "Dr. French." By mid-October, Abbot Raphael was really worried about the suspicious behavior of Dr. French. He therefore contacted an Arkansas abbot for confirmation of his suspicions: "I have heard indirectly that you had him with you also. I would like to get some information so that I might be able to close in on him, since I feel that we must be coming to a showdown one of these days, unless by some act of God's Providence we can get him set straight on many things. The chances seem slight but we might give it a try."[297]

Saint Martin's imposing impostor also turned out to be—among other things—a deserter from both the U.S. Navy and Army. As such he was picked up on campus by F.B.I. agents on November 2.[298] Thus ended the Lacey tenure of Ferdinand Waldo Demarra Jr. (1921–1982) alias "the Great Impostor." Abbot Raphael described the whole affair as "an interesting episode in monastic annals!"[299]

Engineering New Courses

In the fall of 1946, Wally Flynn started teaching engineering for SMC which then as now was a very hands-on job. "Everyone was most enthusiastic," he later recalled, "and I was most happy to be a part of the exciting days ahead." During his five years on the College faculty, he also coached tennis, laid out a running track and initiated the "Saint Martin's Relays," an intercollegiate track and field event. (Cartoon by Frank Sinclair, SMC '47)

MR. W.V. FLYNN AND PLOW

Back around 1940–1941, an SMC faculty committee that included Father Raphael Heider and Father John Raymond among others had been "appointed to investigate what four-year programs beyond liberal arts might be developed economically for an all-male boarding school in the rural more than suburban setting of that time." Two new academic majors were recommended and subsequently approved by the college faculty: civil engineering and agriculture.

In 1928, SMC had begun offering a two-year program variously described in the institution's catalogs as pre-engineering or general engineering. By 1936–1937, courses in engineering drawing and problems and surveying were being offered but those courses were discontinued when World War II shrank the college's enrollment to a token size.[300]

As college president, Abbot Raphael supported the offering of engineering education as part of SMC's expanded postwar curriculum. Father Gerald, the dean of the college, and Father Meinrad, its registrar, also leant their support. Walter W. Flynn, who was about to be separated from the U.S. Army at nearby Fort Lewis, was hired to teach engineering courses starting in the 1946 fall semester. Wally Flynn proved to be an energetic fellow and quickly developed a schedule of preliminary engineering coursework to get the program started. "Everyone was most enthusiastic," he remembers, "and I was most happy to be a part of the exciting days ahead."[301]

Between 1946 and 1951, Flynn worked hard to develop programs in general, civil, traffic and agricultural engineering. He was also "involved in miscellaneous construction projects" on campus and likewise assisted with coaching in a couple of varsity sports. In 1947 Flynn also began the "Saint Martin's Relays," as an invitational collegiate track-and-field event. He found Carl

Reder, chairman of the Athletic Committee of the Olympia Chamber of Commerce, to be especially helpful. Under Flynn's enthusiastic management through 1951, the relays became a popular annual event.

SMC's Engineering Department was handicapped by "a lack of adequate engineering equipment and lab facilities" and a very small faculty.[302] Working under those constraints but with lots of drive from all concerned, the school's incipient Engineering Department set about building itself up for the future.

Father Richard Cebula returned to Lacey in 1947 after four years of graduate study in mathematics at the University of Michigan. He jumped into the engineering program with lots of energy teaching mathematics to engineering students. He also took intensive summer coursework in specific engineering subjects so as to be more flexible in his teaching areas. Forty-some years later, Tom Kane, a very successful 1950 graduate in civil engineering, praised Father Richard as an inspirational teacher who "did a remarkable job putting it all together" for him.[303]

Close student-faculty relations and a high degree of interaction with off-campus engineering professionals—for which SMC's Engineering Department would later become famous—soon developed. The department also quickly touted "an effective placement service" designed "to promote the welfare of its students."[304]

Agriculture on Campus

"Farm Chores" at Saint Martin's was the subject of a May 1939 photo-essay in the *Seattle Sunday Times Rotogravure* magazine. Nine captioned photos showed monks at work producing "most of the food" for campus students and monks. Brother Maurus Baggenstos with a plodding horse named

Dolly cultivated the rhubarb patch while Father Gregory Wall worked on building a calf shed. Brother Adam Richardson extracted honey from its wax frames and Brother Boniface Baggenstos fed his geese and ducks fattening them for "holiday dinners." Brother William Boucher admired his prize porkers while a newly arrived candidate for the brotherhood plowed a field for planting oats. The article displayed more than a bit of artistic license by picturing the monks doing their farm jobs dressed in their long black robes. In fact, they wore coveralls and other appropriate gear when plowing, hoeing, or doing carpentry.[305] Nevertheless, that 1939 newspaper article underscores the fact that Saint Martin's already had a long-established working farm when our College started offering agriculture courses for academic credit in 1946. In February of that year, the abbot informed his junior monks studying in Oregon that "Father Felix [Wirth] has finished lining up a pro-

In this 1950s photo Father Felix Wirth (1913–1984), Saint Martin's farm boss, and ex-lumberjack Father Gregory Wall (1894–1979, on right) are shown with some professional foresters who had been consulting about management of the campus forest After decades of running a farm, the monks' best crop continued to be fir trees! (Saint Martin's AbbeyArchives)

gram for agricultural courses. We expect to include them in the catalog which is being edited at the moment."[306]

The new agriculture program was designed "to provide a basis for intelligent, practical farming, including the principal specialized types of farming suitable to western Washington." Courses offered in other College departments which developed "abilities and qualities for leadership and cooperation in a rural social community" were also recommended. Workshop and laboratory facilities were available "for the student to carry out in practice the theory obtained in the classroom." Courses in animal, poultry and dairy husbandry would be added when demand justified.[307] By 1950, two tracks in agricultural studies—"for students who are interested in agriculture as a way of life"—were advertised by SMC. A bachelor of science degree could be pursued in agricultural engineering focusing on "the problems of drainage, farm structures and mechanical equipment." One could also opt to emphasize agricultural economics and rural sociology as those studies pertained to "farm management, organization and operation" or "rural social problems." Furthermore, it was clearly stated in the College catalog that "the principles of Christian rural life pervade the entire agricultural education program."[308]

Bringing Christian principles into the study and management of agriculture was more than rhetorical at SMC. This objective was demonstrated by an August 1953 experience of Abbot Raphael. Heading east by train, he chanced to encounter a Monsignor Heinz from Beech, North Dakota, who was "on his way to Saint John's [Abbey and University] to talk at the rural life institute being held there." Shortly thereafter, he wrote to his prior back in Lacey: "I would like to have had a representative [of Saint Martin's] there, since I feel that in the not too distant future we should have established rural life institutes for the pastors of our area."[309] This episode demonstrates Abbot Raphael's connection at that time—in spirit if not too much in practice—with the then flourishing

National Catholic Rural Life Conference. That organization, especially strong in the U.S. Midwest from the 1930s to the 1950s, emphasized what today might be termed a holistic approach to the spiritual, social, and economic needs of farmers and farming. Abbot Raphael obviously hoped his monastery and school could help raise the quality of rural life in southwest Washington.

Saint Martin's need to be as self-sufficient as possible was once again challenged in the months following the end of the war. In February 1946, for example, a federal government order "restricting the use of wheat for [animal] feed" was described by Abbot Raphael as being "a serious obstacle to our providing an education for veterans under the G.I. Bill of Rights." Saint Martin's needed "to produce the food consumed in the institution as far as possible to provide the board of our resident students and the faculty," he asserted, "for the sole purpose of keeping the cost of education as low as possible, thus placing the opportunity for an education within the reach of all." Therefore, the campus farm's production had to be greatly "stepped up" by doubling "the size of our flocks and herds" to feed growing numbers of G.I. students. More not less animal feed was needed at Lacey.[310] Lingering wartime food and agricultural regulations had to be either circumvented or trimmed in sensible ways as quickly as possible if SMC was to successfully switch from treading water to growth.

Securing additional funding for new programs is often quite a challenge for small institutions. In January 1946, Abbot Raphael asked his counterpart at Saint Benedict's Abbey in Kansas for information about "some philanthropical agency" which might support "agricultural research, or a school, or something" since Saint Martin's was "thinking along" those lines. He was put in touch with someone at Sears Roebuck in Kansas City, Missouri, and forthrightly solicited that corporation's aid: "We have been discussing and tending somewhat in the direction of offering our students an opportunity to take work in the field of agriculture." Perhaps, he inquired, Sears and Saint Martin's "could work together for the achievement of a distinct contribution to education and agriculture."[311] Nothing is known to have come from that solicitation.

The last listing for agriculture as an academic major was published in the College's 1955–1957 Bulletin. Francis H. Dummer has "fond and full" memories of his participation in SMC's agriculture program in the 1950s including "a great sense of gratitude for the dedicated people that made it possible." He remembers that "many hours were logged on the campus timber lots, in the barns, the gardens, [and] touring the locally selected agricultural industries." Moreover, he believes that "the purpose of the program met the needs of a special group of students of the time." His studies and work on our campus helped him find "contentment, fulfillment, solitude, and many of life's satisfactions close to nature" both then and later.[312]

Campus Housing Concerns

By early 1946, the abbot also realized that Saint Martin's would soon face an acute housing shortage "not only from the college angle but also from the monastic and employee angle."[313] The College turned, therefore, to the federal government seeking emergency housing and additional educational space for returning veterans. "Without any further provision," Abbot Raphael informed Congressman Charles R. Savage in March 1946, "we can house 120 men students and we can teach 350." However, some 200 G.I. students would then have to find off-campus housing in the vicinity of Lacey and there was "nothing to speak of" available.[314] While SMC was awarded ten two-man trailers from a closed Pasco, Washington, federal facility, they were "only a small part of the answer to vet housing" so the abbot immediately requested dormitory units adequate to house about 100 male students. The abbot also asked Seattle architect George W. Stoddard, whom he had employed to guide SMC's general development, to quickly prepare "a plot plan for spotting the trailers" just west of the main building.[315] He also sought to acquire surplus chapel buildings from nearby Fort Lewis "to provide educational space for veterans."[316]

SMC's first shipment of military surplus property had arrived in Lacey back on September 16, 1945, after "infinite details and paper work" had been completed. Abbot Raphael quickly asked his monks still in the military "to get the angles" on the best way to claim additional surplus property for the College: "Let's just quietly go about, wise as serpents, mouths shut and ears and eyes open. It may be a bonanza."[317]

Father John Raymond, the institutional procurator or business officer was kept "extremely busy" scouting out and applying for "donable surplus property" at government salvage depots. Among "prize" items he acquired in 1946 were a "brand new" D-4 Caterpillar with bulldozer and power take-off and a 6,800 cubic foot refrigerator and compressor unit. It seems that almost any donable surplus property item could be put to some use on campus!

Here Come the G.I.s!

The 1944 G.I. Bill of Rights (a.k.a. the Servicemen's Readjustment Act) provided money for college or job training to ex-G.I.s with little cash. Many resumed their studies while others became the first members of their families to go to col-

Ex-servicemen brought a whole new feeling to SMC when their numbers swelled the school's ranks starting in 1946. Joe Peacock's cartoons of GI-Bill students sharing their musings along with lunch and a pipe humorously caught their serious but flippant men-of-the-world posturing. (From 1948 Samarco)

Expecting SMC's student ranks soon to be swelled by returning GIs, Abbot Raphael asked his monks serving as chaplains in the military "to get the angles" on the best way to get a share of government surplus property for the College. Father John Raymond, the institution's "procurator," was kept "extremely busy" scouting out and applying for "donable surplus property" at government salvage depots.

In early 1946, the College acquired ten two-man trailers from a closed federal facility in Pasco, Washington. They were quickly "spotted" just west of the north end of the main building with an added central shower-toilet complex.

SMC's campus housing and instructional space were both very limited as its enrollment surged. The streamlined profile of Benet Hall—opened in 1946— on the south campus frames the SMC's hilltop acropolis.

Other barracks were used for housing as well as instructional and recreational space. This rear-view photo of College, Dunstan, and Eberhard Halls in later decades shows how no-frills this government-surplus "temporary" housing was. SMC continued to use parts of these buildings into the 1970s.

Military surplus Quonset huts were reassembled on campus to provide classroom and storage space to help handle the College's swelling number of GI Bill enrollees.

lege. By 1947, half the people in college in the United States were vets. The original benefits were $500 a year for tuition and fees and $50 a month for living expenses—enough to afford the best of schools.[318]

Getting SMC "on the official list of institutions available to veterans" was a major concern of Abbot Raphael as the College's president. It had been left off such a list recently issued by Washington State's superintendent of public instruction causing "endless confusion and misunderstanding."[319]

Vets swarmed over campuses eager to make up for lost time. "Academic urgency was the order of the day," remembers Jim Ellis. At SMC from 1941 to 1943, he returned to Lacey to finish his degree in 1947 under the G.I. Bill. Highly motivated and intensely competitive for academic honors, the "G.I. students" took heavy class loads year round "feeling a need to make up for lost years." Many thought of themselves as the lucky ones who owed it to their fallen comrades, their families and themselves to make a success of their chance for higher education and the better life it promised and they did.[320]

Other postwar students also felt challenged to succeed at SMC. Ed Niedermeyer and his sometime roommate in the campus trailer park, Mike O'Callaghan, both "wanted the most out of college." They would jog two miles before breakfast, as Ed recalls, attend class and then really hit the books. The College's staff included such imposing individuals as the rough-and-ready ex-logger, Father Gregory Wall. Ed lived for a semester in a barrack dorm prefected by that monk, whose insistence on "punctuality, honesty and fair play" so impressed Ed that he named his first son after Father Greg.[321]

A few weeks into the 1946 fall semester, SMC enrolled a record 272 full-time students—a big majority of them being vets. People scrambled on campus to find space for living as well as for teaching and to process the much increased paperwork. On November 2, Benet Hall residence center finally opened and the College also applied for additional temporary facilities through the Federal Works Agency.[322]

In early 1947, the U.S. Veterans Administration assigned Erik Bromberg, a World War II veteran with a strong academic background, to expedite the backlog of paperwork which had delayed subsistence payments to many G.I. students in southwest Washington. One vet at SMC had been bombarding state and national politicians and newspapers with tales of starving vets. Bromberg was sent in to break up the logjam. He remembers the SMC faculty as "a shy, subdued, unworldly group who showed obvious signs of being overwhelmed by the sudden flood of worldly, experienced, confident, earnest young men." Fathers Marcel and Jerome, "very worldly, confident and outspoken" ex-military chaplains, were the exceptions. "Above all this was the figure of Father Meinrad—a man who obviously relished life and enjoyed himself immensely with his flock of veterans." "To me," Bromberg avers, "Saint Martin's in the late forties is summed up in the personality of Father Meinrad."[323]

A Tacoma Catholic College?

In late July 1945, Abbot Raphael wrote to Father Gerald, who was ensconced on the East Coast trying to complete his doctoral dissertation in sociology for Catholic University. "For your information in thinking about our future, I give you the net result of the Big Question on the [possible Tacoma] college. We approved taking on the proposition. This information was given to the bishop. He answered a short while later that the scheme is abandoned for now. So the net result of it all is that we are just where we were, and that we can go on as if the problem had never come up. Of course, that is just what we wanted to know. We did not want to have such a question dangling in the air, constantly hampering our plans for home base."[324] Somewhat relieved, the abbot commented to a Minnesota colleague a few months later: "Hence we can get along with our business without having the possibility of a new venture hanging over us. I was anxious to bring the issue to a conclusion, one way or another, and now I feel quite satisfied."[325] However, a Tacoma Catholic College did operate for a while in the late 1940s with some Saint Martin's monks on its staff.

Saint Martin's High School

Answering an October 1945 letter from a Seattle pastor, who was pestered by a mother to have him plead with Saint Martin's High School authorities to readmit her son, Abbot Raphael commiserated but declined: "We aim to hold high standards and we do require a satisfactory background for the boys we accept. It is regrettable if the mother has placed undue pressure upon you, but I hope that the net results will warrant the attitude we have taken."[326]

On December 14, 1955, Father Matthew Britt, one of the mainstays of the High School faculty for half a century, died. Both his personality and longevity had conspired to make him a truly redoubtable campus presence as can be seen in the reaction to his death.

Due to a lifelong condition of epilepsy, he used to "fall over clump" (that is, pass out) from time to time so his occasional but temporary "incapacity" was well known in the

Father John Raymond (1911–1974) was a great teacher of mathematics at SMC for a third of a century as well as Saint Martin's chief financial officer for many years. He was also an avid fisherman (shown at left) but the thirty-eight-and-a-half-pound salmon in this photo was caught in 1972 at Sekiu on Washington's Olympic Peninsula by his fishing partner Brother Kenneth Malloy! (Photo courtesy Brother Kenneth)

The desk of California freshman Roger Rasche looks well organized for serious studying in 1953.

During the 1954 freshmen "Hell Week," frosh Bill Naumes shines an upperclassman's shoes as the latter studies at his desk.

Phil Moran's smile from behind the table suggests that "Lelani Seranade" was a social success of the 1954–1955 season. (Was that when the "fountain" leaked on the gym floor?)

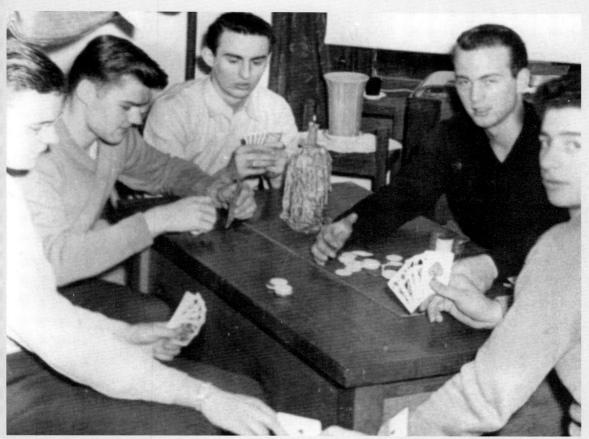

For some reason, these campus cardplayers seem more serious than honest! Well, they couldn't study all the time!

Adjacent to Anselm Hall, "Lake Anselm" mirrors Old Main's facade and the grand staircase in this mid-50s shot. The reappearing body of water was a seasonal feature of lower campus life for many years!

Benet Hall's main entrance with some of the cars of those college men lucky enough to have "wheels"! Anselm Hall is on the right.

(All photos by Reed M. Skibeness, SMC '57)

179

monastery. One morning a young cleric found the elderly priest in his top floor room seated at his desk but rigid and cold to the touch and apparently dead. He rushed downstairs to inform Abbot Raphael. The abbot immediately went to the sacristy, vested in surplice and stole, took out the holy oils used for anointing the dead—but then turned to the younger monk and diffidently asked: "Are you *sure* he's dead?"[327]

Adding Up To Excellence

Good teachers teach their subjects well; great teachers inspire their students for a lifetime. Father John Raymond, O.S.B. (1911–1974), was a great teacher of mathematics at Saint Martin's for a third of a century. For the best of his students, such as Ken Dolan, who became a nuclear physicist, "his lectures were like poetry."[328]

Hailing from Olympia, young Homer Raymond did his High School and Junior College studies at Saint Martin's and then became a novice in the Abbey's Benedictine monastic community in 1929. Given the religious name of *John*, he took his first vows in 1930 and was sent to complete his bachelor's degree at Saint Benedict's College in Atchison, Kansas. Several other young Saint Martin's monks were then studying philosophy or theology at that Benedictine school. He earned his B.A. there in 1932. Upon completing his theological studies in Kansas, he was ordained a priest at Seattle's Saint James Cathedral on June 6, 1936. He gained an M.S. in mathematics from the University of Iowa in 1934 and won his Ph.D. from the University of Washington in 1949.

John Firkins, now himself a distinguished teacher of mathematics and humanities at Gonzaga University in Spokane, Washington, states that four SMC teachers "have had a major impact on my professional life." Those great teachers were Father Meinrad Gaul (whose history lectures were "better than a Steven Spielberg movie!"), Father Henry Rozycki (whose physics classes no one left early!), Mike Contris ("an incredible teacher" who taught him to write) and Father John Raymond, who was his mentor and his example.

"Father John wore several hats. He was Bursar, math professor, priest, friend. He was hard to get to know and for a poor kid from Lacey, somewhat overpowering and scary. In this way he warded us off, but it didn't take too long before we noticed that when he adjusted his glasses his eyes would twinkle and a hint of a smile would start at the corner of his mouth. Ah! This man was human after all."

"As graduation drew nearer, he called me in and informed me that he had sent my name to the National Science Foundation for a possible award. I did not obtain it, but I did hear from twenty-eight colleges offering me an assistantship. The rest is history. Father John had made a decision and he saw to it that the kid he had nurtured was going to grad school."[329]

For thirty-four years Father John Raymond taught mathematics at SMC. He also taught in the High School as needed. He conducted eight government-funded in-service institutes for high school teachers which were widely acclaimed. He also put in three stints as Saint Martin's bursar or treasurer in addition to his teaching but as the years went on a series of heart attacks curtailed his activities. Such great teaching joined with real, personal concern for students always has been at the very core of this College.

Saint Martin's Labor Priest

In 1914, young Lorraine Toner came to Lacey from Eau Claire, Wisconsin, for High School studies at SMC. An older brother, the future Father Martin Toner, O.S.B., had recently made his first vows as a monk of our Abbey. Lorraine became a noted all-around athlete both as a student and later as a young monk. In the summer of 1923, he joined the Abbey's novitiate and was given the religious name *Jerome* by which he was henceforth to be known. He studied theology at Lacey from 1926 to 1930 while at the same time being assigned many other campus duties as was the practice in that hard-working era. He was ordained a Catholic priest on June 14, 1930.

Father Jerome (1899–1977) went on to earn a B.S. in education from the University of Washington in 1932. He then won both an M.A. (1935) and a Ph.D. (1941) in economics at the Catholic University of America in Washington, D.C. One of his teachers at Catholic U. was the famed "labor priest," Monsignor John A. Ryan (alias "The Right Rev. New Dealer"). Father Jerome's extensively researched and groundbreaking study on *The Closed Shop in the American Labor Movement* (1944) was based on his doctoral thesis. He joined the SMC faculty in 1941 and later served as a World War II Army chaplain from 1944 to 1946. President Truman then appointed him a delegate to an International Labor Organization conference in Switzerland after which he shared his insights and concerns about labor issues with both U.S. and Vatican officials. In Washington State in 1956 and again in

1958, Father Jerome effectively marshaled religious and educational institutions against what he considered oppressive anti-union right-to-work initiatives. Both were thrashed by more than 2-to-1 negative votes. Governor Rosellini appointed the well-known cleric to the new State Human Rights Commission of which he later served as chairman.

Father Jerome's avid commitment to workers rights fitted into his over-all philosophy of what he called "Industrial Relations" or "IR" for short. From 1946 through 1968, his "IR" program at SMC had for its purpose "the improving of industrial relations in the state and nation by providing instruction, information, and research in all aspects of industrial, labor, government, and public relations affecting

SMC's "Labor Priest," Father Jerome Toner (1899–1977), studied, taught, and worked to improve "Industrial Relations" in Washington State as well as nationally and internationally. Many of his "IR" students became labor-relations specialists for unions, corporations, and government agencies. (Saint Martin's Abbey Archives)

employers, employees, and the public." Special consideration was given "to the need for cooperation between management and labor through the recognition of and respect for the rights and responsibilities of each, and of the public." Father Jerome saw an SMC degree in industrial relations as providing labor-relations managers to both the private sector and governmental agencies "from the city to international organizations."[330]

Many of Father Jerome's "IR" graduates in fact became noted and respected labor-relations specialists while still others became attorneys prominent in labor law. Father Jerome's work in teaching and fostering good "industrial relations" clearly fulfilled SMC's educational mandate, which aimed "to develop in its students such a vivid realization of their individual and social responsibilities that they may assume leadership in their chosen fields of public and private enterprise."[331]

"The Labor Priest from Saint Martin's" often ruffled feathers but he persisted in tying his labor concepts to papal teachings on the dignity of workers and their rightful place in the economic world. Father Jerome taught his SMC students—and many others besides both regionally and nationally—what he himself strongly believed, namely that "moral integrity had to be found on both sides of the management-labor negotiating table."[332]

Our Musicmakers

Music has long been the companion of religion and this has certainly been true at Saint Martin's. Over the decades as our monks have worked to enrich their celebration of the Mass, the monastic Office, and lesser church rituals, something of the great Catholic liturgical tradition has been displayed on campus. Such services of public worship, in which music played a major part, were (and are) attended by monks, students, and neighbors alike. As an offshoot of this liturgical growth, a succession of boys' and men's choruses developed in our High School and College. The best of these groups performed accomplished concerts of sacred, classical, and popular music. Father Eugene Kellenbenz (1917–1982) was perhaps our most noted chorusmaster and from the late 1940s through the 1960s his ensembles toured extensively and produced a number of records and tapes.

Good Friends Depart

On April 28, 1958, the prioress of the Benedictine Sisters of Saint Gertrude's Convent in Cottonwood, Idaho, sent Abbot Raphael a momentous announcement: "I hereby wish to notify you that we have officially set August 1, 1960, as the date on which we will withdraw our Sisters from Saint Martin's culinary and sewing departments." She had earlier spoken with Father Walter Hellan, the Abbey's business manager, about their forthcoming withdrawal. The Sisters could depart earlier if the monks could find suitable replacements.[333] That decision would bring to a close over half a century of happy collaboration between Lacey's monks and Cottonwood's Sisters. On May 14, 1954, for example, the Sisters' golden jubilee in Lacey had been warmly saluted by a general assembly of College and High School students. The appreciative boys and men of the combined student bodies offered their much-appreciated cooks and menders a lively musical program that day. They also presented the Sisters with a "spiritual bouquet" listing multiple prayers and other spiritual activities offered for them.[334]

Mother Mary Augustine withdrew her Sisters from Lacey in order to reassign them to schools or hospitals closer to home

On June 15, 1959, the last of the Cottonwood, Idaho Benedictine Sisters whose members had managed the campus kitchen since 1904 left Saint Martin's for their own monastic home at Saint Gertrude's Priory to take up new responsibilities. In the absence of Abbot Raphael, the Abbey's Prior, Father James Piotrzkowski, saw them off. Here they kneel to receive his farewell blessing. (Saint Martin's Abbey Archives)

or to have them assume new duties at Saint Gertrude's itself. Abbot Raphael rather blandly noted the Sisters' imminent departure in a letter to the president of the Seattle Saint Martin's Mothers' Club: "The Sisters in the kitchen are practically all packed and ready to leave for their motherhouse early next Monday morning. The professional food service corporation begins operations at breakfast on Sunday morning. So there are plenty [of things] happening."[335]

For quite a few years, the Abbey had also provided a priest-chaplain for the Sisters and their students at Cottonwood as well as various monks to conduct annual spiritual "retreats" for the nuns at Saint Gertrude's and elsewhere. The long Lacey-Cottonwood nexus had been a mutually happy one.

The Sisters left Lacey on June 15, 1959, on the SMC bus and arrived at Cottonwood about 8:00 p.m. the same night. "We were deeply impressed and edified at the gathering of your dear Community for the final good wishes on our journey home," one nun wrote the very next day. However, she added in characteristic style: "Everyone here seems to be as busy as everyone there so I presume we will all get our aprons on and help along." She signed her postcard: "Your loving Sisters in Saint Benedict."[336]

A week later, the prioress forwarded her own kind words to Abbot Raphael and his monks: "Our Sisters have been home a week today and we are so happy to have them with us. All of them will always treasure the many fond memories they brought home from Saint Martin's. May God reward you and your Community for all you have done for them during their years of service to Christ in the monastery at Olympia." She also thanked the abbot for "the generous parting gift" he had given the sisters and assured him of her newly returned Sisters' "lasting impression of true Benedictinism" which they all had received during "the happy years" they had lived and worked at Saint Martin's.[337]

Taking the College Coed

Grace S. Dixon graduated cum laude as valedictorian from SMC in 1953. Already a graduate of Tacoma General Hospital's nursing school, she was one of a handful of Olympia-area women allowed by way of exception to complete her coursework here for a bachelor's degree. Other pioneer women students included Myrtle Six, Marianne Lemon, Marion Dorn, and Eileen Alexander. In addition to being smart and perky, Grace was also blind. She attended classes with her seeing-eye dog, Holly, whom the other students used to pet a lot. Father Meinrad was her special person—her favorite instructor and admired friend.[338] During the decade following Dixon's graduation, a few other women took courses at SMC attempting to complete their degrees. In 1964, the issue was specifically raised whether women, who then attended the College only as "special students," could or should be award-ed their degrees with academic honors. On May 31, the Abbey's Senior Council was sent a memo to Father Richard Cebula, then SMC's dean of instruction, in an attempt to resolve the issues: "Since the present honors winner has expressed the opinion that coeds at Saint Martin's be not in line for distinctions for a variety of reasons, let the policy be adopted viz.: Coeds shall not be eligible for distinctions (at commencement exercises). They are just not eligible for dis-tinctions. This policy shall be brought to the attention of any coeds who may in the future be accepted as special students."[339] ❧

St. Martin's Mothers Club

SCHOLARSHIP BENEFIT   NIGHT of GAMES
APRIL 10, 1964   8:30 p. m.
VISITATION PARISH HALL
South 58th and Warner St.
1st Prize—Admiral 11" New Brief Case Style Portable
With Cover
2nd Prize—2' Outdoor St. Francis Planter Shrine
3rd Prize—$10.00 Cash
Need Not be Present to Win
DONATION $1.00   Door Prizes

For many decades, Saint Martin's Mothers Clubs' activities have benefited students, staff, and monks. In 1964, the Tacoma Mothers Club was as usual hard at work finding small but much appreciated ways to underwrite Benedictine educational programs. (Author's Files)

*The setting and quality of prayer on campus was signifi-
cantly enriched with the completion in late 1970 of Saint
Martin's long-desired Abbey Church. Christmas Midnight
Mass was the first Eucharist to be celebrated in the new
church. Solemnly blessed on April 13, 1971, the structure
was designed to provide flexible worship space suitable to
monastic and school needs in line with liturgical changes
promulgated by Vatican Council II. A quarter-century
later, the Abbey Church remains a beautiful house of prayer
and has been much emulated. (Photo by John Kaiser)*

CHAPTER 7
Changes and More Challenges
(1964–1979)

❖

MAJOR CHANGES IN LEADERSHIP TOOK place at Saint Martin's in 1964 for that summer Father Michael Feeney was appointed president of the College and in December the monks elected Father Gerald Desmond as their new abbot. Overall, the 1960s and 1970s would prove to be both an exciting and a disheartening era for Saint Martin's. The College would surge and then falter; the Abbey would excitedly breathe in the spirit of Vatican Council II renewal but likewise lose a large number of its monks in the resultant agitation; and the High School would experience both its acme and its closure. Meanwhile, the United States itself underwent great turmoil and upheaval centering around the civil rights movement and the war in Vietnam. As a popular song from 1968 put it: "Those were the days, my friends!"

New Leadership and Coeducation for SMC

Father Michael Feeney, forty-five, had already been principal of Saint Martin's High School (1953–1959) and was serving as the monastery's prior when the Abbot Raphael asked him to switch jobs with Father Dunstan Curtis in the summer of 1964. "I never sought a change [of jobs]," he recalls in reviewing his many assignments as a monk, "I took the job as needed." Once appointed its leader, Father Michael felt strongly that SMC had to become "a college among colleges" and that it could not survive if it merely continued to be "a little monastic school."[340] Although College leaders in 1938 had seriously considered but then decided against phasing in coeducation, Father Michael felt that SMC in the mid-1960s was already in fact an "under-the-table coed institution" because it enrolled women in night courses and summer session. Moreover, several women in the early 1950s had been enrolled by way of exception in regular daytime course work. Grace S. Dixon, in fact, had graduated as the valedictorian of the Class of 1953! Taking the College officially and fully coed, therefore, seemed like a logical step for both financial and academic rea-

In 1964, Father Michael Feeney, O.S.B., was appointed president of SMC. During seven years in that position he developed strong contacts with local business and community leaders and took the College coed in 1965. He also inaugurated a Board of Regents to engender broader advice and deeper support for campus programs. (Photo by Forest and Whitmire)

sons. It would immediately double its pool of potential students and also serve to attract and retain male students.

The president's office surveyed SMC faculty, current students, alumni, and local leaders and families about the desirability of the College going coed. One former student responded that while his recent freshman experience at Lacey had been "without a doubt excellent," he had, nevertheless, transferred to a coed, Catholic college after deciding that such a locale was "the best milieu" in which "to associate with the fair sex" in preparation for life.[341] Community leaders and place-bound adult women in Thurston County strongly supported enrolling women in all Saint Martin's programs. "The need for, and interest in, continuing education is surely as great among women as among men," an Olympia woman commented, "and the step Saint Martin's is taking will undoubtedly benefit not only individual young women and their families, but also the whole community."[342]

Members of the College faculty submitted their interestingly varied opinions regarding coeducation at SMC. Father John Raymond, a distinguished professor of mathematics and a former long-time campus business manager, as usual firmly asserted his view: "In whatever area we move, it must be toward excellence. If this includes coeducation, well and good.

By 1966, the Registrar's Office staff included three coeds among its student employees. At the office Christmas party that year were (left to right) Barbara Grigsby, Gene Beauvais, Mary Stoddard, and (seated) Mike McKinnon, Registrar Brother Kilian Malvey, Lois Parcher, Madeline Scott (secretary), Terry Roche, Bill Ording, and Darryl Dyer. (Photo by John C. Scott, SMC '67)

But the basic program must come first Then the other items later. I consider coeducation as one of these later items, to be taken up after the basic excellence [of SMC's programs] is firmly established." He also asked, much to the point, "Can we do the excellent job in educating women that we feel that we can with men?"[343]

Accounting professor Edward Daniszewski, himself a 1952 graduate of the College and a recent addition to its staff, cogently addressed the question: "The founding fathers of SMC followed the then current opinion that only men need be educated because they were the dominant sex in society. Since World War II, this opinion is no longer tenable by facts [for] women have made and are making tremendous advances in their social and economic position. With this progress, there can be no question that they should need the liberal education as well as training in special fields that SMC can provide. If we have an apostolate to give a Christian education, we should want to teach all who want to avail themselves of it, whether they be men or women."[344] Father Ansgar Hallen, who taught French and English on campus and simultaneously served as the Lacey area's Catholic pastor, also approved SMC's moving into coeducation: "We [monks] have a spiritual mission for both men and women, individual[ly] and [monastic] community-wise; socially we can do much [as a coeducational college] for the establishment of Christian and Catholic homes; we must live for the future and not for the past."[345]

However, a young philosophy professor, Father George Seidel, did not like "the speed at which the decision for something as important and as far-reaching in its consequences as co-education" was being taken. Could the proposal "stand up against long-range and careful criticism and appraisal"? Most importantly, "planning with foresight" was necessary. "The *real* reason" we are giving consideration to coeducation at any level at this time," he asserted, "is, frankly, money. It is a matter of pure expediency." Father George also argued that the majority of SMC's faculty—who were monks—lacked both the training and experience of educating women. He further assumed that women would mostly want to study subjects in the liberal arts and humanities—"and rightly so considering the role they will play in society as wives and mothers"—in which areas the College's faculty and offerings were at present very limited. He concluded that increased revenues from an enlarged, coed student body would be more than offset by much higher operating costs due to requirements for additional faculty and facilities.[346]

After various institutional skirmishes, however, once the SMC faculty voted in favor of coeducation "everyone cooperated."[347] A public announcement was made that effective in September 1965 the College would enroll women in all its programs. Father Michael quickly began a search for a dean of women and a teacher for primary education, initially looking for one person to fill both positions. He was seeking "a woman who has a Ph.D. or near it in education and who could serve as a model and guide for the some thirty or forty coeds we expect in September."[348] SMC was fortunate to fill this key and pioneering position with Mrs.(and soon to be Dr.) Elda Brophy, a person of energy, tact, and ability.

Although Father Michael had told the monastic chapter that taking the College coed would be "as good a solution of the problems of the Olympia area" for higher education for women as was presently available, he also had admitted that it was not in his view an "ideal solution." He hoped, rather, to develop in cooperation with the Benedictine Sisters of nearby Saint Placid Priory two cooperating schools—"one men's college and one women's college."[349] His anticipated that the Benedictine Sisters would add college-level offerings for women to the High School curriculum for girls which they had initiated in 1961. That hope was later reiterated for campus and alumni constituencies in an SMC newspaper: "There is somewhat a tradition in the United States that Benedictine Schools solve the problem of 'co-education' by having two neighboring schools—situated close enough to enjoy the advantages of coeducation, but far enough away to avoid the distractions of immediate proximity," the *Saint Martin's News* opined. "We salute our 'sister-school' [Saint Placid High School] and look forward to its growth to collegiate status so that the Benedictine system of 'co-education' can be solved in this happy way."[350] Nothing came of that hope, however, and

SMC therefore proceeded on its own to refashion itself into a permanently and fully coeducational institution.

Seeking New Advice and Support

Father Michael soon found that his various proposals to expand and vitalize the College got bogged down in the Abbey's Senior Council, which functioned as SMC's Board of Trustees. In its deliberations, he observed, "monastic problems always came first" and decisions relating to the College "got delayed." In retrospect, Father Michael candidly admits that this tardy decision-making process along with his own great desire "to get things done" pushed him "to make certain decisions I should not have made" as well as to "spend money we didn't have."[351] Moreover, some monks—in their capacities as College faculty or trustees—viewed certain proposals and administrative actions of Father Michael's as "too terribly aggressive" and so resisted various projects that he wanted boosted.[352]

Father Michael's approach to handling operational deficits was to encourage all monks to help increase College income rather than make cuts in what he saw as already underfunded programs.[353] Income did not grow rapidly enough to overtake outlays, however, so operational "red ink" began to accumulate. Requests for annual subsidies from the Abbey to help underwrite College (and High School) operations grew in the late 1960s and 1970s just at the time that the number of monks declined rapidly. "Serious monastic losses in manpower," which Abbot Gerald attributed in 1967 to "disturbances in the world today," further depleted Saint Martin's human as well as financial resources.[354] The operating deficits which began at this time would continue to plague College budgets into the mid-1980s.

A perceived need on the part of Father Michael to broaden the College's management perspectives and to invigorate its advancement prospects led to the establishment of an advisory Board of Regents in 1966. Knowledgeable, well-placed men and women were to be recruited to serve as Regents and to advise the College administration, staff, and faculty as to the most effective ways of helping SMC grow in quality as well as in size.[355] College personnel would be available to assist the Regents and to help promote the projects of the Board through liaison with its committees. The Associated Students of SMC would also be accorded "participation on the Board through a committee selected by the Student Council."[356] The first group of Regents included several alumni of SMC or

SMHS as well as people otherwise already connected with Saint Martin's. Other members of the new Board, however, were prominent individuals not yet very familiar with the College. The Board of Regents' inaugural meeting, chaired by Tacoma businessman Robert P. Mallon, took place on January 20, 1967, in the Student Union Building on campus.

While the Regents' experience and perspectives were seriously sought and considered by SMC's administration, there was also an expectation that their personal financial assets, or those of institutions with which they were connected, could and would be tapped to financially strengthen the College. In retrospect, it is clear that the Regents as a whole were more generous with their advice than with their treasure. Several former Regents, however, later served on the College's slow-to-be-developed governing body, the SMC Board of Trustees, with distinction.

Largely because of his great energy and drive, Father Michael became the first non-abbot president of SMC to truly function as the school's chief executive officer especially after the 1968 revision of the SMC Bylaws. His seven years in office reshaped the way SMC did its business and provided a plateau from which his successors could attempt to lead the College during their terms. In 1971, he resigned as president but stayed on for almost two years as a fundraiser and community relations officer before accepting a parish assignment.

New Campus Facilities

Major new College facilities were built on campus in the mid-1960s. A Student Union Building largely funded by the Associated Students organization (ASSMC) was erected in 1965. A prankster stole the new building's marble cornerstone from its display in the Library lobby the night before the SUB's dedication and formal opening that May. However, ASSMC leaders quickly secured a temporary replacement cornerstone from a Tumwater memorial company and the ceremony proceeded as scheduled. The Student Council later officially named the facility the Trautman Union Building (also known as the TUB) in honor of Father Bertrand Trautman, ASSMC's longtime faculty advisor. However, that name never really caught on and once the building's exterior sign disappeared the name SUB was commonly used for the much needed and much used facility.

In 1966, the striking three-story Burton Hall residence center, initially reserved for juniors and seniors, was erected near the popular Baran Hall (1957) dormitory. It could house up to 184 students and also provided an apartment for the director of residence. Designed by the noted architect Paul Thiry, a Saint Martin's alumnus, with lots of input from college staff (especially Father Bertrand), its innovative floor plan grouped four two-person bedrooms around a pair of shared bathrooms and a common living room. Unfortunately, its two courtyard-facing stairwell turrets were partially opened to the sky at roof-level and thus occasionally served to divert cascades of rain water down the stairs! While the planners carefully outfitted Burton with extra-long beds (to better accommodate SMC's male basketball players!), they overlooked such necessities as bathroom towel racks or hooks and did not provide for locks on the suites' interior bedroom or bathroom doors. While those oversights were only slowly remedied by later residence hall staff, Burton Hall has proven to be a popular place for on-campus living especially for SMC's international students.

SMC's much-needed and long-awaited health and physical education building, initially called the Capital Pavilion, was

Academic life at SMC remained vigorous during the 1960s and 1970s. In May 1965, Father Bertrand Trautman (1918–1972) as academic vice president led the procession of graduates from the hilltop to the Abbey Theatre for their commencement. Sophomore Jeff Flint carried the flag. (Photo by John C. Scott, SMC '67)

finally completed and dedicated in January 1968. Seeing the long-delayed facility as both a campus asset and a much needed community resource, local businessmen, organized as "Partners In Progress," assisted with the project's completion. Federal financing, however, was the crucial factor in getting a "new gym" for SMC. On December 21, 1966, the Abbey Chapter authorized Father Michael's request to add $38,000 of campus funds "to the $157,000 from the Ford Foundation Funds" so that the new gym could at last be finished.[357]

Vatican Council II and Monastic Renewal

In early October 1962, Abbot Raphael declined an invitation to attend a function of the Seattle Saint Martin's Mothers' Club later that month. "We will be having the first of our regular monthly theological conferences for all the priests of our monastic family [on that date]," he explained. "It is proper that I should remain at home for these conferences."[358] Those conferences were but a small part of a larger movement of renewal and revitalization among American Benedictines and in the Catholic Church worldwide. That same month, the first session of Vatican Council II had been convoked in Rome by "Good Pope John" to stimulate Catholic reform and renewal. The Council directly initiated a period when Catholic religious life underwent "a pervasive and intense transformation" which proved to be both exhilarating and wrenching for all involved.[359]

Although contemporary renewal of Catholic religious life had begun several years before the Council, its "Decree on the Appropriate Renewal of Religious Life" (November 28, 1965) directly brought about "far-reaching changes in organized religious life throughout the world." After Vatican Council II concluded in December 1965, the federation of monasteries with which Saint Martin's Abbey was affiliated held several special meetings to implement Council-mandated renewal. The federation issued "Renew and Create," an updated statement on Benedictine life, along with a set of "Juridic Elements" in 1969. The latter had been prepared to replace the long-outmoded "Statutes" which had regulated monks' lives as a sort of interpretation and application of the *Rule of Benedict*.[360]

The election of Abbot Gerald Desmond, O.S.B., by his fellow monks as their fourth abbot on December 30, 1964, clearly reflected the tenor of the times. Vatican Council II was breathing "fresh air" into the Catholic Church worldwide and Saint Martin's people looked to the new abbot to update and redirect campus operations. He did. (Saint Martin's Abbey Archives)

The election late in 1964 of Father Gerald Desmond, sixty, as Saint Martin's new—and fourth—abbot clearly reflected the tenor of the times. Vatican Council II had awakened in the Roman Catholic Church a spirit of *aggiornamento* or openness which challenged Catholics to renew themselves and their institutions. Many of the Abbey's monks had been excited by that aspect the Council's work and looked for ways to implement "renewal" at Lacey. Abbot Raphael, who had been in office since 1943, seemed to many to be out of sympathy with the prevailing spirit of renewal. In the opinion of one younger Benedictine, a incident in 1964 really spotlighted the abbot's inability to "dialogue" with his monks: "The events leading up to the new abbatial election are fuzzy. [However,] the supposed straw that broke

In the choir loft of Seattle's Saint James Cathedral, Father Eugene Kellenbenz, O.S.B., leads the famed SMC Men's Chorus in song during the solemn abbatial blessing of Abbot Gerald Desmond on March 21, 1965. The Men's Chorus produced several recordings and toured widely in that era. (Photo by John C. Scott, SMC '67)

the camel's back was [when] the final plans for the [proposed Abbey] church were announced to the [monastic] chapter without chapter permission."[361] (In matters of great importance or cost, an abbot must by church law consult the members of his monastery and, in certain specified areas, obtain their consent before undertaking a large debt or otherwise obligating their monastery.) Subsequently, on November 27 Abbot Raphael announced that "the Holy See has given permission to hold an election of a coadjutor abbot" for Saint Martin's.[362] This was clearly a face-saving gesture for the coadjutor abbot would in fact assume full jurisdiction over the abbey upon the confirmation of his election.

"Lately, the theme song of the [monastic] community has been either 'Heavenly Sunshine' or 'We Shall Overcome,'" was how one monk described the mood of Lacey's resident Benedictines in early December 1964. "As the days pass and the election becomes more of a reality, the spirits rise."[363] Father Adrian Parcher, thirty-one, favored Father Gerald for abbot for several key reasons: He had been and was the spiritual advisor to many monks, "both brothers and fathers." He was "able to spend hours listening to the monks," which, "I think, after Raphael, will be a good thing." Furthermore, "Gerald has been attending all monastic exercises faithfully for the past three years," which was an oblique reference to the abbot's frequent absence from morning prayers. Moreover, Father Gerald, who had a Ph.D., while "a college man" was "not against the high school." Looking to the future, an Abbot Gerald would "believe in adequate training and study for the monks, be they brothers or priests." His reputation at the University of Washington "and with State Institutions" would also do Saint Martin's "a good turn." Finally, as "an older man . . . he will not live too long."[364]

An election chapter meeting was scheduled for December 30 and all monks in solemn vows were summoned to attend unless excused for sufficient cause. Sixty chapter members were on hand that day or represented by proxy. The balloting session was called to order at 1:30 p.m. and the election of the new abbot was concluded in about two hours. Father Gerald had led Father Michael Feeney on the first two ballots. He then received on the third ballot one vote more than the two-thirds majority required for election—forty-two of the sixty cast—and accepted the election. "The fact that it only took three

Monks in their overlapping generations have made up the membership of Saint Martin's Abbey's over the past century. In 1969, bearded and ancient Father Mark Wiechman (b. 1875) at the organ in the monastery's community room entertained Father Conrad Rausch (b. 1921), Father Kevin Myles (b. 1942) and Novice Edmund Ebbers (b. 1948). (Photo courtesy Brother Edmund)

ballots seems to indicate that the community had a good understanding of the basic needs at this time," one happy priest reported, "and perhaps Pope John's aggiornamento can be instilled."[365]

"The best way to appraise Father Gerald as Abbot is to say: 'We have a Pope John,'" wrote a jubilant monk early in 1965. "He is really moving—mostly at present in the way of the spirit—open-door policy, free speech, freedom of access. One now sits to speak with the Abbot."[366] The same correspondent expanded on his glowing appraisal a few days later: "We could not have elected a better man: very humble, very sincere, extremely charitable; and most understanding, yet with a fantastic sense of humor. The more I see of him as abbot the more I admire him. He trusts his monks and respects them as individuals. He realizes the necessity of hard work, but [also] the need for relaxation and holidays." Abbot Gerald's remarks at the Mass he celebrated to mark the opening of the new semester also greatly impressed the College's faculty and students.[367]

Equality among Brothers

A very significant event in the history of monks of the modern Benedictine Order took place as a result of a papal indult received by American Benedictines in November 1966. Henceforth, lay brothers in the Order would be able to make solemn profession as Benedictine monks. The long-standing canonical division between "choir monks" and "lay brothers," which had come to be seen as invidious to many American monks, thus came to an end. All monks would now have equal status in their communities whereas previously only ordained priests, or finally professed "clerics" aspiring to be ordained as priests, could be voting members of the monastery's "chapter," which assembly decided all crucial matters for any monastery including the election of its abbot.

One of the items on the agenda for the chapter meeting of December 28, 1966, was a "Motion to Admit Brothers to Solemn Vows." Father Bede "thought it wasn't the right time yet" and that the abbey "should wait about five years." He was also concerned about setting a minimal age before solemn vows might eventually be made by brothers. "Other capitulars raised questions such as where to draw the line, and who will be admitted as Brother Candidates in the future." However, various monks also "thought it would not be good to wait any longer before implementing the move for Solemn Vows" for brothers. When the issue was finally put to a vote, thirty capitulars favored admission of brothers to solemn vows, four voted against the motion, and one person was undecided.[368] A week later, the monastic chapter met again to consider "the applications for Solemn Vows" of seven brothers and all were accepted. It was also announced that "for the present" the Senior Council had "set age twenty-three as a sort of minimum age" for Brother applicants for solemn vows. Also, "all Canonical requirements as to Last Will, etc." were to be fulfilled by all new applicants and an identical formula of profession would henceforth be used by all Saint Martin's monks.

A seemingly trivial but symbolically important matter was also decided that day: "Next [raised] was the question as to whether all Finally Professed [which would include the monastery's "clerics" and also those brothers who had not opted to apply for solemn vows] could recreate with the Fathers. Most capitulars present [there were twenty-one in attendance] seemed to think so, but there was some question as to the value of the non-finally professed, which included postulants, novices, and junior monks in temporary vows, having the same opportunity."[369] The prevailing mood clearly was to functionally integrate all Saint Martin's monks into one community.

At a moving ceremony in the campus chapel on January 22, 1967, Brothers Bernard Anderson, Dominic Hahn, Kilian Malvey, Romuald Laverdiere, Neal Roth, Stephen Johns, and Theodore Vavrek pronounced their solemn vows and thus became full-fledged capitulars of Saint Martin's Abbey. The status boundary had finally and rather easily been crossed in what some monks considered their monastery's own civil rights campaign. For some years thereafter, however, there still remained some confusion and indecision within the ranks of the Abbey as to differing expectations—and qualifications—for

candidates for the monastic life at Saint Martin's. For example, the minutes of a June 5, 1968 chapter meeting contain this telling comment: "At this time no definite policy was decided upon as [regarding] Final Vows in the case of Brothers. Most members thought we might learn something from the [American Cassinese Congregation] General Chapter" scheduled to begin later that month.[370] There was a continuing uncertainty as to the appropriate minimal age and educational attainment for Brother candidates for solemn vows. Indeed, for some years after this official equalization in status, clerical and brother candidates were accepted or rejected for the novitiate and/or for vows according to different criteria. This situation reflected a lingering preconception that future monks who might some day advance to Holy Orders should have higher educational attainments or potential for the same.

At Last, An Abbey Church!

For some fifteen centuries the *Rule of Benedict* has commanded Christian monks to lift up their hearts and voices in the common worship and praise of God. Accordingly, for the past century Lacey's monks have gathered for corporate prayer several times a day. While the place for their shared prayer has changed as successive chapels were built and modified and a church finally constructed, the monks' primary spiritual obligation of performing their prayerful "Work of God" has continued to be fulfilled.

Equality among brothers was at least formally achieved on January 22, 1967, when seven lay brothers were admitted to solemn vows, something only recently authorized for Benedictine monasteries in the spirit of Vatican Council II renewal. Seated (left to right) are Theodore Vavrek, Dominic Hahn, and Kilian Malvey; standing are Bernard Anderson, Neal Roth, Stephen Johns, and Romuald Laverdiere. (Photo by Jeffers Studios)

From the opening of the College in September 1895, daily attendance at Mass was considered normative and other opportunities for growth in the knowledge and practice of the students' Catholic faith were regularly made available. Chapel services, often embellished by vocal or instrumental music performed by monks and students alike, were sometimes further enhanced by outdoor devotional processions. The 1895 all-purpose College building contained a chapel and a principal reason for the construction of its 1904 addition was to provide space for a larger chapel. The campus chapel remained in the expanded original building when the 1913 brick building—the south wing of today's "Old Main" complex—was opened. A Students' Chapel was later built on the second floor of that structure's new west wing and in use by 1920. It remained the center of campus religious activities for the next half-century.

Local Catholics in the then rural Lacey area at first attended Mass on Sundays and holy days in the campus chapel. In 1923, however, an off campus "mission chapel" was constructed just to the east of the College's playing fields by Father Fabian Sexton, O.S.B. Dedicated to the Sacred Heart of Jesus, that chapel slowly evolved into a full-fledged parish (1967) and continued in the charge of priests from Saint Martin's until September 1990.

In May 1959, Abbot Raphael succinctly described Saint Martin's need for an Abbey Church: "I acknowledge your gift to us. I have taken the liberty of adding it to our Abbey Church Building Fund. This is a project which we should like to begin work on in 1961. Since 1895 we have needed an adequate place where we might carry on the public worship of God. Of course, we have always tried to give the liturgy all the splendor of which we were capable, even in limited facilities, but it would help a great deal to have an adequate abbey church. I would appreciate your keeping this project in your prayers. When I first became abbot in 1943, the Visitators urged me to see that this gets done. It is already sixteen years since I received the mandate. Time is running out."[371]

In the late 1950s the great generosity of Mr. and Mrs. Albert Schafer, whose sons were Saint Martin's alumni, provided a very substantial boost for the slowly accruing Abbey Church building fund. A decade later under the leadership of Abbot Gerald, a committee of monks chaired at first by Father Eugene Kellenbenz and then by Father Germain White took the lead in conceptualizing the design for an Abbey Church.[372] Earlier design proposals for an Abbey Church, in 1957 and in 1967, had been rejected by the monks as being "either too expensive or too monumental for their needs."[373] The monks

PICTURED TOP TO BOTTOM: *The Abbey Church immediately became the campus' most important building with its completion late in 1970. Good design, excellent furnishings, and tasteful decoration combine to make it an outstanding example of a Vatican Council II–inspired Catholic worship center: (1) eagle-lectern by Robert Stanton with Bible, altar table, and the distinctive armless Saint Martin chairs; (2) mechanical-tracker organ custom built in Holland by Vermeulen Brothers contains fifteen stops, nineteen ranks, and nearly one thousand pipes; (3) (left to right) Father Germain White, Brother Aelred Woodard, and Father George Seidel were three gifted singers who often enhanced worship in the new Abbey Church. (Saint Martin's Abbey Archives)*

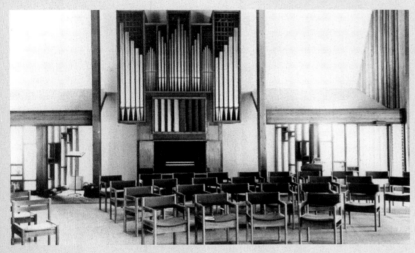

worked with Olympia architects Stephen D. Johnson and Stephen A. Masini in devising a flexible new worship space suitable to monastic and campus needs and in line with liturgical changes promulgated by the Vatican Council II. The monks built their church just to the northwest of the 1959 monastery building on the site of the former convent for the Benedictine Sisters.

On June 5, 1968, after being informed that $384,000 "was on hand for the construction of a Church," the monastic chapter voted forty-four to three to spend not more than that amount "in accordance with a contract with Bennett and Johnson acceptable to the Senior Council."[374] It was almost two years later, however, that final approval for actually constructing an Abbey Church was achieved. At a Chapter Meeting on March 5, 1970, Father Germain, as chairman of the Church Building Committee, "explained about the smaller size of the Church" and its higher cost of $337,000 which included a pipe organ but excluded "other furniture and landscaping." A "turn-key figure" of $362,000 was proposed for approval with the details of the building "to be worked out by the Abbey Building Committee working with the architect." Authority for final contract approval was to be delegated to the abbot and Senior Council.

Various monks at that meeting stated that a church "shouldn't be built now because of uncertainty and insecurity of the times" and others argued that the High School question "should be settled first." However, Father Bede and others "urged the building of a Church, claiming that we tend to put God last" and that a church was "central to our religious life" as monks. Abbot Gerald then stated that despite continuing deficits from its High School and College operations Saint Martin's was "not bankrupt." He then added that there was to be "no stampeding" or ramroding of monks into approving construction of the proposed church. After much discussion, the assembled monks voted to build themselves an Abbey Church by a more than two-thirds favorable vote.[375]

Christmas Midnight Mass was celebrated in the mostly finished Abbey Church in 1970. Most of the $465,000 accrued over so many years for the Church fund had been spent by the time Saint Martin's new worship space was consecrated by Archbishop Thomas A. Connolly of Seattle on April 13, 1971. An inspired design, good workmanship, specially commissioned artwork, careful maintenance, and selective additional embellishment of the Abbey Church have made and have kept it a model for contemporary Catholic worship spaces. Today, students, faculty, and staff as well as neighbors, alumni, and other visitors join their prayers to those of the monks for the church and the world in the serenely beautiful Abbey Church of Saint Martin's.

High School's Acme and Closure

Saint Martin's High School probably reached its acme in the mid 1960s when its enrollment was increasing and the quality of its academic, athletic, and extracurricular programs was self-evident. On October 19, 1966, with just "a bit of discussion" and by a thirty-two to three favorable vote, the Abbey Chapter placidly approved the borrowing of some $1,400,000 for the construction of the first two units of a new High School campus.[376] The new facilities were to be built in the woods northeast of the hill across a large meadow from the closed Abbey farm. A two-story residential building would house 320 boys four-to-a-room and include student common rooms and suites for several monk-prefects. The nearby cafeteria and recreation facility would also contain a small chapel and a principal's suite. In December 1966, the Chapter further authorized the SMHS administration "to draw from the High School reserve fund up to $75,000 for utilities" work at the new site.[377] A month later, a hurried request to also build a new High School classroom facility was turned down when a quick study by the campus finance office projected an annual deficit of some $50,000 from that additional construction.[378] However, a modest proposal in June 1967 to build a sixty-by-thirty-five-foot swimming pool at the new High School site, "said pool to have a bubble covering, and the entire project not to exceed $20,000," was readily approved by the Abbey Chapter. Funds accumulated over the years by Father Leonard's successive High School snack bar operations would cover most of the pool's cost.[379] A fine and popular outdoor pool was speedily built in the central quadrangle of the new SMHS residential complex but it never did get its "bubble" for cold-weather swimming!

At a boarding school for adolescent males, discipline at SMHS was essential and close supervision a necessary regime. Of course, over the years the boys tried their best to get away with as much as possible as far as the rules were concerned! Get an old High School prefect such as Father Urban Feucht talking and he will almost inevitably recount some elaborate ploy that one or more of his charges pulled off to his consternation but also—at least after the fact—to his admiring delight. Writing years later to Father Conrad Rausch, the principal at the time of his enrollment, a 1964 High School alumnus summarized the disciplinary techniques in vogue in his era: "You did it with stares. Father Kenneth with his paddle." He then added a not uncommon hindsight: "I think of Saint Martin's often, although when I was there I hated it. Much like the armed forces, it had a character building quality for those who met the challenge."[380]

Father Leonard Feeney especially enjoyed all the noise and fun of his adolescent charges. He took them seriously and for thirty years worked hard to steer them in good directions. One product of Father Leonard's nurturing realized only in later years how the priest transformed "his" awkward boys into self-sufficient young men. By means of "generous doses of example, compassion, and discipline," George G. McKnight now understands, the savvy monk built up "a moral and ethical center in his 'boys' that would shield them from the traumas that life unfailingly provides."[381] Bob Hull, 1970 SMHS graduate, fondly remembers that Father Leonard was "the person who had the most impact on me." Their special relationship allowed him "to question, to discuss (I never won an argument with him)," and to get help with "the problems of growing up." Bob worked for the amiable priest in the student snack bar and as a projectionist for High School movies in the Abbey Theatre. "Saint Martin's shaped my life into what it is today," he gratefully asserts.[382] Many other High School alumni likewise acknowledge the positive influence of Father Leonard and other monks in the formation of their character.

Dark Clouds On the Horizon

Campus ledgers in the late 1960s showed more and more "red ink" for both High School and College operations. At a June 1968 Abbey Chapter meeting, for example, the College president, Father Michael Feeney, the new High School principal, Father Alfred Hulscher, and the campus' finance officer, Father Peter Sand, "stressed the importance of an all-out effort to get more students for both College and high school." At that same meeting, the budget for the forthcoming fiscal year was accepted by the monastic chapter (the schools' "corporate body") only after the motion to do so "was amended to the effect that a committee be established to study realistically what we want to do, and what we can do, as regards our [academic] apostolate."[383] In terms of the continuing viability of the High School and/or the College, three urgent questions presented themselves: "How much to charge our students? How to get more money from benefactors? How to get more financial aid from Government?"[384]

Sports are a very important component of any all-boys school. This late 1940s SMHS catalog photo depicted the major sports offered.

This mid-1950s view of the "Student Refectory" shows the High School boarders chowing down and their aproned "flunks" or waiters serving up the calories!

Both instrumental and choral music was taught, played, and enjoyed by our High School boys although Father Michael Feeney (left) and Father David Prebula and the young members of the "Ranger" band look mostly serious in this circa 1950 photo.

These boys seem focused on their pool game in the basement High School rec room, circa 1962. Was this a lesson in applied geometry?

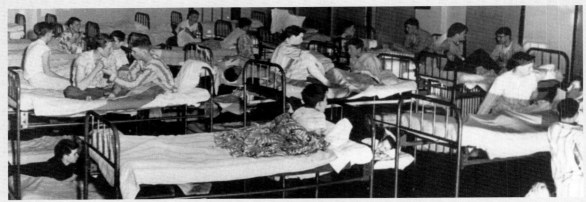

Bedtime in one of the High School dorms, circa 1950s: Even the boisterous young needed their rest as did their hardworking monk-prefects!

Some of SMHS's Benedictine staff in the 1960s: (left to right) Fathers Terence Wager, Leonard Feeney, Nicholas Rausch, Cletus Bradley, and Urban Feucht; seated: Father Conrad Rausch, principal.

The new Saint Martin's High School residential complex boasted a fine outdoor pool in its central courtyard when it opened in 1967 and its principal, Father Conrad Rausch (on right) was mighty pleased with what he saw!

To the great concern of all involved, more deficits were reported later that year. Father Peter informed the Abbey chapter on October 15 "that the College and High School both went in the red" during fiscal year 1967–1968, "but that the College had better prospects financially for the [current] year so that it might be able to make up the losses of last year." Sadly, the High School was "in even worse circumstances for the present year due to decreased enrollment of only about 180 boarders." What funds the Abbey had available should therefore "preferably go to the High School which will be down $100,000 to $120,000." The total combined deficit for the campus schools for 1967–1968 was $125,000. It was covered with $75,000 from Abbey restricted funds and a $50,000 bank loan.

Nevertheless, on November 29 a representative of the institution's outside auditing firm reported that while there were "a few red flags up" Saint Martin's overall was "still in sound financial condition." However, the auditors also noted "that [the College's] lay faculty salaries had risen from $170,000 in 1966 to over $300,000 in 1968" and that about 60 percent of the College faculty now consisted of lay persons.[385] Among other things, the employment of more lay people by the College reduced the amount of income that stayed on campus which in turn diminished the Abbey's ability to subsidize its schools without going into debt. Typically, a significant part of the "salaries" assigned to Benedictine teachers and administrators was routinely used to subsidize the schools' operating budgets. In 1972, the College's president, Father Matthew Naumes, explicitly recognized this crucial monastic support by asserting that "the single greatest asset SMC has is the support and involvement of Saint Martin's Abbey in its work of education and Christian formation of the young." Moreover, he added, "the continued impact of the monastic family on the college is certainly essential to its survival and its success."[386]

The financial condition of the High School's operations continued to deteriorate. Its principal, Father Alfred, reported in May 1969 that there had been "no surge in applications" for the coming school year and that a debt of $185,000 for the current operating year had accumulated. Moreover, a $10,000 shortfall remained even after the High School "dormitory fund" had been exhausted to cover that deficit. Yet he also pointed out that there would be a long-term debt requiring an annual payment of about $105,000 even if the High School were closed and that the tax exemption on the new plant would then cease. Therefore, two hired [lay] teachers had been released for the coming year and "a new, more professional recruiter" had been hired to attempt to boost High School enrollment and gifts.[387] Little good news was available by October 1969, however, for enrollment was down by a dozen boys and even more "red ink" was reported. Father Alfred hoped to have a final report of what further might be done as well as specific recommendations by January 5, 1970. He insisted, however, that "The specific decision, if the High School will have to be closed, is *not* to be revealed until those in authority decide upon the time of revelation."[388]

Gloom began to settle in as all possible steps to save the High School were considered including adding seventh and eighth grade programs, "affiliating more closely with SMC and with Saint Placid High School," a nearby girls school, and asking the Catholic Archdiocese of Seattle for help. Possible "alternate uses" for the new High School facilities were likewise frankly discussed. It was also noted that monks employed in the High School were greatly overworked and that was perhaps why only two younger monks were "at present coming up for H.S. teaching." Another monk "maintained that our [monastery's] Apostolate should first be decided upon very definitely before making final decisions as regards our H.S."[389] Harrowed by the continuing deficits, the Abbey Chapter decided in March 1970 to support one more year of SMHS operations with certain strict conditions. The rescue package was predicated on anticipated higher enrollment as well as an increase in fees, a substantial contribution from the College to assist in paying debt service on the new High School facilities, and "immediate steps" to increase operating income through a real estate development program involving the Abbey and its two schools.[390] Most of Saint Martin's "endowment" at that time consisted of its campus acreage in Lacey. How to put that "fixed" endowment to use in helping to subsidize Saint Martin's educational and religious activities was a complex question.

The monks assembled on November 27, 1970, to resume their painful deliberations concerning the future of their High School. During the past summer, the new SMHS dormitory and cafeteria-recreation buildings had been evacuated. The much reduced number of High School boarders was once again being housed in rooms in Old Main's west wing. Father Conrad, back on the firing line as the school's principal, told the chapter members that currently there was "no real way of knowing how much it really costs to run the High School." He also insisted that many of the charges for which it was currently being assessed for joint use of parts of the campus physical plant were "way out of line." However, some $300,000 was still needed to operate SMHS for 1970–1971 "exclusive of [new] dorm debt service" of some $105,000. How to get additional students was unclear although local alumni and their parents had "promised to get us more day students" provided that the school returned to a five-day week. Begging letters had so far garnered just $6,000 and recruiting efforts in various Northwest metropolitan areas had not yet produced many new or even prospective high school boys.

Father John Raymond, the institutional treasurer, then presented two options: close the High School or continue it. Due to "locked in" costs, however, the institutional finance committee had come to the conclusion that closing the High School "cannot be recommended from a financial point of view." He therefore proposed trying to continue operating SMHS with a program and budget "acceptable to most of the [monastic] high school personnel." Some "genuine possibilities" in terms of a newly configured High School program might be discovered by increased effort. After extensive discussion in which "many, many opinions were expressed," Abbot Gerald concluded the meeting by stating that the Chapter "should not act too hastily" concerning the future of its High School.[391]

When the Chapter again took up the future of SMHS in mid-December 1970, the picture had been somewhat clarified. Pending rental of the closed "new" high school plant to an outside user promised "to come close to covering" future obligations to the insurance company which held the mortgage on the facility. Furthermore, the results of a careful analysis of general campus operations had again recommended against closing the High School "at this juncture." The best option seemed to be "to increase the number of day students" by returning to a five-day class week and lowering the tuition. While such a program "over the next two to three years" might "improve income without increasing expenditures," it was also conceded that the High School administration's enrollment and budget estimates "include a guess element." Abbot Gerald then spoke about the High School's usefulness as a place for monks to work productively and gave assurances that the assessments currently charged to SMHS for overall campus operations would be studied with a view to decreasing them. The Chapter then voted 28-20 to continue the High School for an unspecified period.[392]

In April 1971, the new Washington State Department of Ecology signed a lease with Saint Martin's Abbey to rent three-fourths of the former SMHS residence facility for its headquarters offices.[393] This arrangement would later be expanded to involve Ecology's use of the entire new High School plant and would continue for over twenty years to the mutual satisfaction of both parties.

Conditions did not improve for SMHS during "the Boeing bust" of the early 1970s when the entire Pacific Northwest's economy was deflated. In October 1971, Father Conrad forthrightly recognized that the future of the High School was clouded. Only seventy-two of a hoped for one hundred day students had been enrolled while residential student enrollment had declined to ninety-three. Higher enrollment in either category was uncertain with parents pleading an inability to pay required fees. Younger Saint Martin's monks were not much interested in working in SMHS and some of its current monk-teachers were "getting to the age where they cannot carry full loads." Use of "stop-gap measures" in staffing the High School could not continue indefinitely. Raising $20,000 during the present school year to help subsidize High School operations—as stipulated by the Chapter—was "totally unrealistic." The principal ended his remarks on an ominous note: "Some of this report is not so encouraging, but I have tried to give it honestly. Everyone has to draw his own conclusions."[394]

Increasing doubts within the monastic community itself about the High School's viability were dramatically indicated in October 1971 by the Chapter's twenty-five to twenty-one vote *against* a proposal to resolve the SMHS deficit for the *previous* fiscal year. That vote had come after lengthy and emotional discussion about "the finances and the significance of the high school apostolate."[395] The monks spent "many hours of discussion" on the future of their High School on November 10, 17, and 24, 1971, under the leadership of a "Works of the [Monastic] Community Committee" chaired by Father Martin Anderson. The Chapter met again on November 26 to consider a proposal that the High School be continued but "only as a predominantly day school" and in close cooperation with SMC "to strengthen the academic program and to facilitate advanced placement of high school students" in College classes. A long discussion ensued in which all the positive and negative conditions affecting SMHS were yet again rehearsed. After some final clarifications on the issue of "unbalanced budgets," the monks voted by the narrow margin of thirty to twenty-six to support the operation of a reconfigured High School for 1972–1973.[396]

Protracted worry over the High School's future understandably "caused a multitude of tensions" among its staff and really hurt their morale. By the spring of 1972, however, Father Conrad—delighted to be once again retiring as SMHS' principal—reported that the High School staff's spirits were up and they were determined to make their school succeed. Father Terence Wager had been appointed principal, the curriculum had undergone a "re-construction" with a view of making it a real preparatory school, and a "heavy recruiting program" had already shown "some good response." However, Father Conrad with his usual candor also reported that parents did not seem "anxious to send their sons away for their high school education to the tune of $2,200 per year when they can get good 'free' education in the public schools, *unless* there is some type of problem at home." He further advised the Chapter "to accept the fact that we are not going to have 'hordes' of students knocking at our doors."[397] Father Terence then "pleaded for optimism" toward the High School's prospects and also for "the continued material and spiritual support" of the monastic community. He also pledged that cooperation with Saint Placid High School would be "continued in every feasible manner." The Chapter after much additional discussion voted twenty-five to seventeen in favor of the Abbey underwriting the High School's deficit for 1972–1973.[398]

The High School suffered a further decline in enrollment in the fall of 1972 including the loss of an ominous 42 percent of the previous year's nongraduating students. In response, Father Terence appointed the ever enthusiastic Father Robert Renggli to be "on the road full time for admissions work" to increase SMHS's ranks. The principal and several other monks met with a public relations and development firm to get ideas about the advancement of the High School. Father Terence also objected to the reduction of the number of monks working in SMHS by their reassignment to positions in Saint Martin's other operations.[399]

Late in the evening of October 16, 1973, at the end of a long session of meetings held that day, the Abbey Chapter voted thirty-five to fifteen to close SMHS effective June 30, 1974. "A vote of confidence in and gratitude to the high school staff, both present and past" was also unanimously adopted. The wrenching decision to shut down Saint Martin's High School program came only after years of "red ink" and despite the best efforts of the High School monks themselves and Abbey leaders.

Some Benedictines at the time felt betrayed by what they saw as a coalition of non-High School monks and College administrators to close *their* High School. However, the blunt fact that SMHS had ended its 1972–1973 business year with another operating deficit of $52,000 and already "owed the Abbey $444,000" which was "more than its total assets, which in the business world would mean bankruptcy" simply could not be ignored.[400] After-the-fact attempts to come up with a viable way of transforming the closing Benedictine institution into an Olympia-South Sound regional Catholic high school came to naught. Forty boys, including several juniors who had accelerated their studies in order to finish their secondary education at SMHS, made up the final High School graduating class on May 18, 1974.[401] Hundreds of SMHS alumni were saddened by the termination of an institution which had been an important part of their lives. Eventually, most High School monks recycled themselves successfully into jobs in the Abbey's other areas of service. Some became successful pastors or hospital chaplains while several added their talents and energies to the staff of Saint Martin's College. However, in some cases the integration of former SMHS monks into the ranks of the SMC staff or faculty was insensitively handled.

Shown in his College office in March 1972, Father Matthew Naumes, O.S.B., served as president of SMC from 1971 to 1975. He pushed academic changes in order to consolidate curricular offerings and sought to have the College play a more significant role in the cultural life of the capital city region. (Saint Martin's Abbey Archives)

Progress in the College

In June 1972, at the end of his first year as SMC's president, Father Matthew Naumes "expressed great disappointment on the failure of either church or state to give aid to private higher education." He had written strong letters of protest to the state's congressional delegation concerning their refusal to support pending federal legislation. He was also very annoyed with Archbishop Connolly of Seattle who "not only refused to allow pulpit solicitation for financial aid to SMC and Seattle University [a Jesuit-sponsored Catholic school], but even forbade recruitment of students by priests at the parish level."[402] That October Father Matthew had to report to a

shortfall in anticipated College enrollment for despite a healthy 79 percent retention rate from the previous term the number of freshmen and transfer students was "below a healthy minimum." He also reiterated his position that "curriculum changes were mandatory" since "nineteen majors are seven too many" for a school the size of SMC. Furthermore, he was annoyed that neither the curriculum committee nor the general faculty had actively taken up this important matter.[403] Abbot Dunstan, as chairman of the College's board of trustees, then promised support for a "cool-headed, realistic review" of the SMC curriculum and "a reasonably prompt implementation" of whatever changes would increase the College's "viability."[404]

In the 1960s and the 1970s, Father Richard Cebula, O.S.B., served two terms as SMC's chief academic officer. He brought military Bootstrap students to Lacey and set up successful extension programs at Fort Lewis and McChord AFB. For a long while, he was also the heart and soul of the College's Civil Engineering Department. (Saint Martin's Abbey Archives)

In 1973–1974, SMC's academic programs were reorganized in what the president thought was a "reasonably effective" way into three academic divisions: Humanities, Natural Sciences, and Social Sciences. Long-range academic planning was also initiated with strong faculty leadership. The College's faculty and administration numbered forty-four and they served 476 full-time and part-time students. One hundred and five degrees were conferred at the May 17, 1974 commencement and eighty other persons had earlier received their SMC degrees at August and December 1973 convocations. Sixteen monks worked in the College and the Abbey had supported the school's operations "with a gift of over $100,000" during the just concluded academic year.[405] Abbot Dunstan thanked the College's administration and faculty "for their heroic efforts to carry on a strong Christian institution amid so many difficulties." He also urged even stronger support "in the immediate years ahead" by the monks for *their* College.[406]

In the early to mid-1970s, a new but temporary cohort of students enhanced SMC academically and also contributed to its never-too-full coffers. Popularly called the "Bootstrap" program, it was a degree-completion opportunity for U.S. military personnel available on several campuses around the country. Father Richard Cebula, the college's academic vice president, was responsible for bringing the Bootstrap program to SMC where it mostly involved commissioned officers given time off with pay (typically from nine to fifteen months) to complete their college degrees. Highly motivated individuals, these military men came to Lacey eager to learn and to excel. Perhaps a typical faculty appraisal of them was that applied by Father Meinrad Gaul to December 1972 graduates: "The Bootstrappers are excellent students, and we are sorry that their stay at Saint Martin's is so limited."[407] Serious and generally gung-ho, many Bootstrappers later became some of the College's most dedicated alumni.

The well-organized and energetic Father Richard was also principally instrumental in setting up SMC degree completion programs for military personnel and their dependents at Fort Lewis, a very large Army post about a dozen miles from Lacey. The veteran Benedictine educator "understood the needs and possibilities of continuing education" and bravely entered into "the battle for non-traditional education." The Army civilian administrator in charge of developing the Fort's postsecondary educational programs in the 1970s ascribes to Father Richard "the most credit for the long lasting and high quality" SMC programs then instigated on post and which continue there to this day. In his work with Boostrapppers at Lacey and with Fort Lewis and, later, McChord Air Force Base academic programs, Father Richard wisely and successfully built "a new segment of the College alumni that would cover the world."[408] The Bootstrap and military extension centers initiatives of Father Richard significantly helped to stabilize the College's finances in fluctuating times.

Seeking to involve SMC more significantly in the cultural life of the capital city region, Father Matthew had become a director and vice president of CAAPA (Capital Area Association for Performing Arts). With his assistance and support, in May 1974 CAAPA made a formal request to the Abbey Chapter "to lease college-owned property for the building of a $1 million Performing Arts Center." Up to ten acres would be needed for the facility which would be erected on a campus site to be designated by James Chiarelli, a noted Seattle architect and SMC trustee. Terms of the lease would be $1 a year for forty years with an option to renew the lease for two twenty-year periods. The request was approved by a thirty-six to five vote "with details to be worked out and brought back to the Chapter later."[409] Nothing came of that project, however.

The College president's October 15, 1974 report to the monastic community was serious but upbeat. SMC's previous fiscal year had ended "in a surplus position." Certain necessary capital improvements had been made, "notably lighted parking west and south of the hill" and some "modest remodeling in the main building, utilizing space hitherto used by the High School." The fall 1974 enrollment was up from the previous year's and represented "a gain on maintaining SMC as a four-year institution rather than as a degree completion institution serving graduates of state-operated junior colleges." The McChord and Fort Lewis programs were maintaining strength and making a significant contribution to the College. While Father Matthew reported the initiation of what he hoped would be stronger financial undergirding for SMC (such as the initiation of a deferred gifts program), he also stressed that "certain modifications" in the College's academic programs still had to be made to consolidate the institution's future. The national "trend of inflation" was very serious as was the need for Saint Martin's to offer a more attractive academic program to prospective students. A key to the latter goal was "to find an academic vice president sensitive to these needs."[410]

Abbot Dunstan complimented Father Matthew and his College staff for "their very effective work during the past year" which had resulted in both a balanced budget for the current year and "a sizable surplus" for the past year. However, at the same meeting the always gentlemanly abbot also tried to suture the open wound resulting from the October 2 dismissal of Father Richard Cebula from his position as SMC's academic vice president. There had been "an essential disagreement" between two monk administrators and "it was clear that the Board of Trustees would require that the President be upheld." So the abbot in his capacity as Board chairman, with much regret, had relieved the AVP of his duties. Abbot Dunstan also strongly reminded the monks that it was "vital that we give a sense of solidarity and unity to our publics, especially to our students" concerning the recent administrative confrontation and change.[411]

New Leadership for SMC

For several years a good portion of the student activities fees collected by the College had been turned over to the student government (ASSMC) for its use in providing extracurricular programming. However, Father Matthew announced in June 1973 that "during the next academic year the student activity fee" would be used to support a "lecture-concert pro-

PICTURED TOP
TO BOTTOM:
*Campus life at SMC in
the 1970s had much about
it that was congenial.
(1) A Burton Hall student
enjoys a quiet moment in
his room and (2) a pickup
football game west of the
Student Union Building
attracts a small crowd that
includes popular Director
of Residence Judy Sharpe
(in right background in
white shirt) and (3) student
chaplain Father Martin
Anderson (center) presides
at an outdoor Mass behind
Baran Hall; Fathers Blaise
Feeney (left) and John Scott
concelebrate. (SMC Office of
Communications)*

gram more fitting to the academic and cultural mission of the school than the program mounted by ASSMC" in recent years.[412] Whatever its other merits, this change would bring about an angry and, eventually, bitter response from SMC's student leaders. The issue became so contentious that student government leaders in 1974–1975 initiated a lawsuit against the College administration over its withholding of those fees. Their actions in making public a campus dispute mirrored other tensions at the College.

By the spring of 1975, Saint Martin's College had become a rather fretful place. Several key administrators resigned, tempers flared and campus tensions grew more acrimonious until Father Matthew resigned in late May. What went wrong for SMC's leader? Despite some impressive accomplishments during four years in office, his management style and personality finally seemed to many College people to displace his other qualities. Shortly after he resigned the presidency, he was quoted in a local newspaper as saying: "I ruled with an iron first."[413] In a close-knit community like Saint Martin's that could and would be tolerated for only so long.

At Abbot Dunstan's request, four of the Abbey's priests applied for the job of running SMC. Apparently the involvement of three of them in recent campus disputes inclined the abbot and other College trustees to choose the youngest and least controversial candidate to take over the helm. The monk selected, Father John Scott, had been pursuing doctoral studies out of state since 1973.[414] The new president took over the administration of the College toward the end of June and soon described his vision for SMC in a hopeful and forthright way: "Saint Martin's collegial life," he asserted, "should be seriously academic, comfortably familial, person-centered and clearly demonstrative of those Christian values which have nourished the Catholic tradition over the centuries." He believed that his principal task as president was "to oversee, encourage and facilitate" co-responsibility within the school's "community" of faculty, staff, students and alumni. His chief goal was to help SMC become more truly "a proud, happy center of mutual growth and learning."[415] Having at age thirty become the youngest college president in the United States, Father John applied a comment of the American humorist Mark Twain to his new job: "There is nothing that [so] saps one's confidence as the knowing how to do a thing." He then set to work to ease campus tensions while continuing his predecessors' efforts to improve off-campus relations.[416]

Father John believed that the SMC's Catholic and Benedictine "element," which emphasized interdependence,

Abbot Dunstan Curtis, O.S.B. (1921–1981), was a true gentleman. Through his contact with Father Alcuin Lawrence, one of the Abbey's priests serving as a World War II Army chaplain in California, he converted to Catholicism and came to Lacey after the war as a candidate for the monastic life. He made his first vows in 1947 and was ordained a priest in 1951. He earned a doctorate in education from Stanford University and started SMC's teacher education program with key help from Roger J. Feeney. He served as College president from 1959 to 1964 and then as prior of the Abbey. Elected our fifth abbot in May 1972, ill health forced his resignation in November 1977. He bore his extended illness gently and died on July 28, 1981, esteemed by all who knew him. (Saint Martin's Abbey Archives)

did and should shape the school's educational philosophy. It was essential, therefore, for teachers and students alike to be involved "in a mutual quest for both conscience and competence." He hoped that their time at SMC would help each of its alumni "to become a man or woman definitely committed to working for a humane future . . . that will hold in store for all of us at least a little increase in beauty and at least a little decrease in injustice."[417]

In 1976, Father John "moved" the College "back" to Lacey and the Abbey also simultaneously changed its address! This administrative action was necessary because some thirty years earlier the U.S. Post Office had required Saint Martin's to begin using Olympia as its official mailing address. SMC's annual academic *Bulletin* (the school's catalog) had first indicated that change of address in 1948 and subsequently people had taken to referring to Olympia as Saint Martin's location. Father John's decision to "relocate" SMC was immediately prompted by the purchase by the City of Lacey (incorporated in 1966) of some Saint Martin's owned acreage adjacent to the campus for the site of its new City Hall. However, even more to the point was the fact that the Benedictine monastery and school had in fact physically been in "Lacey" for some eighty years! The publicly minded College president also took this step in order to emphasize that SMC *was* Lacey's College and that it should be proud to be in the "heart" of a growing community.

In an era of unbalanced budgets when SMC's future was being much discussed, the school's president shared his thoughts with alumni at a February 1978 Homecoming luncheon: "What does the future hold for your school? Are we committed to continuing our educational services, in updated yet personal ways? Financially, SMC is having some hard times—as many colleges presently are. We are working energetically to attract students to our programs, to heighten awareness of the college in our primary service area (southwest Washington), to find new sources of support, and new ways of being a good, small, Catholic college." Thus, "SMC needs your help—your money, of course, but also your good will and your good words in referring students to us, and speaking positively about what you received [here]." With help from its alumni and other friends, he pledged, everybody currently at the school was committed "to perpetuate this special place and the kinds of education it can provide. The future is challenging for SMC," he admitted, "but there will be a future!"[418]

By the fall of 1979, Father John was increasingly frustrated with his own inability to come to grips with the College's budgetary problems. He was also very much concerned to complete his Ph.D. dissertation and thus to get back into teaching history at SMC. Therefore he followed the advice of the Abbey's temporary administrator, Father Hilary Thimmesh of Saint John's Abbey, and submitted his resignation as president of SMC effective January 3, 1980. As he concluded his administrative service at his alma mater, he offered some quietly optimistic thoughts: "No individual can possibly be the paragon of wisdom and virtue, the management wizard or the public-relations and development superstar that SMC would seem to need. Yet when this College's Board [of Trustees] and its president and staff work together to support and develop each others strengths and to compensate for inevitable weaknesses, Saint Martin's will succeed in its efforts to continue to offer a quality education with practical and humanizing results for both its students and its staff."[419] ⚜

As College president from 1975 to 1980, Father John Scott, O.S.B., sought to keep campus life at SMC seriously academic yet comfortably familial. He encouraged alumni to support their alma mater both financially and by way of recruiting more students for its programs. Father John also "moved" the school from Olympia "back" to Lacey by the simple expedient of changing its address! (Photo by Andy Hagara)

The vital interplay between the perennial prayer and work of the Abbey's Benedictine monks and the mutual teaching and learning of the College's faculty and students is embodied in the Society of Fellows, SMC's academic honors organization. Student inductees, circa 1994, pose with Faculty Fellows Father Kilian Malvey and Professor Norma Shelan (second row, first and third from right) after the annual spring Awards Convocation in the Abbey Church. (Photo by Gant W. Eichrodt)

CHAPTER 8
From Yesterday to Tomorrow (1980–1995)

WHEN DR. JOHN D. ISHII WAS NAMED president of Saint Martin's College in January 1980 he became the first layperson to lead the Benedictine College in the school's eighty-five-year history. However, as an alumnus of both SMHS ('38) and SMC ('42), he knew the "tradition" of the institution. Himself a Catholic, he valued the Christian and monastic spirit the Benedictines had sustained on campus as well as the school's family-like culture. Furthermore, during a career in international relations he had gained a broad perspective on life as well as a fine family. Dr. Ishii's personal and professional experiences thus served to make him at age fifty-nine an ideal transitional leader.[420]

Jack Ishii returned to Lacey in 1973 to take a job teaching international relations in his alma mater's Government [now Political Science] Department, a challenging undertaking for he had no formal teaching experience. He therefore considered himself very lucky to have some Vietnam War veterans in his first courses because "they had lots of opinions on everything and really ran the classes." Dr. Ishii also worked to help develop programs for international students on campus in order to help bring a more global perspective to SMC. In mid-1979, he was asked by the College's president, Father John Scott, to take on the duties of vice president for academic affairs "for a few weeks." Some months later he himself was offered the presidency. He accepted because "he wanted very much to try to give to students the same inspiration and humane perceptions of a troubled world that he had [earlier] gained under the Benedictine monks."[421] His wife, Lillian Ishii, who thereupon became the College's first "First Lady," quickly became an invaluable asset in her own right for she added a touch of class to everything she helped with on and off campus.

The new president faced the daunting task of running SMC in a period of both economic stringency and diversifying educational demands. The really "tight" financial position of the College was noted by SMC's chief financial officer, Alan Spence, in comments he made to the Abbey Chapter in May

As SMC's first non-Benedictine president, Dr. John D. Ishii brought to his challenging new job both deep familiarity with the school's tradition as an alumnus and broad experience in international affairs. Starting in 1980, he helped turn the College in a more outward direction by emphasizing international programs while working closely with the Abbey's leadership to assure increased involvement of monks in campus services. (SMC Office of Communication)

1980. While the College had "been able to stop our decline" it did "not presently have the financial means for institutional growth." SMC also lacked, Spence stated, "available funds for major repairs or renovations" and had "as yet been unable to implement our retirement program."[422] The College, moreover, was too dependent on student-derived income as about 80 percent of its revenues came from tuition, room and board, and other fees. Comparable institutions derived only about 70 percent of their operating income from such sources.[423] Yet competition for other types of "supportive funds" was so "fierce" that Dr. Ishii would have to spend ever more of his time searching for additional operating funds and endowments. A Gifts-in-Kind program was initiated in 1981 to encourage alumni, friends, and businesses to donate everything from mini-computers to laboratory equipment to furniture. Donation of personal or professional skills such as in electrical and plumbing work for on-campus jobs was also invited.[424]

In his interactions with students, the new president observed that many of them were looking for "meaning, purpose, directions and values." Dr. Ishii therefore made it a priority to work with Father Adrian Parcher, his chief academic officer, "to re-introduce Christian ideals and values" into the school's programs. He also told the monks that he would like to see as many of them as possible "involved in the work of the College." The president also believed that SMC needed to broaden its curriculum to offer degree programs attractive to more students including older men and women involved in career changes. Improving the retention rate among current students would likewise be critical in stabilizing the College. At the end of his first year as president, and despite the many challenges of managing a small private college in troublesome times, Dr. Ishii was confident that "we will become the fine college we all want to become."[425]

Holy Names Sister Katherine Gray was appointed vice president for academic affairs by Dr. Ishii in 1981 with a mandate to update the College's curriculum. A seasoned administrator, she worked with the school's faculty on programs that would better respond to local and regional academic needs and stimulate enrollment growth. With an increasingly "older" population entering or returning to higher education, she observed that there would have to be a "greater emphasis on community related programs." More of SMC's departments would be including internships in their degree requirements and some carefully crafted interdisciplinary studies would be tried. Institutional needs for "computerization" for management and instructional purposes would be quickly assessed. (The College established a microcomputer center for its students in May 1982. Under the joint direction of math professor Sheryl Blix and Patrick McIntyre of the Education Department, it quickly became a regional resource for teaching computers-in-education.) Graduate programs in engineering and in business might be ready within two years. "There are going to be exciting new programs in many areas," Sister Katherine promised, and SMC is "sure to have a greater impact on the community."[426] Starting in the summer of 1982, a Spiritual Life Institute was established under the joint sponsorship of the College and Abbey. It was conceived by Institute director Father Kilian Malvey as a program that would allow "participants from all faiths" to share with the campus' monastic and academic community as they study "developments in theology, religious education, spirituality, and the religious life." The Spiritual Life Institute has reconfigured its format over the years yet it continues to provide in-depth theological reflection on and spiritual consideration of important topics—and not entirely without controversy.[427]

"Red ink," however, continued to blot SMC's ledgers. The College's "long-standing short-term debt" with its "quite substantial" interest payments demanded extraordinary attention by the 1983 fall semester. A special task force of College trustees and Abbey financial advisers prescribed stern solutions. Short-term debt was strangling the College, they reported, and "must be liquidated at the earliest possible date." Therefore "an aggressive management system" for Saint Martin's–owned properties was needed along with "a fund development program headed by a top-level individual" jointly undertaken by the Abbey and College. In addition, a "management audit of the internal financial operation of the College" was imperative plus the appointment of a campus-based "high-level financial controller." SMC's academic programs also had to be examined "to see which are viable."[428] Their sobering advice served as a wake-up call for the campus at large.

By the summer of 1984, Abbot Adrian, in his dual capacity as the monastery's superior and the College's chancellor, was reporting some initial progress in the financial restoration of Saint Martin's overall operations. Some valuable property not adjacent to the campus was being sold to retire "two short-term debts entered into for cash flow" and no additional loans had been needed because of "careful fiscal management" by a new budget manager. The Abbot also expressed his optimism that a reinvigorated land development program "could become a strong factor" in stabilizing Saint Martin's operations along with the renewed quest for endowments and expected additional tuition fees.[429]

Once that high-powered "restoration" program for SMC had been launched, President Ishii requested a sabbatical leave through December 31, 1984 on which date his five-year term would end. It was granted and he thereafter intensified his activities as chairman of Governor John Spellman's recently established Advisory Council on International Trade Development for the State of Washington. Dr. Ishii had long argued "that our American public and commercial entities must become more aware of the Pacific Rim people" and "not only in trade but in culture." Earlier he had recruited Pacific Rim students for SMC and now he would have the chance to promote his home state's transpacific commercial and cultural outreach.[430]

A New Abbot

On June 19, 1980, the monks of Saint Martin's Abbey elected Father Adrian Parcher, forty-seven, to be their new—and sixth—abbot. He thereupon succeeded Father Hilary Thimmesh, who had served as the monastic community's interim superior for the previous two years. A monk of Saint John's Abbey in Collegeville, Minnesota (which had founded Saint Martin's in 1895), Father Hilary was highly respected by the Lacey monks and very likely would have been elected their abbot had he not emphatically announced his plans to return to Saint John's.

Of necessity, Abbot Adrian took immediate steps to better shore up the financial stability of Saint Martin's overall operations. He also voiced his support for Dr. Ishii's management of SMC and especially for the president's stated "hope and resolve" to re-emphasize the school's Catholic and Benedictine heritage by enlarging the importance of theology and philosophy in its curriculum. The almost tangible sense of *caring* on campus, Abbot Adrian asserted, must be maintained by all of

Abbot Adrian Parcher, O.S.B., was chosen by the monks as their sixth abbot on June 19, 1980. He immediately worked to shore up the financial stability of Saint Martin's overall operations and to reemphasize the College's Catholic and Benedictine heritage. He also initiated an Abbey Church Events series of classical music concerts and theological lectures. (Saint Martin's Abbey Archives)

the Saint Martin's community for we must not forget that "cure without care is meaningless."[431]

The new abbot also underscored the importance of Benedictine monastic "observance" (that is, of the prayer and work which the monks shared daily) and of the general environment of the "cloister" in which "the common life" of the monastic community was lived. Abbot Adrian soon established a series of Abbey Endowment Funds the interest on which would be used to fund monastic retirement, a new Abbey Church Lecture/Events series, and to help support other monastery needs and programs.[432]

The abbot also sought to develop within the Abbey a more aesthetic tone or focus. The 1980 observance of the 1500th anniversary of the birth of Saint Benedict provided the occasion for the initial scheduling classical music concerts in the Abbey Church. Abbot Adrian then appointed Brother Elias Lien to plan a series of concerts and lectures for subsequent years. Knowingly or not, he thereby brought to fruition a dream of Abbot Raphael Heider, who in November 1945 had shared a hope with one of the Abbey's priests serving overseas as a military chaplain: "Last Wednesday we had a lecture by Dr. Gabor de Bessenyey, Catholic journalist, commentator, and teacher at DePaul and Fordham. He came through a bureau and seems to be well received. His talk was quite satisfactory, I thought, and I would like to see a way to have more lectures and some concerts. Some day maybe we will have a tradition of such offerings."[433] In 1990, Brother Boniface Lazzari assumed the direction of the Abbey Church Events program and has maintained its high standards. Thus under the patronage of Saint Martin's Benedictines, for over fifteen years impressive lecturers and gifted musicians have enriched campus audiences with their insights and performances. The programs remain open to the public without charge.

On Easter Sunday 1985, a front-page story in *The Olympian* reported Abbot Adrian's statement that "people forget" that Saint Martin's "is a monastery as well as a college." Yet he also asserted that the monks' religious spirit was a unique influence that penetrated Saint Martin's College and gave it a special ethos. The abbot himself was described as a "realist" determined to see his monastery remain vital and stable as it went through its necessary "metamorphosis." He explained that the Abbey lost thirty-four of its ninety-six monks between 1974 and 1978 and that "only eleven are in the cemetery." Those who defected were principally "in their 30s and 40s, most with master's degrees, many with Ph.D.'s" and most of them were truly missed. "In that period of uncertainty, the joy was lost" but the abbot was "now trying to rekindle the joy." Abbot Adrian concluded his interview by making one thing very clear: "We [monks] have a reason to be here: 'to seek God.'"[434] Therefore the religious quest of the monastic life was and had to be central to the lives of the Abbey's monks. On the other hand, individually or as a community the "labors" of Saint Martin's monks could profitably be employed in many tasks within SMC and off campus as well.

Abbot Adrian brought to his pivotal job much energy and many talents along with a real elegance of style as a liturgical celebrant. With his extensive scriptural and monastic studies and several years in the classroom as a scholarly and precise teacher of English, he was also a very fine preacher. Perhaps as a break from his many stressful duties he "collected and subsequently refurbished many art pieces previously lost and forgotten" in the nooks and crannies of the campus. He also acquired an important collection of the works of leading artists of the Pacific Northwest and displayed them in various Abbey and College sites.[435] Likewise his patronage of the arts and inauguration of the Abbey Church Events concert and lecture series reconnected his monastery and school with the centuries-old Benedictine tradition of fostering the arts and culture. Eventually, however, aspects of his policies and activities came to severely hamper his ability to effectively lead his monastery. His own personal circumstances became more adverse. He resigned as Abbot of Saint Martin's on March 15, 1986, because of ill health and has since pursued various forms of pastoral service in other locations.

Abbot Conrad Rausch, O.S.B., was elected by the Abbey's monks as their seventh abbot on May 23, 1986. His solid personal example and quiet leadership helped restore balance to the life of the monastic community. Earlier in his career, he had happily been an SMHS teacher and principal. Since retirement in 1993, he has maintained his decades-long involvement in campus beautification projects. With the help of Abbey Clippers volunteers and various monks, he continues to cultivate the hilltop's rose garden and flower beds. (Saint Martin's Abbey Archives)

Abbot Conrad Settles Things Down

On May 23, 1986, the Abbey Chapter elected Father Conrad Rausch as the monastery's next—and seventh—abbot. At sixty-five, he was a tried-and-true veteran of monastic life and a man interested in much less sophisticated activities than his immediate predecessor. For some twenty years he had worked happily in Saint Martin's High School as an energetic teacher, prefect, coach, advisor, and principal. After SMHS was closed in 1974, he accepted other assignments on

campus and then served a two-year stint as headmaster at a Benedictine prep school in Colorado. Extensive weekend pastoral assistance over the years at a number of Catholic churches and chapels also allowed him to extend his ministry off campus. Work to him is a pleasure so since retiring as abbot in 1993 he has happily labored to keep the Abbey's hilltop precincts a site of beauty as well as prayer. The Abbey Clippers garden club and other monks have aided him in maintaining our little bit of "paradise."

A Monastic Mission Statement

Over the centuries Benedictine monks have sought to follow an ordered pattern of prayer and work as the spiritual and material matrix for their shared life. In 1992 the Benedictines of Saint Martin's approved a new Abbey Mission Statement as a means of restating their purposes and goals. They reaffirmed their commitment to "lifelong formation in vows, common liturgical prayer and work in response to God's invitation to follow Christ" as the major focuses of their shared life "so that in all things that we do, God may be glorified." They also declared that their monks' work in Saint Martin's College would continue as their principal apostolate. They likewise endorsed the "generous sharing and service to the larger community" shown by those Abbey monks who worked in pastoral care of the sick and parish ministry.[436]

Environmental stewardship is also an important value for Lacey's monks. For example, Saint Martin's obligation to care for its campus "woods" was very well described by Brother Boniface Lazzari in 1992: "We recognize the value of conserving our wooded environment for our Saint Martin's community and for the [Lacey] community at large," he said, for "not all people are afforded the opportunity to live and work in such an environment which provides for quiet, solitude, and nourishment for the soul."[437] Saint Martin's thus continues to maintain its campus as a creditable part of the "Evergreen State"!

Spangler Comes on Duty

On August 17, 1984, Dr. David R. Spangler, chairman of SMC's Civil Engineering Department, was appointed by the Board of Trustees as the College's next president. At forty-four, he was evaluated by the presidential search committee "young, yet mature" and "knowledgeable about the various peculiarities of our College and its monastic connection." While enthusiastic he was "not naive about the future of SMC" and, very importantly, brought to the presidency "managerial experience of great significance." His considerable administrative and academic experience, as well as a humane and wise approach to complex issues, can be attested by the Committee."[438]

A savvy West Pointer, he soon engineered a management plan that included long hours for himself of detailed study of every aspect of the institution's operations. His objective was to assure the school's immediate operational stability while also strategizing its future growth and development. Cuts would be carefully made as needed so as to assure future growth after the institution's resurgence. Already "a careful, diligent and tireless worker," that disposition served Dr. Spangler and the College well through his very troubling initial years as president. Of necessity, balancing the budget became the watchword. SMC Registrar Mary Conley Law remembers the hard times and appreciates Spangler's pivotal role in stabilizing and then turning around the College's operations: "He had to make many unpopular decisions; spending cuts, program cuts, and lots more, to keep the school afloat."[439] But such tenacity paid off and a renewed commitment to SMC's survival and future growth slowly developed on and off campus.

By 1989 enrollment growth was seen as the best way to more fully rejuvenate the College. Having stanched the hemorrhage of "red ink," the president announced that the school next had "to concentrate on a sizable increase in student enrollment" to create a larger on-campus population for its educational services. "Regional growth provides not only

Dr. David R. Spangler was appointed president of SMC in August 1984 by a Board of Trustees seeking someone with managerial experience to reconfigure the school's programs and expand its resources. Through hands-on management and lots of hard work, he secured operational stability for the institution and gradually led it into a period of solid growth. (SMC Office of Communication)

Building on academic outreach programs initiated in the 1970s, SMC further developed its offerings at the Fort Lewis and McChord AFB education centers in the 1980s and 1990s. The College's solid and thriving satellite programs involve dedicated faculty and highly motivated students who develop into avid alumni. (SMC Office of Communication)

opportunities for expansion," Dr. Spangler believed, but also "demands for our programs." And those needed enrollment increases did come! In fact, the College grew by 53 percent in full-time equivalent student headcount between 1984 and 1994. For example, in the 1991 fall semester 748 people were enrolled in main campus courses, 420 full-time while 1995 fall semester enrollments at Lacey numbered 923 people, 298 part-time. SMC's offerings at its Fort Lewis and McChord AFB military extension centers (which operate on different schedules) attracted 585 students for their fall 1991 classes compared with 727 in 1995. Dr. Spangler saluted the College's faculty and staff for being primarily responsible for the resurgent enrollment. He also believed that SMC "will assure its place in the future" by continuing to offer effective "education based on personal interaction."[440]

In 1984 Mike Contris, an English professor who had long embodied the Humanities at SMC, described the mission of SMC as being "to give men and women not only competence in professional careers but, more importantly I think, help them develop a conscience that judges that professionalism and all contacts with the world at large with Christian and humane values." While Contris admitted that such goals were "most difficult to integrate into the pressing curricular demands for careers," he insisted that they were nonetheless vital to "the Saint Martin's experience."[441] Dr. Spangler also stated his belief that a college education must be more than just a training ground for jobs. "Having a sound education, a questioning mind, communication skills, and admirable personal values" are what he thought would shape any real personal or professional "success." Personal contact and continuing interaction with learned faculty, he believed, was one feature of SMC that helped develop such success.[442] Whether a vital liberal arts focus and such personal contact could be adequately maintained as the College entered upon a period of growth and expansion remained to be seen.

While SMC was getting itself back into the "black" financially, its administration, faculty and staff also worked on developing programs that might attract more students and also wider sources of support for the College. One such outreach looked to the Far East.

Michael J. Contris (1910–1985) lived at the heart of two communities—Saint Martin's and the capital city of Olympia—and lavished his concern and compassion on both.

For half a century a prodding, exhilarating teacher of English, journalism, and humanities at SMC, he taught his students to think and to write and to care.

An alumnus of both our High School ('28) and College ('30), he thoroughly embraced the Benedictine motto of "Prayer and Work" for the glory of God and the betterment of society. He was awarded an honorary doctor of letters degree in 1960 by the College to mark twenty-five years of meritorious academic service. Mike's interests beyond the campus were widespread and his numerous volunteered services important and effective.

For forty-five years a writer, editor, and columnist for The Olympian, *Mike both reported the news and supported the needs of this region's educational, religious, artistic, healthcare, and athletic agencies and projects. His lengthy dual career as teacher and journalist constructively stimulated the minds of several generations of Saint Martin's students and illuminated the needs of the two communities he loved so much. His classroom, like his long-lived newspaper column, was a crucible of concern and learning.*

Mike is pictured here in the 1960s and assisting a student in the 1980s. (Photos from Saint Martin's Abbey Archives)

Building on earlier work by President John Ishii, SMC instituted its Institute of Pacific Rim Studies in 1988. The Institute was conceived, explained Director Josephine Yung, as "an umbrella for several international programs aimed at exposing Pacific Rim students to American language and culture, and eventually, American students to the Pacific Rim." It initially included a three-month Semester-In-Residence program inaugurated by students from Japan's Reitaku University, who could earn academic credits at their home campus while studying written and conversational English as well as American history, literature, and culture at Lacey. A Pre-College Language Program in cooperation with the Academy of International Education in Japan made available a year of intensive English-language training. There was also an arrangement that permitted students after completing two years at Nagoya YMCA College to transfer to SMC. A fine exchange program with Mukogawa Women's University would later be established. The College's Puget Sound area location made these Japanese academic tie-ins a natural development for a growing school.

SMC's Institute of Pacific Rim Studies has developed diversified trans-Pacific cultural and educational programs. Short-term visitors and resident students alike are involved first-hand in experiencing the differences and the richness that exists on both sides of the Pacific. In 1994, Toshiyuki Onoda (back left) and Hitomi Kobari worked with local Girl Scouts during a "Japanese Culture Day" on campus. (Photo courtesy IPRS)

Eventually the Institute hoped to place SMC students and faculty at Pacific Rim campuses in East Asia. An initial opportunity in that direction occurred when seven SMC students and staff participated in a ten-day study visit to Japan in May and June 1991. In addition to promoting international friendships, the Institute seeks to develop an understanding among its students and alumni that we all are "economically interdependent and that the challenge of the future is to achieve economic growth through cooperation."[443] SMC's relatively small size turned out to be an advantage for attracting international students as it more easily allowed them to feel at home.[444] Within a few years, the staff and students of the Institute of Pacific Rim Studies had become a welcome segment of the SMC campus. SMC's International Club was soon co-hosting with the Institute an annual International Open House for the campus community. It was considered a good way to help people feel more comfortable "in the culturally-diverse and mercurial smaller world" that was quickly developing. It was also a lot of fun![445]

Building for a Second Century

The initial high point in the rebirth of SMC's physical plant came with the successful 1989–1992 "Entrance To Excellence" project to refurbish the Saint Martin's Pavilion and the College's dowdy south entrance off Pacific Avenue. The institutional courage to initiate such a package of highly visible campus improvements was greatly stimulated by the generosity of one individual. Grateful for the education he had received at Saint Martin's, Thomas B. O'Grady pledged $1 million in 1988 to strengthen SMC's academic programs and scholarship endowment and to help support physical plant improvements.[446] By the summer of 1989, O'Grady's generosity had been parlayed into a south campus renovation and expansion project initially estimated at $1.5 million. It included "a major building addition [to] and renovation work" in the Pavilion itself as well as paved, landscaped, and lighted parking areas.[447]

Thomas B. O'Grady (HS '44; SMC '45) credits the individual support and quality education he received at Saint Martin's as "a consistent and major reason" for his later personal good fortune. His generosity has stimulated other alumni as well as old and new benefactors to take a second look at SMC. (SMC Office of Communication)

Completion of the expanded $3.2 million, three-phase, three-year "Entrance To Excellence" project was celebrated on August 6, 1992, with the dedication of the renovated Saint Martin's Pavilion and the adjacent Norman Worthington Conference Center.[448] The stunning new Worthington Center was a real crowd pleaser! In attendance were many project donors including Trena Belsito Worthington, a retired Olympia attorney, who made the naming gift in memory of her late husband, a forestry scientist of great renown. Tom O'Grady, whose vision and financial assistance had stimulated the entire south campus renaissance, made some typically brief and modest comments.

The Conference Center's four subdivisions were named for the late Father Meinrad Gaul, longtime history professor and alumni priest; the late Mike Contris, a renowned English and journalism professor; Father Michael Feeney, former SMC president; and current Abbot Conrad Rausch, who had also once served as the principal of Saint Martin's High School. Gary Mulhall, the College's director of development who spearheaded the project, heartily thanked the many individuals and corporations whose generosity had supported the key campus renewal project.

During the alumni reunion activities the weekend following the Pavilion and Conference Center dedication, the new Art Acuff Fitness Center was officially opened in the locker room section of the Pavilion. Between 1955 and 1982 Acuff

The dedication of SMC's new Norman Worthington Conference Center on August 6, 1992, highlighted the College's successful south campus rejuvenation. (1) Happily participating in the formal opening ceremony are (left to right) SMC President David R. Spangler, Lacey Deputy Mayor Earlyse Swift, SMC Trustees' immediate past chairman Robert P. Mallon, major donor Trena Belsito Worthington for whose late husband the Center is named, SMC Board Chairman Hal Marcus, Alumni Association President Jim Schwarz, Abbot Conrad Rausch, ASSMC President Helen Miller, and ace Saint Martin's booster and major donor Thomas B. O'Grady. (2) The versatile new facility—and the remodeled Saint Martin's Pavilion adjacent to it—has since been heavily booked by both campus and community organizations. It provides a fresh face for the College on busy Pacific Avenue. (Photos by Paul Peck)

was an SMC coach, physical education teacher and director of athletics. He was saluted for consistently displaying his concern and offering his help to the College's students and staff and for pointing many people in the right direction.[449]

234

First and foremost, SMC faculty are teachers who communicate their special expertise and personal concern through close faculty-student relationships. *(Photos from Saint Martin's Abbey Archives)*

Math prof Peter Murray teaches hot theorems on a campus hillside on a hot day.

Civil Engineering's Chris Allaire shares some roadway recipe with future practitioners.

Political Science's Roger Snider keeps trying to make sense of government for students who are also citizens.

Computer Science's Doug Ford shares know-how and seeks knowledge with his students.

Sociology and Community Services' Norma Shelan finds that all-around involvement leads to effective learning.

Better Learning Sites Needed

A library is the heart of any academic institution, a symbol and center of learning. For many years Saint Martin's has needed a "new" library and more recently its growing enrollment has made that need imperative. What SMC requires, to put it more precisely, is a state-of-the-art structure to house current and expanded "learning resources" in printed and other formats as well as much more adequate study and administrative space. Moreover, given the competitive and changing higher education market in the Pacific Northwest, the adequacy of a school's library holds a "strategic importance" in its long-term success and advancement.[450] So with the completion of SMC's publicly acclaimed south campus improvements in 1992, an excited College administration took up the task of planning and funding new or renewed facilities—emphatically including a new library—to accommodate the school's recent and future enrollment growth.

In 1993, a major first step in the remodeling of SMC's hilltop complex was completed when Old Main's vast roof structures were thoroughly reconstructed. The Abbey and College jointly undertook the upgrading of campus infrastructure and facilities for the institution's second century of service. A November 15, 1994 fire in the basement kitchen's dishwasher room caused over a million dollars in damage and subsequently fast-tracked the overall updating of Old Main starting in 1995. (SMC Office of Communication)

A funding feasibly study for a proposed Saint Martin's Library was conducted in the fall of 1993. If and when undertaken, it would almost certainly be the largest fundraising endeavor in the College's hundred-year history. Therefore funding potential must be evaluated carefully to see if it could match construction costs. Preliminary assessment of what a new library would need in terms of facilities was already underway. There was growing excitement on campus especially among faculty and students.

The library campaign feasibility study yielded positive results. Hopes on campus and among institutional alumni and friends were high that the new library campaign—if approved by the College's Board of Trustees—would be "key to a higher level of educational service and broader recognition" for Saint Martin's.

The SMC Board of Trustees in June 1994 unanimously approved a new library fundraising program under the rubric of "Building for Our Second Century."

Dr. Spangler announced with pleasure that Michael Graves, an internationally renowned architect, had been retained "to begin conceptual planning for the new library building."[451] Undoubtedly years of planning, fundraising, and construction lay ahead before the new campus library would be a reality but the most important project for Saint Martin's second century had been launched.

Also demanding immediate attention was renovation of "Old Main," the 110,000-square foot brick acropolis built in 1913–1922. Access, utilization, and safety considerations made its updating imperative and the task would be costly. Furthermore, since the large hilltop structure housed most of the College's classrooms and offices as well as the library, kitchen, and dining rooms, any major overhaul would be quite disruptive of the school's programs and the campus denizens' peace of mind. Therefore, and only after careful study and lots of shrewd hard work by SMC staff and advisors, an extensive renovation of Old Main was agreed on to be principally financed through borrowing.[452]

President Spangler often spoke about building momentum as Saint Martin's set its course for a second century of service. He initially hoped to have both the campaign for a new library and Old Main's renovations substantially finished by or during SMC's 1994–1995 Centennial celebration. While both vital projects have been initiated, planning, approval, and fundraising activities had taken more time, energy, and funding than expected so they remain some distance from completion as this book goes to press.

A Tough But Successful First Decade

In 1993, with the College's finances restored to good health and further opportunities for institutional growth on the horizon, Dr. Spangler described "integrating the many activities, plans, goals, and ideas existing within" the College as the "most challenging requirement" now facing the institution. Creating an updated and prudent institutional vision—also known as long-range planning—thus became an important and, indeed, an urgent task. The College's Board of Trustees therefore mandated the development of a strategic plan for the first decade of SMC's second century. The planning process would evaluate "as a cohesive whole" the choices, opportunities, and practical limits confronting SMC. The "ideal" size of a student population for the College (a thousand full-time-equivalent headcount was a working assumption), the "mix" of undergraduate and graduate offerings, and the facilities needed to appropriately accommodate students, faculty and staff would have to be prudently assessed.[453] A comprehensive SMC strategic plan was expected to be available for consideration, adoption, and initial implementation sometime in 1996.

Dr. David Spangler brought many assets to a tough and trying job not the least of which was his spouse. During her dozen years as the unofficial leader of the school's boosters,

Jeanne Spangler, SMC's winsome second "First Lady, has provided gracious, positive support to the institution's faculty, staff, and students and for many of their programs. She seems to attend more campus functions than almost anyone else and has even spent part of her wedding anniversary on campus for several years because it usually occurs during the week of the College's new students orientation. In 1993, the Saint Martin's Alumni Association saluted Jeanne Spangler for her many and real contributions to the greater Saint Martin's community.

Reactivated Alumni

In 1984, a small cadre of SMC and SMHS alumni ("a choice few" Father Meinrad, that earlier guru of graduates, would have called them) set out to reinvigorate Saint Martin's Alumni Association. New bylaws recommitted alumni "to promote, support, and enhance the educational and monastic community" on campus through "various events that bring people together to form a bond and show interest in Saint Martin's."[454] Besides assisting with on-campus events and services, Alumni Association activities soon included participation in regional celebrations such as Olympia's annual Capital Lakefair. Each July an Alumni food concession (housed since 1995 in a spiffy red trailer-kitchen) can be found along the fair's midway. In addition to its savory menu items, which have

varied in Olympia and at other fairs over the years, the Saint Martin's Alumni eatery has offered thousands of regional fair-goers year by year a delicious reminder that SMC is "really cookin'!"

Alumni Association leaders soon began looking for a large-scale "event" that would specifically showcase Saint Martin's College. They hoped such a festival might become a benchmark community event as well as a hearty scholarship fundraiser for SMC students. On October 28, 1989, with equal parts sweat and bravado, they inaugurated—with lots of help from friends and neighbors—the first Capital Food and Wine Festival. "It was a circus and had something for everyone." Some thirty-two hundred people including Washington's Governor and First Lady, Booth and Jean Gardner, strolled the Pavilion that day with "music, wine and food their common joys" in a "festival of fun." The

The Capital Food and Wine Festival has enlivened the campus each October since 1989. Organized by Saint Martin's Alumni Association with strong help from many community and campus volunteers, the Festival draws thousands of participants during its one-day run and engenders lots of scholarship dollars for current SMC students. It's also a lot of fun! (Photo by Paul Peck)

delicacies of twenty-five local eateries and vintages from thirty Washington wineries were featured at fifty-eight booths. The venue was draped throughout in burgundy and silver and jazz music from several performers enlivened the proceedings. Appearing courtesy of Saint Martin's alumni superstar Tom O'Grady, country music superstar Charlie Daniels "gave festival-goers a rousing set of ballads." The dozens of delighted but exhausted volunteers joined festival chairman Al Eckroth (HS '62, C '66) in pronouncing the event a real success.[455] For many South Sound residents, the now annual Capital Food and Wine Festival has become something to look forward to each October. While the Festival provides SMC students with much appreciated scholarships (for example, twenty-four were awarded to returning students and ten to new enrollees for the 1994–1995 school year) it has also become an example of "friend raising" writ large!

The earnest and expanding work of Saint Martin's reborn Alumni Association buoyed spirits on campus. Its activities also provided additional ways and means to promote SMC both in its capital city hometown area and elsewhere in southwest Washington. As the College regained its economic footing and began again to grow in enrollment and offerings, the SMC administration sought to structure a more focused program of "networking" between former students and current people and programs on campus. The term adopted by 1994 for SMC's expanded alumni outreach was "friend raising" and it pointed up how crucial its alumni were for the College's long-term success as its turned the corner into its second century.

Saint Martin's Athletic Foundation

SMAF's annual golf tournament on the first Friday of August is a very popular event and provides scholarship support for SMC's student athletes. In 1994 lining up a putt was serious work for (front to back) Bob Grisham, SMC athletic director and Saints men's basketball coach; sports information officer and alumnus Adolfo Capestany; Jeff Paulson; and Ray Peters, Saints women's basketball coach. (SMC Office of Communication)

The reactivation of the Alumni Association indirectly influenced the establishment of another campus-related booster organization. The Saint Martin's Athletic Foundation was established in 1985 "to encourage and enhance the quality" of SMC's intercollegiate and intramural athletic programs. SMAF recruited its members from the ranks of campus alumni, current and former students' parents, and local business people and sports enthusiasts. It immediately began a vigorous advocacy of the College's athletic programs and athletes. During its first decade the Athletic Foundation raised thousands of dollars for SMC athletic scholarships principally through its annual golf tournament. SMAF also inaugurated a Saint Martin's Athletic Hall of Fame and began inducting former campus sports stand-outs at the College's 1990 Homecoming celebration.[456]

Extracurricular Activities Offered Fun and Experience

Extracurricular activities have long been a vital part of school life at Saint Martin's. Clubs, musical groups, sports teams, campus journalism, and other kinds of student associations have been and are vehicles for recreation, service, exercise, and just plain fun. They have provided healthy and happy diversions from the "grind" of academic pursuits and the occasional loneliness of being away from home. While especially important among younger resident students, over the years commuter students (once known as "Day Dogs") have also vigorously participated in these important campus-life activities.

For many Saint Martin's alumni, their happiest school memories center around their participation in extracurricular activities. It might therefore be surmised that much of the student-to-student "bonding" that occurred at Saint Martin's over the past century was cemented by nonacademic interactions among campus contemporaries.

Participation in sports, varsity or intramural, certainly shaped people's campus experience. Student government organizations developed skills and attitudes in our alumni. Discovering and sharing ones talent in campus-based musical or theatrical productions was more than just entertainment. Speech and debate activities brought postgraduate confidence by sharpening thought processes and honing vocal skills. By donating time and energy to Sigma Mu Kappa service projects did fraternity alumni go on to discover the reward of service above self after college?

And what about the old student crews of "Ranger Radio" broadcasts over SMC-founded KGY, the South Sound's premier radio voice? Did any of them or other products of Father Meinrad's radio speech courses end up in broadcasting? Surely putting out a good issue of our *Samahi* or *Samarco* yearbooks or writing for *The Arrow* or *The Bell Tower* and other campus papers was involving and satisfying work when shared with classmates and teachers. Did many campus "hacks" end up as publicists or print journalists?

How many alumni got initiated into business procedures by working in the campus Bookstore for Brother Hugh or Bertha Smith or Shirley Crews?

Which "bookish" alumni belong to that honorable corps of former library student-workers who toiled for Father Luke or Mrs. Bonnifield or Mrs. McIntyre? How many students became close friends while cooking, serving, or cleaning up for the campus food service under the eye of the good Benedictine Sisters or SAGA or, in recent years, Marriott?

PICTURED BOTTOM LEFT: *The Lady Saints basketball team earned an incredible thirty-one wins in 1994–1995 and traveled to nationals for the first time. Fan support spurred them on to victory after victory as crowds of two thousand or more rooted for them in the Saint Martin's Pavilion. From the back, row one (left to right): Assistant Coach Michelle Noel, Head Coach Ray Peters, and Sports Information Director Adolfo Capestany. Row two: Heather Frost, Sue Stier, Davina Bergman, Kristen Zellar, Aretha Williams, and Jenny Malhstedt. Row three: Andrea Leons, Junita Mebane, and Renee Kuehner. Front and center with team ball: Olivia Carrillo. (Photo by Ed FitzGerald)*

Beginning in the late 1920s as a campus social fraternity, Sigma Mu Kappa (alias EMK) later developed into the College's service fraternity. It played a dynamic role in campus life when SMC was an all-male institution. This late-1950s photo of the organization's membership also shows a young Father Christopher Abair (1924–1981) as their moderator. (Saint Martin's Abbey Archives)

Pictured Bottom Right: *Brother Hugh Evans, O.S.B. (1900–1957), attended SMHS from 1916 to 1918 and then followed a diverse business career. After the death of his wife, he returned to Lacey in 1951 and became a monk. He turned the campus bookstore into a real emporium. He also was instrumental in acquiring the large plaque of Saint Martin that was installed in the alcove of the outside grand staircase in 1953. (Photo by Dave Boyle, SMC '62)*

Did our preprofessional student organizations—such as those associated with SMC's Education, Industrial Relations, Accounting, Chemistry, and Engineering Departments—help students more easily transition into professional relationships? How many business or professional partnerships started here on campus due to extracurricular as well as academic interaction? Who from that large corps of residence hall "prefects" (latterly called residence assistants) under Father Bertrand, Father Placidus, or Judy Sharpe later found jobs in student services on other campus? How many student staffers of the SMC Admissions Office or Registrar's Office ended in enrollment management jobs on our own and other campuses?

Student life at Saint Martin's was and is more than just classes and labs and unending reports! Past and present, people on this campus learn together and from each other when they study in a place big enough to help yet small enough to care.

A Celebration for the Future

In 1993, Father John Scott, SMC history professor and institutional historian, was named to chair the campus' Centennial observance. He thereafter spoke frequently on Saint Martin's history to a variety of audiences and began publishing historical vignettes in *Insight*, the College's alumni and friends newspaper, to stir up interest in the institution's one hundredth anniversary observance. Campus and alumni leaders quickly agreed that the observance ought to be "A Celebration for the Future" rather than a eulogy for the past. They chose to highlight the themes of "Community, Spirituality and Education" as three enduring aspects of life at Saint Martin's. All of Saint Martin's "constituencies"—its College students, faculty and staff as well as its monks, oblates, alumni, the parents and families of past and present students, parishioners of Catholic churches served by Lacey's monks, and area neighbors and friends—were to be involved in and saluted at one or more of the Centennial events scheduled between July 11, 1994 and November 11, 1995.

During 1994 and 1995, a Centennial "touch" was also added to ongoing Abbey and College programs such as the monastery's highly regarded Abbey Church Events concert and lecture series and the school's annual Homecoming and Reunion celebrations. The Saint Martin's Alumni Association also embellished such popular public events as its annual Capital Food and Wine Festival with Centennial touches. Very attractive publications saluting our Centennial, including the covers of the 1994–1995 Seattle archdiocesan Catholic directory and a Centennial poster featuring past and present campus faces and places, were produced using the design talent of SMC staff graphic artist Holly Harmon. The SMC Faculty-Staff Network published a Centennial cookbook to add tasty calories to the century of memories. Overall planning and coordination for the Centennial celebration was wonderfully handled by Centennial Manager Becky Wonderly (SMC '77).

A Centennial inaugural celebration on July 11, 1994, consisted of a special sung Evening Prayer in the Abbey Church and a festive picnic for some three hundred guests in our hilltop quadrangle. That November 11, the feastday of Saint Martin of Tours, Abbot Timothy Kelly of Saint John's Abbey and University (Saint Martin's parent institutions), was presider and homilist for the feastday Eucharist. He also gave

EVENING PRAISE FOR THE FEAST OF BENEDICT OF NURSIA, PATRIARCH OF WESTERN MONASTICISM

11 July 1994

The Opening of the Centennial of Saint Martin's Abbey and College

A liturgical expression of our gratitude to God for graces received opened Saint Martin's sixteen-month Centennial observance on July 11, 1994. The service was followed by a festive picnic involving monks, SMC students, faculty and staff, and campus alumni as well as civic dignitaries and many other neighbors and friends. (Saint Martin's Abbey Archives)

The Saint Martin's Women's Auxiliary in recent years has been a focal point for campus help and improvement. Countless hours of volunteering by a couple of dozen dedicated members have provided both scholarship dollars and classy touches for College and Abbey special events. In 1989 this quartet of Auxiliary go-getters posed in the Abbey Church's belltower garden: (lower row, left to right) Rose Hammond and Virginia Coomes; (upper row, left to right) Jeanne Wohlers and Teresa Hillier. (Photo by Paul Dunn)

a November 12 public lecture on lifelong education and the Benedictine qualities that nurture it and spent some time getting acquainted with Lacey's monks.

On March 21, 1995, the monastic community hosted Seattle Archbishop Thomas Murphy and about fifty diocesan and religious order priests at a Mass and luncheon. In mid-July, Rome-based Abbot Primate Jerome Theisen (a monk and former abbot of Saint John's Abbey) graced our community with a five-day visit. He gave a public lecture on "Saint Benedict's Gift for the Next Century" on July 10. The next day, some seventy-five sisters representing communities with whom Saint Martin's monks have worked were our guests for a Eucharist at which Abbot Jerome was celebrant and homilist. A festive luncheon was then served at which Benedictine women from our neighboring monastery, Saint Placid's Priory, and from Saint Gertrude's Monastery in Cottonwood, Idaho (whose Sisters had staffed our Lacey kitchen and dining rooms from 1904 to 1959) were warmly saluted.

Abbot Neal Roth and SMC President David Spangler were the grand marshals for the July 15, 1995 Lakefair Parade held in our adjacent capital city of Olympia and witnessed by some twenty thousand people. Also marching in that parade was a group of one hundred students, monks, staff, faculty, alumni, and friends dressed in red Centennial shirts and carrying five-foot-high red or white "candles" crafted from sturdy cardboard tubes and lighted with gold "flames." This third and last annual appearance by our "Centennial Candle Corps" got rave reviews!

Hundreds of alumni returned to campus between August 2 and 6, 1995, to happily and vigorously participate in a user-friendly schedule of Centennial Reunion activities. They were warmly greeted by both the monks and the College's staff. A cruise Wednesday night on sections of lower Puget Sound provided a low-keyed kick-off. Amiable shipmates and pleasant summer weather created ideal conditions for leisurely chats and shared saltwater sightings.

Large numbers of alumni—many accompanied by family and friends—arrived on campus on Thursday. Many attended the casually swank Presidents' Reception that evening hosted by SMC's Board Chairman Frank Owens and his wife Brenda at their stunning "new" home on Olympia's fashionable Cooper Point. (New for the Owens but actually a newly

SMC's Centennial Commencement on May 13, 1995, was blessed with spring sunshine as 349 graduates gathered on and below the grand staircase (1925) in front of Old Main. College Registrar Mary Conley Law directs the happy hood-and-gowned graduates during their stately procession toward the Saint Martin's Pavilion. They were greeted by the thrilling strains of Norm Wallen's "Saint Martin's Fanfare" in its premier performance. (Photo by Steve Bloom) restored classic 1940 residence designed by prominent Northwest architect and Saint Martin's alumnus Paul Thiry.) Former SMC and SMHS student body presidents, past and present members of the College's Board of Trustees and of its predecessor, the Board of Regents) and current and former Alumni Association and Athletic Foundation presidents were the guests of honor. They were joined by other very special friends of Saint Martin's for a perfect midsummer night's dream of an evening.

More good weather attended the Saint Martin's Athletic Foundation's twelfth annual golf tournament, which provided some 250 golfers lots of opportunity for vigorous exercise and hearty camaraderie on the Tumwater Valley links. Their awards banquet that evening was a well attended and tasty feed at which many fine (and a few funny) prizes were presented. Several anniversary classes also held private reunion gatherings on campus Friday evening. Our High School classes of '55 and '70 were the most voluble!

Saturday morning began overcast and deposited a few sprinkles but soon warmed up as that day's reunion activities were launched. A midday luau featured tasty Polynesian foods and family-oriented Samoan music and dance. After a passage of years or of decades, incredulous groans of recognition between old campus buddies filled the gathering followed by boisterous and emotion-choked conversations. A Centennial tree planting was presided over by that campus gardener deluxe, Abbot Conrad Rausch. Campus tours led by Father John Scott provoked many memories for all involved.

A very classy "Reunion of the Century" banquet and program had to be moved into the Pavilion on Saturday night due to the large attendance. After dinner, honored SMC and SMHS classes were saluted and several special guests recognized. Of our many very accomplished alumni, an initial ten were presented (three posthumously) with Distinguished Alumni Awards by Abbot Neal and Dr. Spangler. Each recipient or his representative then gave a personal response. After some final greetings and several photo sessions, dancing and more reminiscing concluded the happy evening.

A Sunday Eucharist celebrated by Father Kilian Malvey at 11:00 a.m. in the Abbey Church was well and prayerfully attended and featured some extra-special music by the Abbey Schola. Dozens of alumni then joined several SMC staff and monks for a stylish brunch in the Norman Worthington Conference Center as the Reunion drew to a close.

On September 11, 1995, our exact Centennial Day, we hosted a campus open house and dedicated a memorial to

Father Bede Ernsdorff (1909–1982), a sterling monk, renowned chemistry professor, and beloved friend to generations of students and alumni. About 250 guests joined the monks for an early celebration of Evening Prayer in the Abbey Church. Afterwards, upwards of 700 people enjoyed a festive meal with live music and Centennial salutes from campus and civic leaders in our SMC Pavilion.

On November 4, the SMC faculty hosted a public forum on world population issues as a way of focusing our College community's academic insights on a key contemporary issue. By design, our Centennial observance ended rather quietly on November 11, the feast of our patron, Saint Martin of Tours, with a Mass of thanksgiving and rededication and a celebratory meal for the monks and key Centennial leaders.

Our extended Saint Martin's family—both off and on campus—is grateful to God for a century of challenges and blessings. We have now energetically entered into a second century of service at this very special place called Saint Martin's. ✤

References to archives cited in this volume are abbreviated as follows:
SMAA-Saint Martin's Abbey Archives, Lacey, Washington
ASJA-Archives of Saint John's Abbey, Collegeville, Minnesota
ASVA-Archives of Saint Vincent Archabbey, Latrobe, Pennsylvania
ACAS-Archives of Catholic Archdiocese of Seattle, Washington
ASSA-Archives of Sisters of Saint Ann, Victoria, B.C., Canada

1. Between the Years (1945), pp. [2–3]. Saint John's Abbey's "Chapter Minutes" for August 3, 1891 note that letters concerning Tacoma were read by Abbot Bernard to the monastic chapter on that date and that he also reported on the June 14, 1891 meetings held in Tacoma. (ASJA)
2. Rev. Peter Hylebos to Abbot Bernard, Tacoma, July 17, 1891. (ASJA)
3. Father William Eversmann to Abbot Bernard, Tacoma, July 21, 1891. (ASJA)
4. Father William to Abbot Bernard, Tacoma, August 5, 1891. (ASJA)
5. *Tacoma Daily Ledger*, Monday, August 10, 1891, Father William to Abbot Bernard, Tacoma, September 3, 1891, and *Holy Rosary Diamond Jubilee* booklet (1966), p. [9]. (SMAA)
6. Father William to Abbot Bernard, Tacoma, August 5, 1891. (ASJA)
7. Father William to Abbot Bernard, Tacoma, September 21 and 25 and December 1, 1891. (ASJA)
8. Father William to Abbot Bernard, Tacoma, April 26, 1892. (ASJA)
9. Father William to Abbot Bernard, Tacoma, April 26, 1892. (ASJA)
10. Father William to Abbot Bernard, Tacoma, September 21, 1891. (ASJA)
11. Archbishop Charles J. Seghers to Abbot Alexius Edelbrock, Portland, October 7, 1881; Abbot Alexius to Archbishop Seghers, San Francisco, December 18, 1881. (ASJA)
12. Rev. Peter Hylebos to Abbot Bernard, Tacoma, July 17, 1891. (ASJA) Articles of Incorporation for SMC, however, were in fact not filed until 1904.
13. Rev. Peter Hylebos to Abbot Bernard, Tacoma, August 14, 1891. (ASJA) On Father Hylebos see Wilfred P. Schoenberg, S. J., *History of the Catholic Church in the Pacific Northwest, 1743–1983* (Washington, D.C.: Pastoral Press, 1987), p. 273.
14. Abbot Oswald to Abbot Peter, Lacey, January 21, 1919. (ASJA)
15. Father William to Abbot Bernard, Tacoma, October [?], 1891. On Father Wolfgang see Alexius Hoffmann, O.S.B., "Autobiography," Vol. 4, citing his diary entry for July 26–27, 1892. (ASJA)
16. *Between the Years* (1945), p. 2. See also Father William to Abbot Bernard, Tacoma, April 8 and 26, 1892. (ASJA)
17. Abbot Peter diary entry for May 8, 1898; Bishop O'Dea to Father Demetrius, Vancouver, Washington, December 15, 1899. (ASJA)
18. Father Matthew Britt to Abbot Peter, Lacey, May 23, 1901; Abbot Oswald to Abbot Peter, Lacey, June 3, 1915. (ASJA) See also Bishop Shaughnessy's Memorandum of August 11, 1939, concerning Abbot Lambert's August 9 visit to the Chancery in Seattle and their discussion about various matters including Holy Rosary Parish. (ASSA)
19. *Holy Rosary Diamond Jubilee* booklet (1966), p. [9]. (SMAA)
20. Father William to Abbot Bernard, Tacoma, December 1 and September 25, 1891, and March 10, 1892. (ASJA)
21. Father Demetrius Jueneman to Father Fielis Lucking, Vancouver, Washington, March 30, 1898. (ASJA)
22. J. Kingston Pierce, "The Panic of 1893," *Columbia* 7 (Winter 1993/94): 38.
23. *Morning Olympian Tribune*, September 28, 1893, p. 4.
24. *Morning Olympian Tribune,* January 24, 1894, p. 1. As it turned out, while many "provisions" were locally purchased most major items used in the construction of the new College were secured in Tacoma from contractors known to the Benedictine priests stationed in that much larger city.
25. Father William to Abbot Bernard, Tacoma, September 16, October 7, November 28, 1892, and January 20, 1893. See "Chapter Minutes, Saint John's Abbey," Vol. 2, 1876–1895. (ASJA)
26. *Morning Olympian,* April 22, 1894, p. 4.
27. Father William Eversman to Abbot Bernard Locknikar, Tacoma, June 9, 1894. (ASJA)
28. *Between the Years*, pp. [5–6]. See also Father William to Abbot Bernard, Tacoma, March 19, 1994. (ASJA)
29. Father William Eversman to Abbot Bernard, Tacoma, April 23, 1894. (ASJA)
30. *Morning Olympian*, April 22, 1894, p. 4.
31. Father Demetrius to Abbot Peter, September 1895 (?), Lacey P.O., Washington, cited in Hoffmann, "History of Saint John's" (unpublished), Vol. 3, pp. 216–217. (ASJA)
32. Father Demetrius to Abbot Peter, September 1895 (?), Lacey P.O., Washington, cited in Hoffmann, "History of Saint John's (unpublished), Vol. 3, p. 216. (ASJA)
33. *Samarco* (1927), "History of Saint Martin's College," p. 13. The 1927 College annual was the first to be called *Samarco*, a contraction of the institutional name. It contained a well-written eleven-page history of Saint Martin's by John M. Gaul, '27, our future illustrious history professor, Father Meinrad.
34. See Alexius Hoffmann, O.S.B., "History of Saint John's Abbey, 1856–1931" (unpublished), Vol. 3, citing an unspecified letter of Father Demetrius; Father Cornelius Wittmann's file where this circa 1930 assertion is reported; and Abbot Peter's diary entry for that date. (ASJA)
35. Joel Rippinger, O.S.B., *The Benedictine Order in the United States* (Collegeville, Minnesota: Liturgical Press, 1990), p. 116.
36. Peter Beckman, O.S.B., *Kansas Monks: A History of Saint Benedict's Abbey* (Atchison, Kansas: Benedictine College Press, 1957), p. 173.
37. About this assumption see Rippinger, p. 117, citing Albert Kleber, O.S.B., *History of Saint Meinrad Archabbey* (Saint Meinrad, Indiana: Archabbey Press, 1954), p. 122.
38. *Daily Olympian*, July 31, 1895, p. 2.
39. "Prospectus of Saint Martin's College, Lacey P.O., Railroad Station, Woodland, Washington." (Tacoma, Washington: Pacific Printing Company, 1895), pp. 3 and 4. (SMAA)
40. First Annual Catalogue of the Faculty and Students of Saint Martin's College (1897), p. 8. (SMAA)
41. Joel Rippinger, O.S.B., *The Benedictine Order in the United States* (Collegeville, Minnesota: Liturgical Press, 1990), p. 118.
42. See SMC Prospectus (1895). (SMAA)
43. *Between the Years*, p. [8].
44. Father Oswald Baran to Abbot Peter Engel, Lacey P.O., September 11, 1895. (SMAA)
45. Frater Benedict Schmit to Abbot Peter Engel, Lacey, January 21, 1896. (ASJA)
46. Frater Benedict Schmit to Abbot Peter Engel, Lacey, April 8, 1896. (ASJA)
47. See his diary entry for September 17, 1896. (ASJA)
48. *Washington Standard*, October 4, 1895, p. 3.
49. Alexius Hoffmann, O.S.B., "History of Saint John's Abbey" (unpublished), Vol. 3, 217. (ASJA)
50. Information on Brother William Baldus extracted from his obituary file and Father Alexius Hoffmann's unpublished "Autobiography" and "History of Saint John's Abbey." (ASJA)
51. See Johann Krell's original waiver of compensation, August 7, 1884. (ASJA)
52. Letters of Johann Krell to Abbot Peter (February 19, 1899) and to Prior Herman (March 6, 1899), both from Salem, Oregon. (ASJA) Krell wrote to Abbot Innocent Wolf, praeses (president) of the American Cassinese Congregation, O.S.B., on July 2, 1899, requesting to be officially released from his monastic vows. His request was granted. (ASVA)
53. Father Benedict Schmit to Abbot Peter, Lacey, January 21, 1896. (ASJA)
54. Father William to Abbot Peter, Tacoma, February 1, 1896. (ASJA)
55. Father Oswald to Abbot Peter, Lacey, November 29, 1895. (SMAA)
56. Father Justin Welz to Father Fidelis Lucking, Lacey, November 7, 1896. (ASJA)
57. Father Cornelius Wittmann to Abbot Peter, Lacey, December 24, 1896 and April 30, 1899. (ASJA)
58. Father Cornelius to Abbot Peter, Lacey, March 17, 1900. (ASJA)
59. Abbot Peter to Father Cornelius, Collegeville, July 28, 1900. (ASJA)
60. See Abbot Peter's diary entry for December 28, 1896. (ASJA)
61. *Northwest Catholic* (Tacoma), Vol. 25, pp. 261f., September 2, 1897. (ASJA)
62. Father Oswald to Abbot Peter, Lacey, March 29, 1897. (SMAA)

63. Father Demetrius to Abbot Peter, Lacey, November 1, 1897. (ASJA)

64. Father Justin Welz to Father Fidelis Lucking, Lacey, January 17, 1898. (ASJA)

65. Father Demetrius Jueneman to Father Fidelis Lucking, Vancouver, Washington, March 30, 1898. (ASJA)

66. See his diary entry for May 4, 1898. (ASJA)

67. Father Benedict Schmit to Abbot Peter, Lacey, August 10 and 28, 1898. (ASJA)

68. See, for example, the Sixth Annual Catalogue [1901], p. 33. (SMAA)

69. Comments by Father Alexius Hoffmann in Brother Florian Mehren's file and Dr. H. Vidal to Abbot Peter, Tacoma, September 28, 1896. (ASJA)

70. Father Matthew Britt to Abbot Peter, Lacey, June 9, 1901. (ASJA)

71. Father Mark Wiechman to Abbot Peter, Lacey, December 28, 1902. (ASJA)

72. Comments by Father Alexius Hoffman in Father Andrew Straub's file. (ASJA)

73. *Between the Years*, p. [11].

74. Father Wolfgang Steinkogler to Abbot Peter, Lacey, September 12, 1900. (ASJA)

75. Father Oswald to Abbot Peter, Lacey, March 8 and June 7, 1896. (SMAA)

76. Father Matthew Britt to Abbot Peter, Lacey, May 7 and May 23, 1901. (ASJA)

77. Father Mark Wiechman to Abbot Peter, Lacey, December 31, 1901. (ASJA)

78. Father Ulric Scheffold to Abbot Peter, Lacey, December 21, 1901. (ASJA)

79. Father Matthew Britt to Abbot Peter, Lacey, May 7, 1901. (ASJA)

80. Joel Rippinger, O.S.B., *The Benedictine Order in the United States* (1990), p. 118.

81. Rippinger, p. 118 citing Peter Beckman, *Kansas Monks* (1957), p. 147.

82. Father Ulric Scheffold to Abbot Peter, Lacey, December 21, 1901. (ASJA)

83. Father Mark Wiechman to Abbot Peter, Lacey, December 31, 1901. (ASJA)

84. Father Matthew Britt to Abbot Peter, Lacey, May 7, 1901. (ASJA)

85. "Memoirs of Adolph Dingmann, O.S.B.," October 28, 1935. (ASJA)

86. Bishop O'Dea to Abbot Peter, Vancouver, Washington, January 10, 1901. (ACAS)

87. Father Ulric Scheffold to Abbot Peter, Lacey, June 2, 1902. (ASJA)

88. Father Matthew Britt to Abbot Peter, Lacey, May 23 and June 9, 1901 and June 11, 1903. (ASJA)

89. Abbot Baldwin Dworschak, O.S.B., to author, Collegeville, Minnesota, August 28, 1984. (Author's Files)

90. Bishop O'Dea to Abbot Peter, Vancouver, Washington, July 20, 1900. (ACAS)

91. Father Cornelius Wittmann to Abbot Peter, Lacey, January 20, 1903. (ASJA)

92. James T. Covert, *A Point of Pride: The University of Portland Story* (Portland: University of Portland Press, 1976), p. 33.

93. Alexius Hoffmann, O.S.B., "Autobiography," Vol. 4, citing his diary entry for March 14, 1902, and Father Mark Wiechman to Abbot Peter, Lacey, May 12, 1902. (ASJA)

94. Father Matthew Brit to Abbot Peter, Lacey, November 30, 1902. (ASJA)

95. Father Mark Wiechman to Abbot Peter, Lacey, December 28, 1902. (ASJA)

96. Alexius Hoffmann, O.S.B., "Autobiography," Vol. 4, citing his diary entry for August 21, 1903. (ASJA)

97. Abbot Peter Engel to Bishop Edward O'Dea, Collegeville, Dec. 5, 1899, and Bishop O'Dea to Abbot Peter, Vancouver, Washington, December 13, 1899. (ASJA)

98. Father Oswald Baran to Abbot Peter Engel, Tacoma, December 22, 1910. (ASJA)

99. Father Alexius Hoffmann, "History of Saint John's" (unpublished), Vol. 3, p. 218. (ASJA)

100. Comments by Father Alexius Hoffmann in Brother Edward Karge's file. (ASJA)

101. *Between the Years*, pp. [13–15].

102. Father Demetrius to Abbot Peter, August 15, 1906. (SMAA)

103. Curtis, Dunstan E., O.S.B. "The Historical-Philosophical Bases for Teacher Education in a Benedictine College," unpublished doctoral dissertation, Stanford University, 1960, p. 285.

104. See Father Leonard Kapsner's several letters to Abbot Peter from Lacey, September 1906 to August 1908. (ASJA)

105. Prior Demetrius to Abbot Peter, Lacey, January 8, 1906. (SMAA)

106. Paperwork dealing with this case is found in ASVA. In this and in certain other cases, I have used anonymity in discussing certain individuals as a courtesy to their relatives or descendants.

107. Father Justin Welz to Abbot Peter, Lacey, December 6, 1908. (ASJA)

108. See SMC's first annual catalogue, 1896–1897, p. 1 and the identical statement in several subsequent annual issues. (SMAA)

109. Alexius Hoffmann, O.S.B., *Saint John's University, A Sketch of its History* (Collegeville, Minnesota: Record Press, 1907), p. 133.

110. Abbot Oswald to Abbot Peter, Lacey, November 24, 1918. (ASJA)

111. Abbot Oswald to Abbot Peter, Lacey, May 6, 1917. (ASJA); *Between the Years,* p. [14].

112. Hoffmann, *Saint John's University*, p. 142.

113. See 1907–1908 SMC catalog, p. 31. (SMAA)

114. Abbot Oswald to Abbot Peter, Lacey, February 23, 1917. (ASJA); see 1916–1917 SMC catalog, pp. 70f. (SMAA)

115. 1905–1906 SMC catalog, pp. 26–32. (SMAA)

116. *Washington Standard*, November 28, 1913, p. 1.

117. 1905–1906 SMC catalog, p. 29, and 1909–1910 SMC catalog, p. 32. (SMAA)

118. 1908–1909 catalog, p. 35, and 1910–1911 catalog, p. 39. (SMAA)

119. 1913–1914 SMC catalog, pp. 69–70. (SMAA)

120. *Between the Years*, p. [11]. See also Mike Oakland's article on Carpenter in "Totem," *The Olympian*, Sunday, January 30, 1983, pp. 3–5.

121. Hoffmann, *Saint John's University*, p. 144.

122. 1909–1910 SMC catalog, p. 31, and 1913–1914 catalog, p. 69. (SMAA)

123. 1907–1908 SMC catalog, p. 32. (SMAA)

124. 1911–1912 SMC catalog, pp. 9–10. (SMAA)

125. 1911–1912 SMC catalog, p. 9; and 1912–1913 catalog, pp. 43–44. (SMAA)

126. 1906–1907 SMC catalog, p. 5. (SMAA)

127. 1912–1913 SMC catalog, p. 49. (SMAA)

128. Interview with Agnes Franz Stebbins Button by author, Lacey, July 8, 1991. (Author's Files)

129. Father Benedict Schmit to Abbot Peter, Lacey, March 10, 1896. (ASJA)

130. Father Demetrius to Abbot Peter, Lacey, June 15, 1905. (ASJA)

131. See SMC catalogs for 1908–1909 (p. 10) and 1911–1912 (p. 11). (SMAA)

132. Father Demetrius to Father Alexius Hoffmann, Lacey, June 15, 1905. (ASJA)

133. Father Demetrius to Abbot Peter, Lacey, July 8, 1908. (ASVA)

134. Father Justin Welz to Abbot Peter, Lacey, December 6, 1908. (ASJA)

135. Documentation about "the Prior affair" and its outcome is found in the American Cassinese Congregation's archives at Saint Vincent Archabbey, Latrobe, Pennsylvania. (ASVA)

136. See SMC's catalogs for 1896–1897, p. 6; 1902–03, p. 3;

137. A. J. Ruth's Diary, 1901–1902; see entries for January 1, 1902; October 30, 1901; and November 4 and December 20 and 25, 1901. Copy in Father Sebastian's papers. (SMAA)

138. SMC catalog for 1908–1909, p. 11; see also 1911–1912 catalog, p. 11. (SMAA)

139. SMC catalog for 1911–1912, p. 11. (SMAA)

140. *Between the Years*, p. [20].

141. *Between the Years*, pp. [21–22]; see also comments in Curtis, *Historical-Philosophical Bases*, pp. 287ff. and his references to *Benedictine Monachist*, Vol. 3, No. 8, p. 1; Father Justin to Abbot Perter, Lacey, August 16, 1913. (SMAA)

142. See Prior Justin to Abbot Peter, Lacey, August 16, 1913. (ASJA)

143. *Washington Standard* (Olympia), August 29, 1913, p. 1.

144. *Between the Years*, pp. [21–22].

145. *Washington Standard* (Olympia), August 29, 1913, p. 1.

146. Father Justin to Abbot Peter, Lacey, November 20, 1913. (SMAA)

147. *Washington Standard* (Olympia), March 7, p. 5, and April 11, 1913, p. 5. By happy coincidence, a great-niece of this Mr. Cady, Dr. Lillian Cady, after a distinguished career in public educational administration, became a professor, and then chair, of SMC's Education Department in the 1980s. She now serves on the College's Board of Trustees.

148. *Between the Years*, pp. [21–22].

149. *Washington Standard* (Olympia), November 21, 1913, p. 1.

150. Abbot Oswald to Abbot Peter Engel, October 12 and to Father Alexius Hoffmann, December 22, 1914. (ASJA) "Culpa" was a gathering of monks at which they admitted their "faults" against the common life and asked the pardon and help of their brethren.

151. 1914–1915 SMC catalog. (SMAA)

152. Abbot Oswald to Abbot Peter, Lacey, January 26, 1915. (ASJA)

153. Abbot Oswald to Abbot Peter, Lacey, November 9, 1914. (ASJA)

154. Abbot Oswald to Abbot Peter, Lacey, December 16, 1914. (ASJA)

155. Abbot Oswald to Abbot Peter, Lacey, January 26, 1915. (ASJA)

156. 1917–1918 SMC catalog, p. 27 and 1920–1921 catalog, p. 11. (SMAA)

157. Abbot Oswald to Abbot Peter, Lacey, January 26, 1915, and November 15, 1916. (SMAA)

158. *Saint Martin's News*, November–December, 1974, p. 3. (SMAA)

159. Abbot Oswald to Abbot Peter, Lacey, October 23, 1917. See also his comment about Peter Engel as Lacey's true founder in his November 29, 1919 letter to same. (SMAA)

160. Abbot Oswald to Abbot Peter, Lacey, December 4, 1916. (SMAA)

161. Abbot Oswald to Abbot Peter, Lacey, December 16, 1914. (ASJA)

162. Abbot Oswald to Abbot Peter, Lacey, July 23, 1918. (SMAA)

163. Abbot Oswald to Abbot Peter, Lacey, July 17 and February 9, 1917. (SMAA)

164. Abbot Oswald to Abbot Peter, Lacey, no date but probably 1916. (SMAA)

165. Abbot Oswald to Abbot Peter, Lacey, November 15, 1916. (SMAA)

166. Abbot Oswald to Abbot Peter, Lacey, December 4, 1916. (SMAA)

167. Abbot Oswald to Abbot Peter, Lacey, November 9, 1920. (SMAA)

168. Abbot Oswald to Abbot Peter, Lacey, July, 1917. (SMAA)

169. Abbot Oswald to Abbot Peter, Lacey, February 16, 1918. (SMAA) Born in a section of the Austrian Empire in 1866, he had come to the U.S.A. with his family as a child. In that era, minor children usually automatically became American citizens when the head of their household was naturalized.

170. Abbot Oswald to Abbot Peter, Lacey, June 29, 1918. (SMAA)

171. Abbot Oswald to Abbot Peter, Lacey, July 23, 1918. (SMAA)

172. Carlos A. Schwantes, *The Pacific Northwest* (Lincoln, Nebraska: University of Nebraska Press, 1989), pp. 283f.

173. Abbot Oswald to Abbot Peter, Lacey, November 24, 1918. (ASJA)

174. See original MO Ruth, Rev. Sebastian. F.5, Misc. No. 2 file. (SMAA)

175. Rev. Lewis R. O'Hern, C.S.P., Catholic Army and Navy Chaplain Bureau to Father Sebastian, Washington, D.C., October 17, 1917. (SMAA)

176. Bishop Edward J. O'Dea to Archbishop P. J.. Hayes, Bishop Ordinary of the Catholic U.S. forces, Seattle, September 7, 1918. (SMAA)

177. Abbot Oswald to Archbishop P. J.. Hayes, Lacey, September 10, 1918. (SMAA)

178. Rev. Joseph M Gleason, Vicar General for Army and Navy Catholic Chaplains, to Father Sebastian, Palo Alto, California, September 27, 1918. (SMAA)

179. Adjutant General, U.S. Army to Rev. Sebastian Ruth, Washington, D.C., October 26, 1918. (SMAA)

180. Captain William A. Shaw, Assistant Camp Adjutant, to Rev. Sebastian Ruth, Camp Lewis, American Lake, Washington, November 4, 1918. (SMAA)

181. Alexius Hoffmann, O.S.B., "History of Saint John's Abbey," (unpublished), Vol. 3, p. 254. (ASJA)

182. Father Matthew Britt to Father Alexius Hoffmann, Lacey, June 10, 1929. (SMAA)

183. Abbot Oswald to Abbot Peter, Lacey, September 18, 1919. (ASJA)

184. Father Prior [James] to Abbot Raphael, Olympia, September 1, 1956. (SMAA)

185. See his comment in "Retreats" information in Father Sebastian's files. (SMAA)

186. Abbot Oswald to Abbot Peter, April 1 and 15 and June 8, 1919. (ASJA)

187. Abbot Oswald to Abbot Peter, May 13 and September 18, 1919. (ASJA)

188. Abbot Oswald to Abbot Peter, October 12, 1919; Bishop Edward J. O'Dea "To Whom It May Concern," Seattle, October 15, 1919. (ASJA)

189. Abbot Oswald to Abbot Peter, Lacey, November 19, 1919. (ASJA)

190. Abbot Oswald to Abbot Peter, Lacey, January 2, 1920. (ASJA)

191. Abbot Oswald to Abbot Peter, Lacey, March 21, 1920. (ASJA)

192. See 1920–1921 SMC catalog, p. 26 and subsequent annual catalogs. (SMAA)

193. Abbot Oswald to Abbot Peter, Lacey, November 9, 1914. (ASJA)

194. Abbot Oswald to Abbot Peter, Lacey, May 9, 1920. (ASJA)

195. Abbot Oswald to Abbot Peter, Lacey, September 17, 1916. (ASJA)

196. *Washington Standard* (Olympia), November 19, 1920, p. 1.

197. *Washington Standard* (Olympia), October 15, 1920, p. 1, and October 22, 1920., p. 1.

198. *Washington Standard* (Olympia), December 1, 1916, p. 4.

199. *Washington Standard* (Olympia), April 8, 1921, p. 1.

200. *Between the Years*, p. [80].

201. Tacoma Mothers' Club Constitution, 1946 revised edition.

202. *The Martian* [then an SMC monthly campus newspaper], April 1921, n.p.

203. Alexius Hoffmann, O.S.B., "Autobiography," Vols. 9 and 10, *passim*. (ASJA)

204. Father Augustine Ogsniach to Bishop O'Dea, Lacey, May 22, 1923. (ACAS)

205. Abbot Oswald to Abbot Peter, Lacey. May 3, 1915. (ASJA)

206. Story related by Richard Mitchell (Emmett's son) to author at SMC on April 12, 1995.

207. Abbot Oswald to Abbot Peter, November 24, 1918; comments by Father Alexius Hoffman in Father Justin Welz's file. (ASJA)

208. Peter Beckman, O.S.B., *Kansas Monks: A History of Saint Benedict's Abbey* (Atchison, Kansas: Abbey Student Press, 1957), pp. 324–325 and 331.

209. Beckman, *Kansas Monks*, p. 325.

210. James M. Vosper, "Changes in the Educational Philosophy of Saint Martin's College, 1940–1973 (M.A. thesis, University of Nebraska, 1971), pp. 2 and 30.

211. Curtis, "Historical-Philosophical Bases," p. 393.

212. *Between the Years*, pp. [42–43].

213. See Beckman, *Kansas Monks*, p. 224.

214. Vosper, "Changes. . . ," p. 30.

215. Abbot Lambert to Father Leonard Feeney, Lacey, May 31, 1937. (SMAA)

216. Father Leonard Feeney to Abbot Lambert, Washington, D.C., October 29, 1936, and Abbot Lambert to Father Leonard, Lacey, November 7, 1936. (SMAA)

217. Father Leonard Feeney to Abbot Lambert, Washington, D.C., November 22, 1936. (SMAA)

218. Abbot Lambert to Father Leonard Feeney, Lacey, November 7, 1936. (SMAA)

219. Father Leonard Feeney to Abbot Lambert, Eua Claire, Wisconsin, probably late June 1938. (SMAA)

220. Father Leonard Feeney wrote an autobiography in 1937 at his family's request. The typescript of that document is fifty-eight double-spaced pages in length and these quotes are from p. 35 of that document. (SMAA)

221. Father Leonard Feeney, "Autobiography," p. 36. (SMAA)

222. Father Leonard Feeney, "Autobiography," p. 42. (SMAA)

223. Father Leonard Feeney, "Autobiography," p. 44. (SMAA)

224. Father Leonard Feeney to Abbot Lambert, Washington, D.C., March 31, 1937. (SMAA)

225. Father Leonard Feeney to Abbot Lambert, Washington, D.C., June 16 and August 17, 1939. (SMAA)

226. Father Leonard to Abbot Lambert, Washington, D.C., January 14 and 19, 1940; Abbot Lambert to Father Leonard, Lacey, January 19 and 20, 1940. (SMAA)

227. Abbot Lambert to Frater Alcuin Lawrence, Lacey, October 4, 1932. (SMAA) See also *Between the Years*, p. [46].

228. Interview with Corinne Schilling Farmer by the author, Seattle, February 2, 1993. (Author's Files) *See also* "Saint Martin's First Fraternity" by Mike Contris in *Insight*, Vol. 11, No. 1, January 1981.

229. Imelda Bergh to Abbot Lambert, Lacey, November 24, 1939. (SMAA)

230. See, for example, his typed notes, "For private information—Taken to [Seattle] Mothers' Club Tea, October 11, 1932" and his handwritten notes for a 1942 visit in Olympia with mothers of current SMC students. (SMAA)

231. See, for example, Abbot Raphael to Corrine Connolly (Olympia Club president), December 11, 1943. (SMAA)

232. Gertrude McCoy to Abbot Lambert, Seattle, September 9 , February 2, and December 1, 1932. (SMAA)

233. Mary E. McDermott to Abbot Lambert, Seattle, December 7, 1937. (SMAA)

234. See, for example, the letters to Abbot Lambert from Seattle Mothers' Club treasurers Eugenia A. Poirier (November 12, 1930) and Teresa E. Farrell (April 20, 1931) (SMAA)

235. Teresa E. Farrell to Abbot Lambert, Seattle, January 1, 1934. (SMAA)

236. Bonita Crowley Smith to Abbot Lambert, Seattle, November 24, 1931. (SMAA)

237. See his outline notes for that talk, "Mothers' Day at Saint Martin's, May 9, 1938." (SMAA)

238. Holy Rosary, 1891–1966 Diamond Jubilee booklet (1966), p. [11] and Holy Rosary, 1891–1991 Centennial booklet (1991), p. 16. (SMAA)

239. Visitation Parish information based on text in the parish's history scrapbooks circa 1992.

240. Queen of Angels Convent chronicle, October 29, 1928. (ASSA)

241. Father Bernard Neary to Rev. Mother Provincial, Port Angeles, May 15, 1933. (ASSA)

242. Provincial Superior to Father Bernard Neary, Victoria, British Columbia, May 19, 1933. (ASSA)

243. Memorandum by Bishop Shaughnessy, Seattle, May 1, 1936; Archbishop Pietro Fumasoni-Biondi to Bishop Edward J. O'Dea, Washington, D.C., January 2, 1931. (ACAS)

244. Abbot Lambert to Bishop Gerald Shaughnessy, Lacey, January 14, 1938. (SMAA)

245. Bishop Gerald Shaughnessy to Abbot Lambert, Seattle, January 20, 1938. (ACAS)

246. Memorandum by Bishop Shaughnessy, November 7, 1940. (ACAS)

247. Discussion of author with Father Michael Feeney, O.S.B., October 18, 1994.

248. Father Matthew Britt to Father Alexius Hoffmann, Lacey, February 8, 1938. (ASJA)

249. See various "Oil and Gas Lease" documents and related paperwork. (SMAA)

250. Taped interview with Gwin Hicks by author, Lacey, May 31, 1991. (Author's Files) *See also* Grove Webster, "The Civilian Pilot Training Program," *Aerospace Historian* (May 1979) 34–39.

251. Gladys Buroker to Gwin Hicks, Athol, Idaho, April 18, 1991, and see her June 4, 1995 memo to author. (Author's Files) *See also* Gladys Buroker and Sue Hailey, "War Time Pilot Training at Weeks Field" in *Museum of North Idaho* [*Bulletin*] (Fall 1990) [p. 2]

252. Father Meinrad's Diary, June 8, 1945. (SMAA)

253. Father Meinrad to Father Bede, Lacey, September 19, 1944. (SMAA)

254. Father Meinrad's Diary, April 18, 1945. (SMAA)

255. Father Meinrad's Diary, May 22, 1945. (SMAA)

256. Father Matthew Britt to Father Bede Ernsdorff, Lacey, January 1, 1945. (SMAA)

257. Father Meinrad's Diary, May 30, 1945. (SMAA)

258. Abbot Raphael to Olympia Saint Martin's Mothers' Club (c/o Corrine Connolly), Lacey, October 1, 1943. The Club had sent him flowers during his short stay at Saint Peter Hospital in Olympia. (SMAA)

259. Belle H. O'Neill to Abbot Raphael, Seattle, September 12, 1943; Abbot Raphael to Belle H. O'Neill, Lacey, May 18, 1944; Marcella M. Mooney to Abbot Raphael, Seattle, July 26, 1944. (SMAA)

260. Abbot Raphael to Loretta M. Baldwin, Lacey, September 9, 1944. (SMAA)

261. See Father Meinrad's 1945 diary for those dates. (SMAA)

262. Father Meinrad to Father Bede, Lacey, January 11, 1945. (SMAA)

263. Abbot Raphael to Abbot Primate, Lacey, October 23, 1945. (SMAA); and see *Between the Years*, p. [49].

264. Father Meinrad's Diary, July 11, 1945. (SMAA)

265. Abbot Raphael to Father Gerald, Lacey, July 28, 1945. (SMAA)

266. Father James Piotrzkowski to Mother M. Eugenia, O.S.B., Lacey, September 29, 1943. (SMAA)

267. Information on Saint Martin's World War II military chaplains and their work is found in their Army personnel files in National Record Center, Suitland, Maryland. (U. S. National Archives)

268. Chaplain Ltc. Anselm M. Keefe to Father Marcel Berthon, (n.p.), March 14, 1946. (U.S. National Archives)

269. Abbot Raphael to Pfc. James E. Dickinson, Lacey, December 5, 1945. (SMAA)

270. Abbot Raphael to Dean E. Miller, Lacey, February 12, 1946. (SMAA)

271. Abbot Raphael to Vincent Govorchin, Lacey, December 9, 1945. (SMAA)

272. Abbot Raphael to Frater Patrick Hollern, January 16, and to Father Martin Pollard, Lacey, January 17, 1946. (SMAA)

273. Abbot Raphael to B., Lacey, December 2, 1946. (SMAA)

274. Abbot Raphael to Father Prior [James]. Saint Meinrad, Indiana, August 16, 1952. (SMAA)

275. Father Matthew Britt to Father Bede Ernsdorff, Lacey, November 18, 1944, and January 1, 1945. (SMAA)

276. Father Prior [James] to Father Bede, Lacey, January 1, 1945. (SMAA)

277. Abbot Raphael to Father Bede, Lacey, January 2, 1945. (SMAA)

278. See Father Meinrad's diary entry for July 11, 1945, and Abbot Raphael to Rose Lemoine, Lacey, July 20, 1945. (SMAA)

279. Abbot Raphael to Father Marcel Berthon, Lacey, November 30 and to Father Richard Cebula, December 5, 1945. (SMAA)

280. Abbot Raphael to Father Jerome Toner, Lacey, December 17, 1945. (SMAA)

281. Father Matthew Britt to Father Bede Ernsdorff, Lacey, January 1, 1945. (SMAA)

282. Frater Eugene Kellenbenz to Father Bede Ernsdorff, Mount Angel, Oregon, March 16, 1945. (SMAA)

283. Abbot Raphael to Frater Clement Pangratz, Lacey, March 4, 1946. (SMAA)

284. Father Prior [James] to Abbot Raphael, Olympia, August 17, 1951. (SMAA)

285. Abbot Raphael to Father Prior [James], Newark, New Jersey, August 21, 1953. (SMAA)

286. Father Meinrad's Diary, June 9 and 15, August 17, and September 4, 1945. (SMAA)

287. Father Matthew Britt to Father Bede, Lacey, January 1, 1945, and on same date Father Prior [James] to Father Bede. (SMAA)

288. Abbot Raphael to Father Jerome Toner, Lacey, September 17, 1945. (SMAA)

289. On September 17, 1945, Abbot Raphael sent similar letters to Fathers Alcuin, Jerome, Robert, and Marcel. (SMAA)

290. Abbot Raphael to James T. Albers, Lacey, February 28 and also to Leon, January 16, 1946. (SMAA)

291. See, for example, Abbot Raphael to Teacher Placement Bureau, University of Oregon, Lacey, March 22, 1946, and a similar request to California State Employment Service of same date. (SMAA)

292. Abbot Raphael to James T. Albers, Lacey, February 28, 1946. (SMAA)

293. Abbot Raphael to Edward Sricherz, Lacey, March 25, 1946. (SMAA)

294. Abbot Raphael to Herb Buroker, Lacey, January 14 and March 9, 1946. (SMAA)

295. Abbot Raphael to Father Prior [James], Peru, Illinois, August 12, 1947. (SMAA)

296. Abbot Raphael to Father Prior [James], Atchison, Kansas, August 22, 1949. (SMAA)

297. Abbot Raphael to Abbot Paul Nahlen, Lacey, October 23, 1946. (SMAA)

298. *Daily Olympian*, November 3, 1946.

299. Abbot Raphael to Abbot Paul Nahlen, Lacey, November 11, 1946. (SMAA)

300. Rev. Richard S. Cebula, O.S.B., P. E., "History of Engineering at SMC" [August 1973]. (Author's Files)

301. Walter W. Flynn, "Some reminiscences of SMC, 1946–51" *Insight*, Vol. 10, No. 13, April 1980, p. 1.

302. Flynn, "Some reminiscences," p. 4.

303. Cited in Owen Vande Velde's cover story on Thomas A. Kane in *Insight*, Vol. 30, No. 2, Spring 1993, p. 2.

304. See Walter W. Flynn to author, Alexandria, Virginia, January 17, 1992 (Author's Files) and 1947–1948 SMC *Bulletin*, p. 52.

305. *Seattle Sunday Times Rotogravure*, May 21, 1939, p. 3. (Author's Files)

306. Abbot Raphael to Saint Martin's clerics at Mount Angel Seminary, Lacey, February 17, 1946. (SMAA)

307. See 1946–1947 *SMC Bulletin*, p. 34.

308. See 1950–1951 *SMC Bulletin*, p. 30.

309. Abbot Raphael to Father Prior [James], Newark, New Jersey, August 20, 1953. (SMAA)

310. Abbot Raphael to person unknown, Lacey, February 23, 1946. (SMAA)

311. Abbot Raphael to Abbot Cuthbert McDonald, January 19 and to E. W. Poor, January 26, 1946. (SMAA)

312. Francis H. Dummer to author, Dayton, Oregon, June 10, 1993. (Author's Files)

313. Abbot Raphael to "Fratres Clerici SMC" (namely, those Saint Martin's monks studying Theology at Mount Angel Seminary in Oregon), Lacey, February 17, 1946. (SMAA)

314. Abbot Raphael to Congressman Charles R. Savage (Washington, D.C.), Lacey, March 11, 1946. (SMAA)

315. Abbot Raphael to Father Edward Weckert February 2, 1946, and to George W. Stoddard, January 30, 1946. (SMAA)

316. Abbot Raphael to Federal Public Housing Authority (Seattle), March 14, 1946, and to Army Corps of Engineers (San Francisco), March 11, 1946. (SMAA)

317. Abbot Raphael sent similar September 17, 1945 letters to Father Robert Wippel and to Father Alcuin Lawrence. (SMAA)

318. See "G.I. Bill: It changed life in America," *Olympian*, June 23, 1994.

319. Abbot Raphael to S.P.I., Lacey, September 5, 1945. (SMAA)

320. Jim Ellis to author, San Ramon, California, February 16, 1992. (Author's Files)

321. Ed Niedermeyer to author, Portland, Oregon, January 19, 1990. (Author's Files)

322. *Daily Olympian*, November 2, 1947. See Curtis, "Historical-Philosophical Bases," p. 407.

323. Erik Bromberg to author, Albuquerque, New Mexico, May 13, 1989. (Author's Files)

324. Abbot Raphael to Father Gerald, Lacey, July 28, 1945. (SMAA)

325. Abbot Raphael to Mother Rosamond, O.S.B., Lacey, October 16, 1945. (SMAA)

326. Abbot Raphael to Rev. Joseph Conway, Lacey, October 24, 1945. (SMAA)

327. Information based on a June 22, 1994 interview at SMA of the author with Father Thaddaeus Arledge, who as a young man had discovered Father Matthew's remains.

328. Ken Dolan (HS '58, C '58–60) conversation with author, February 13, 1992.

329. John Firkins (CG '57) to author, Spokane, Washington, August 4, 1992. (Author's Files)

330. See *SMC Bulletin*, 1952–1953, p. 50.

331. See *SMC Bulletin*, 1950–1951, p. 23.

332. From Mike Contris' salute to his old colleague, "Father Jerome, Saint Martin's Labor Priest" in "The Crucible," *Daily Olympian*, February 27, 1977.

333. Mother Mary Augustine, O.S.B., to Abbot Raphael, Cottonwood, Idaho, April 28, 1958. (SMAA)

334. Abbot Raphael to Archbishop Thomas A. Connolly, Lacey, May 5, 1954. (SMAA)

335. Abbot Raphael to Mrs. Joseph Partington, Olympia, June 12, 1959. (SMAA)

336. Postcard from an unidentified Sister to "Benedictine Fathers, S.M.C.," Cottonwood, Idaho, June 16, 1959. (SMAA)

337. Mother Mary Augustine to Abbot Raphael, Cottonwood, Idaho, June 22, 1959. (SMAA)

338. Edythe Dixon (Grace's daughter-in-law) to author, Eureka, California, October 26, 1992. (Author's Files)

339. Copy of May 31, 1964 memo. (Author's Files)

340. Father Michael Feeney, O.S.B., interview with author March 14, 1994, at SMA. (Author's Files)

341. Douglas G. Hall to Father Michael, Seattle, February 14, 1965. (SMAA)

342. Alison M. Matthews to Father Michael, Olympia, February 16, 1965. (SMAA)

343. Father John Raymond, memo on coeducation, undated but early 1965. (SMAA)

344. Edward Daniszewski, memo on coeducation, undated but early 1965. (SMAA)

345. Comments by Father Ansgar Hallen on coeducation cited in a compilation of opinion issued by the president's office, undated but early 1965. (SMAA)

346. Father George Seidel to president and College faculty, January 9, 1965. (SMAA)

347. Father Michael Feeney, O.S.B., interview with author, taped March 14, 1994. (Author's Files)

348. Father Michael Feeney to Father John Fitterer, president-elect, Seattle University, Lacey, April 2, 1965. Similar letters were sent to presidents of five other regional Catholic colleges. (SMAA)

349. Father Michael Feeney's "[Notes] to [Monastic] Community re Coeducation," February 2, 1965. (SMAA)

350. From an undated clipping on "Saint Placid Priory and High School" in *Saint Martin's News* (c. 1965) (SMAA)

351. Father Michael Feeney, O.S.B., interview with author, taped March 14, 1994. (Author's Files)

352. Observation of Robert P. Mallon, first chairman of the Board of Regents, in taped interview with author, February 2, 1993. (Author's Files)

353. See, for example, his statement on in November 24, 1967 Chapter Minutes. (SMAA)

354. See comment by Abbot Gerald in November 24, 1967 Chapter Minutes. (SMAA)

355. Memo of Father Michael to administrators, faculty, and staff of SMC, January 17, 1967. (SMAA)

356. Bylaws, Board of Regents of SMC, Articles 7 and 9. (SMAA)

357. Saint Martin's *Abbey, Chapter* Minutes, December 21, 1966. (SMAA)

358. Abbot Raphael to Louise C. Rast, Olympia, October 1, 1962. (SMAA)

359. Colman J. Barry, O.S.B., *Worship and Work*, expanded edition, Collegeville, Minnesota: Liturgical Press, 1993, p. 349.

360. Barry, *Worship and Work,* pp. 350, 354, and 355.

361. Father Kenneth Keller to Father Maurus Keller, Olympia, February 14, 1965. (Author's Files)

362. Abbot Raphael to "Dear Confreres," December 7, 1964. (SMAA)

363. Father Adrian Parcher to Father Maurus Keller, Olympia, December 10, 1964. (Author's Files)

364. Ibid. [viz., December 7, 1964, Adrian to Maurus]

365. Saint Martin's Abbey, Chapter Minutes, December 30, 1964. (SMAA) Father Kenneth Keller to Father Maurus Keller, Olympia, December 30, 1964. (Author's Files)

366. Father Adrian Parcher to Father Maurus Keller, Olympia, January 5, 1965. (Author's Files)

367. Father Adrian Parcher to Father Maurus Keller, Olympia, January 8, 1965. (Author's Files)

368. Saint Martin's Abbey, Chapter Minutes, December 28, 1966. (SMAA)

369. Saint Martin's Abbey, Chapter Minutes, January 4, 1967. (SMAA)

370. Saint Martin's Abbey, Chapter Minutes, June 5, 1968. (SMAA)

371. Abbot Raphael to Sister Mary Alice, Olympia, May 25, 1959. (SMAA)

372. Interview with Tom White (formerly Father Germain), Seattle, March 10, 1993. (Author's Files)

373. Comment by Father Eugene Kellenbenz, September 14, 1967. (Author's Files)

374. Saint Martin's Abbey, Chapter Minutes, June 5, 1968. (SMAA)

375. Saint Martin's Abbey, Chapter Minutes, March 5, 1970. (SMAA)

376. Saint Martin's Abbey, Chapter Minutes, October 19, 1966. (SMAA)

377. Saint Martin's Abbey, Chapter Minutes, December 21, 1966. (SMAA)

378. Saint Martin's Abbey, Chapter Minutes, January 18, 1967. (SMAA)

379. Saint Martin's Abbey, Chapter Minutes, June 21, 1967. (SMAA)

380. Richard L. Capistrant to Abbot Conrad Rausch, Carson City, Nevada, July 23, 1991. (Author's Files)

381. George G. McKnight (S.M.H.S. '51) to *Insight* editor, Hilton Head Island, Florida, April 12, 1996. (Author's Files)

382. Robert L. Hull to Abbot Conrad Rausch, Kent, Washington, May 14, 1992. (Author's Files.)

383. Saint Martin's Abbey, Chapter Minutes, June 5, 1968. (SMAA)

384. Saint Martin's Abbey, Chapter Minutes, November 29, 1968. (SMAA)

385. Saint Martin's Abbey, Chapter Minutes, October 15, 1968. (SMAA)

386. Father Matthew [Naumes], "Annual Report to the Saint Martin's College Corporation," May 23, 1972. (SMAA)

387. Saint Martin's Abbey, Chapter Minutes, May 29, 1969. (SMAA)

388. Saint Martin's Abbey, Chapter Minutes, October 21, 1969. (SMAA)

389. Saint Martin's Abbey, Chapter Minutes, November 28, 1969. (SMAA)

390. Saint Martin's Abbey, Chapter Minutes, March 9, 1970. (SMAA)

391. Saint Martin's Abbey, Chapter Minutes, November 27, 1970. (SMAA)

392. Saint Martin's Abbey, Chapter Minutes, December 16, 1970. (SMAA)

393. Saint Martin's Abbey, Chapter Minutes, April 28, 1971. (SMAA)

394. Father Conrad Rausch to Membership, High School Corporation, October 17, 1971. (SMAA)

395. Saint Martin's Abbey, Chapter Minutes, October 19, 1971. (SMAA)

396. Saint Martin's Abbey, Chapter Minutes, November 26, 1971. (SMAA)

397. Father Conrad Rausch, "Report on the High School," June 1, 1972. (SMAA)

398. Saint Martin's Abbey, Chapter Minutes, June 1, 1972. (SMAA)

399. Father Terence Wager, "Progress Report—SMHS," November 24, 1972. (SMAA)

400. Saint Martin's Abbey, Chapter Minutes, October 16, 1973. (SMAA)

401. *Saint Martin's News*, Summer 1974, p. 1. (SMAA)

402. Saint Martin's Abbey, Chapter Minutes, June 1, 1972. (SMAA)

403. Saint Martin's Abbey, Chapter Minutes, October 17, 1972. (SMAA)

404. Abbot Dunstan Curtis, "Report of the Chairman of the Board of Trustees of SMC," October 17, 1972. (SMAA)

405. Father Mathew [Naumes], "Report to the SMC Corporation," May 24, 1974. (SMAA)

406. Abbot Dunstan E. Curtis, "Report to Members of the Abbey Corporation," May 30, 1974. (SMAA)

407. *Saint Martin's News*, December 1972, p. 1. (SMAA)

408. James M. Greenhalgh to Phillip Carbaugh, Tacoma, January 17, 1992. (Author's Files)

409. Saint Martin's Abbey, Chapter Minutes, May 30, 1974. (SMAA)

410. Father Mathew [Naumes], "Report to the SMC Corporation," October 15, 1974. (SMAA)

411. Abbot Dunstan Curtis, "Report of the Chairman of the Board of Trustees of SMC," October 15, 1974. (SMAA)

412. Father Matthew [Naumes], "Report to the Saint Martin's Corporation," June 4, 1973. (SMAA)

413. See "Ken's Corner" column in *Lacey Leader*, June 18, 1975. (Author's Files)

414. Yes, the author of this history is the "subject" of this segment. It seemed to him more appropriate to narrate his own activity from a third-person perspective. *Caveat lector!*

415. *Lacey Leader*, June 25, 1975, p. 1.

416. See *Catholic Northwest Progress* (Seattle), June 27, 1975, pp. 1–2 and also the retrospective profile of Father John by Melinda Bell

Howard in *Insight*, Vol. 9, No. 1, September 1978, p. 6.

417. Father John Scott, "Remarks at August 1975 SMC Commencement." (Author's Files)

418. Father John Scott, "Homecoming '78—Luncheon Remarks," February 11, 1978. (Author's Files)

419. Father John Scott, "The Work and Role of the President of SMC," November 1, 1979. (Author's Files)

420. These and other observations are based partially on an interview with John D. Ishii, May 7, 1993. (Author's Files)

421. See Mike Contris's "Close-up" appreciation of Dr. Issii, *The Olympian*, June 1, 1984.

422. Saint Martin's Abbey, Chapter Minutes, May 19, 1980.

423. See *Insight*, Vol. 12, No. 2, April 1982, p. 1.

424. See *Insight*, Vol. 12, No. 1, January 1982, p. 1.

425. See Mike Contris's interview with Ishii in *Insight*, Vol. XI, No. 1, January 1981, p. 1 and Saint Martin's Abbey, Chapter Minutes, May 19, 1980.

426. "New Vice-President for Academic Affairs" in *Insight*, Vol. 11, No. 3, July 1981, p. 1.

427. See *Insight*, Vol. 12, No. 2, July 1982, p. 7.

428. Saint Martin's Abbey, Chapter Minutes, January 23, 1984.

429. See "New Directions," in *Insight*, Vol. 14, No. 3, July 1984, pp. 1 and 2.

430. See "Dr. Ishii Recruits Pacific Rim Students" in *Insight* Vol. 12, No. 3, July 1983, pp. 1 and 7 and "Sabbatical," in *Insight*, Vol. 14, No. 3, July 1984, p. 1.

431. See Abbot Adrian's comments in *Insight*, Vol. 10, No. 4, July 1980, p. 2 and Vol. 11, No. 4, October 1981, p. 1.

432. Saint Martin's Abbey, Chapter Minutes, May 21, 1981.

433. Abbot Raphael to Father Marcel Berthon, Lacey, November 30, 1945. (SMAA)

434. *The Olympian*, April 7, 1985, pp. 1A and 5A.

435. See *Insight*, Vol. 16, No. 1, Spring 1986, p. 1.

436. Abbey "Mission Statement" (May 21, 1992) and "Value Statement" (April 22, 1992).

437. Brother Boniface Lazzari's remarks are found in a 1992 document relating to construction of a new State of Washington Ecology Department headquarters building adjacent to Saint Martin's campus. (Author's Files)

438. Abbot Adrian (as chairman of SMC Board of Trustees) to "Members of the SMC Community," September 7, 1984. (SMAA)

439. See *Insight*, Vol. 31, No. 4, Fall 1994, pp. 1 and 2, on Spangler's ten years in office.

440. See *Insight*, Vol. 26, No. 2, Spring 1990, p. 2 and Vol. 31, No. 4, p. 2. Comparative satistics courtesy SMC Registrar.

441. See Mike Contris's "Close-up" column, *The Olympian*, June 1, 1984.

442. See *Insight*, Vol. 25, No. 2, Spring 1989, p. 2 and Vol. 25, No. 4, Fall 1989, p. 2.

443. See *Insight*, Vol. 29, No. 1, Winter 1993, p. 12.

444. See *Insight*, Vol. 25, No. 1, Winter 1989, pp. 3 and 7.

445. See *Insight*, Vol. 27, No. 1, Winter 1991, p. 9.

446. See *Insight*, Vol. 25, No. 1, Winter 1989, p. 1.

447. See *Insight*, Vol. 25, No. 3, Summer 1989, pp. 2 and 4.

448. See *Insight*, Vol. 28, No. 4, Fall 1992, pp. 1, 8–10 and 15.

449. See text of Acuff Fitness Center dedicatory plaque.

450. Comment by Director of Development Gary Mulhall in *Insight*, Vol. 28, No. 3, Summer 1992, p. 2.

451. See *Insight*, Vol. 29, No. 4, Fall 1993 , p. 4 and Vol. 31, No. 3, Summer 1994, pp. 1–2.

452. See Dr. Spangler's comments in *Insight*, Vol. 29, No.1, Winter 1992, pp. 1–2 and 15.

453. See *Insight*, Vol. 29, No. 4, Fall 1993, p. 16.

454. Saint Martin's Alumni Association By-Laws (July 1984), p. 1. (Author's Files)

455. *Insight*, Vol. 26, No. 1, Winter 1990, pp. 1, 8, and 9.

456. *Constitution and By-Laws of Saint Martin's Athletic Foundation* (1985). See also *Insight*, Vol. 25, No. 1, Winter 1989, p. 5.and Vol. 26, No. 2, Spring 1990, p. 11.